PARANORMAL AMERICA

Paranormal America

Ghost Encounters, UFO Sightings,
Bigfoot Hunts, and Other Curiosities
in Religion and Culture

SECOND EDITION

Christopher D. Bader,
Joseph O. Baker, *and*
F. Carson Mencken

NEW YORK UNIVERSITY PRESS
New York

NEW YORK UNIVERSITY PRESS
New York
www.nyupress.org

References to Internet websites (URLs) were accurate at the time of writing. Neither the author nor New York University Press is responsible for URLs that may have expired or changed since the manuscript was prepared.

ISBN: 978-1-4798-1965-2 (hardback)
ISBN: 978-1-4798-1528-9 (paperback)

For Library of Congress Cataloging-in-Publication data, please contact the Library of Congress.

New York University Press books are printed on acid-free paper, and their binding materials are chosen for strength and durability. We strive to use environmentally responsible suppliers and materials to the greatest extent possible in publishing our books.

Manufactured in the United States of America

10 9 8 7 6 5 4 3 2 1

Also available as an ebook

CONTENTS

ACKNOWLEDGMENTS

We have so many people to thank for their help in this endeavor that we fear the attempt. Someone will certainly be forgotten.

The quantitative data presented in this book are partially based upon three waves of the Baylor Religion Survey fielded in 2005, 2010, and 2014. The Baylor Religion Survey project was originally supported by a grant from the John Templeton Foundation. The development of survey content was the result of a collaborative effort in the Department of Sociology at Baylor University. Finally, the Gallup Organization provided valuable feedback on the final questionnaire and ultimately collected these data.

Other data presented in this volume originate from two waves of the Chapman University Survey of American Fears (2014 and 2015). The development of the survey instruments involved the efforts of many Chapman students and, in particular, Dr. Ed Day of Chapman's Department of Sociology and Dr. Ann Gordon of Chapman's Department of Political Science. We also must thank the staff at Knowledge Networks, who provided valuable feedback on the survey and gathered these data.

Throughout the book we frequently use pseudonyms for those we spent time with, and these names are in quotation marks for the first mention. We do so when the person has not publicly disclosed their paranormal beliefs and/or experiences, unless they have expressly stated a willingness to be identified.

The late Datus Perry of Carson, Washington, spent many hours ushering the first author through the woods looking for Bigfoot. We greatly appreciate Laura Cyr's willingness to tell us of her many supernatural and paranormal experiences. We are equally grateful that the UFO Contact Center International opened its doors to our questions and to Paul Ingram for telling us his harrowing experience with the Satanic panic of the 1990s. We greatly appreciate the efforts of Ernie Alonzo of Haunted Orange County in arranging a ghost hunt at Chapman University and allowing one of us to follow it. The North American Wood Ape Conservancy (NAWAC) was extremely patient dragging three sociologists through the woods on one of its field operations, and we greatly enjoyed getting to know the group's members.

Numbers can only get you so far—we did not believe we could tell a story about American paranormal beliefs without hearing from people who have experienced the paranormal for themselves. We are greatly in debt to the many people who gave us their trust and their time.

Finally, engaging in such a project requires support at home. The authors would like to thank their spouses—Sara Bader, Kim Mencken, and Amy Edmonds—for their love, patience, and understanding as we spent the night in haunted houses, chased Bigfoot, and delved into UFO abductions and psychic phenomena.

1

The Interrupted Lecture

Professors love to talk.

It takes something dramatic to interrupt one during an impassioned lecture. But such an event happened to Bill at Chapman University in Orange, California.[1] It was mid-semester and Bill was about halfway through a lecture in Smith Hall 211, standing before his class in front of the chalkboard. Thirty students sat in rows of tables, studiously taking notes.

"All of the sudden there was a large creaking sound right to my left like a large footstep." The loud noise caused an astonished Bill to jump to the right and look down at the spot on the floor from where the sound originated. Some students near the front of the class heard this noise and noticed Bill's surprise. They also looked toward the floor.

Bill composed himself and continued the lecture. But several seconds later a second footstep, not quite as loud as the first, echoed further to his left. The students could now tell that something strange was occurring and many stood up at their desks. About a second later, three more footsteps sounded at an accelerated pace, seemingly moving between Bill and the wall. According to Bill, the sounds were "so pronounced that I expected to see something, perhaps depressions in the carpet."

The students became very excited, chattering with one another about what just happened. "It was very clear to all of us that the sounds were in the room with us." By this point class was entirely disrupted, and Bill and his students spent the rest of the period trying to reproduce the sounds. Bill went into the classroom next door (which shared a common wall) and stomped back and forth, yelling to students who remained in Smith 211 to see if the sounds were repeated. They were not. Students walked back and forth in the hallways and up and down the stairs. After several such experiments, Bill related, "we convinced ourselves that we could not reproduce it."

Bill and his students remain flummoxed by the incident.[2] The story has since been shared around campus and the local community. Before

Bill's experience, there did not appear to be tales of ghosts in Smith Hall. Since then, it has become notorious as one of Chapman's haunted locations. Some employees have added their stories of feelings of dread and strange noises when working in the building late at night.

Paranormal America

In more than two decades of studying people who claim paranormal experiences, I (Christopher Bader) have had many fascinating experiences. Some have been alone, others with my co-authors. In the fall of 2015, I joined an all-star team of ghost hunters from popular paranormal television shows such as *Fact or Faked*, *Ghost Hunters International*, and *Ghost Mine* as they attempted to communicate with the spirit of Smith Hall at Chapman University.

I have also observed support groups for people who report abductions by alien beings and visited with therapists who claim to have recovered memories of vast Satanic conspiracies to control the planet. I have heard all manner of outrageous conspiracy theories, and wandered the aisles of innumerable New Age and paranormal book stores. My coauthors, F. Carson Mencken and Joseph Baker, have joined me on hunts for Bigfoot, visits to psychic fairs, and trips to haunted houses.

During this time we have noticed an interesting trend in how Americans relate to the paranormal: they are simultaneously fascinated and repulsed, intrigued and dismissive. The paranormal has permeated our culture, and the fascination Americans have with the paranormal appears to be growing.

A key indicator of the increasing popularity of the paranormal is the availability of related entertainment (see figure 1.1). Americans have long been entertained by fictional television shows with paranormal themes such as *Supernatural*, *Medium*, *Ghost Whisperer*, and *The X-Files* (which reappeared as a miniseries in 2016). In an earlier era our parents tuned in daily to watch the exploits of Barnabas Collins, the protagonist vampire on *Dark Shadows*. These shows may simply seek to entertain, but they also disseminate paranormal beliefs. Far more popular of late are paranormal "reality" shows that present documentaries about famous cases and/or related investigations. There is a bewildering variety of such programming. In the past few years, viewers with an interest in monsters

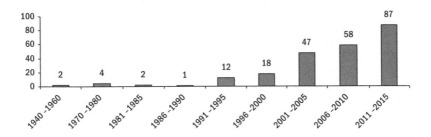

Figure 1.1. Paranormal Television: Number of Paranormal "Reality" Shows by Premiere Date (1940–2015) (Sharon A. Hill, "Paranormal TV Show Listing," *Doubtful,* https://idoubtit.wordpress.com)

could choose from *Finding Bigfoot* (Animal Planet) or simply leave the television on Destination America, which offered *Monsters and Mysteries in America, Monsters Underground, Mountain Monsters,* and *Alaska Monsters.* The venerable *Ghost Hunters,* which premiered in 2004, still airs new episodes on the SyFy channel. It has produced spin-off shows such as *Ghost Hunters Academy* and *Ghost Hunters International,* but also faces stiff competition from dozens of other ghost-related shows, including *The Demon Files, Ghost Stalkers,* and *Amish Haunting* (all on Destination America). Paranormal researcher Sharon Hill maintains a list of paranormal television shows and their premiere dates at her website.[3] Of the 231 shows listed in 2015,[4] 101 of them (44%) premiered since the first edition of this book in 2010.

If a viewer's interest is piqued by such fare, she can delve into the large New Age/paranormal book sections of Barnes & Noble or Amazon.com, or join one of the nearly three million regular listeners of *Coast to Coast AM,* a nightly paranormal radio show carried on over six hundred stations. A variety of paranormal podcasts including *Mysterious Universe, Jim Harold's Paranormal Report, Anything Ghost, Sasquatch Chronicles,* and *Expanded Perspectives* provide paranormal information on demand. Even more paranormal websites and forums allow users to swap ghostly tales and learn about Bigfoot and other phenomena.

Further, a significant number of Americans spend their weekends at UFO conventions hearing whispers of government cover-ups, at New Age gatherings learning the keys to enlightenment, or ambling around historic downtowns learning about resident ghosts in tourist-targeted "ghost walks." Cities have learned to capitalize on their mysteries. Rumors of the 1947 crash of a flying saucer draw tourists to Roswell, New Mexico, which holds an annual UFO festival[5] and sports its own UFO museum. Willow Creek, California, proclaims itself the "Bigfoot Capital of the World" and cashes in on the hairy beast through gift shops, museums, and festivals. Barefoot Campus Outfitters, a small retail business in Whitney, Texas, was able to expand its operation into a multi-state retail clothier by selling UFO-themed merchandise after a national story broke about multiple UFO sightings in nearby Stephenville in 2008.[6] The former luxury liner *Queen Mary*, now docked in Long Beach, California, offers an entire suite of paranormal activities. Visitors can take the "Haunted Encounters" ghost tour and wander the ship on a scavenger hunt to find twelve plaques marking the location of ghost sightings.

Paranormal Tourism: The Lights of Marfa, Texas

Paranormal tourism has indeed become a ubiquitous aspect of American popular culture. Consider the many locations around the United States that seek tourist dollars by promoting local "ghost lights." Unexplained lights regularly appear in a number of locations in the U.S., such as Brown Mountain, North Carolina; Summerville, South Carolina; and St. Louis, Missouri. But one of the most popular ghost light locations is in Marfa, Texas.

The famous Marfa ghost lights dance across the Mitchell Flats of the Chihuahuan Desert floor on most nights. In July 2013, I (Carson Mencken) and my family took a vacation to Big Bend National Park and spent the Fourth of July in Ft. Davis, home of the McDonald National Observatory. Marfa, being a mere hundred miles from Big Bend (just right around the corner in Texas terms), and being myself in the midst of a writing a book on the paranormal, I convinced a somewhat reluctant family to take a slight detour.

There exists an abundance of information debunking the very existence of the Marfa lights. I, too, was skeptical. In total, I spent three nights in 2013 (July 2, July 3, and July 5) waiting for the lights to appear and for my skepticism to fade. A few minutes east of Marfa proper, sits an adobe viewing center with a back porch that overlooks the desert that it is nicely appointed with ample seating and paved parking. The grounds are well-maintained with a mix of desert fauna. Each night people gathered around sundown (roughly 9:30 p.m. that time of year). On night one there was a sparse crowd of fifteen to twenty—a mix of men and women, some with children in tow. Some had clearly visited the Marfa Dairy Queen for frosty snacks before stopping for the evening's entertainment. The night was cloudy and visibility was limited. At first there appeared to be some lights across the desert and the crowd became excited. Unfortunately, I could not discern what they were, even using high-powered binoculars.

The second night was very clear and a larger crowd (over thirty people) inhabited the viewing platform. About 10:15 p.m., lights appeared on the horizon. The other visitors and I saw them very clearly. They were bright white orbs that gave the sensation of moving toward our location, but disappearing as they reached the edge of the desert near the viewing platform. The lights would then reappear on the horizon and start moving again, sometimes in odd patterns, sometimes changing colors and sometimes moving quite slowly, as if someone were walking across the desert carrying a lantern or flashlight. The crowd cooed as if watching fireworks. Children became excited and all jockeyed for better views.

Bolstered by the second evening's events, I bribed my spouse and son with Dairy Queen treats to return with me on the third night. Sure enough the lights appeared again. The movement patterns were somewhat different this time and I was convinced that the colors were different than on the second night that I visited. At first, it appeared that I was watching a car back down a mountain in the distance, but there are no roads or paths in the mountains that flank the desert floor. The mountains in this range contain jagged rock outcroppings, far too rugged for even a four-wheeler to traverse. The strange lights then appeared to randomly dance across the desert floor, until we finally tired and returned to our hotel for the evening.

So, what are these lights that I and thousands of others have witnessed? There are nearly as many explanations of the ghost lights as there are people who have observed them. The lights were first noticed by cowboys in 1883, and were assumed to be the campfires of Native American scouting parties in the Chinati Mountains. Two universities in Texas (Texas State University and the University of Texas at Dallas) have conducted scientific observations. One possible explanation is that the lights are a by-product of meshing hot and cold air in the high desert (the desert near Marfa sits at an elevation of over four thousand feet). The UT-Dallas team correlated light activity with the volume of traffic on Highway 67, a surprisingly busy two-lane road that connects the towns of Marfa and Alpine. Other scientists have hypothesized that the lights are quick fires caused by methane gas escaping from the ground. Others claim that they are reflections from luminescent phosphorous minerals in the desert, or a phenomenon known as "ball lightning," itself an unexplained phenomenon.

None of these explanations has been scientifically verified. Most of the observers are quick to point out that the lights were first witnessed in the 1800s. Moreover, the lights are seen year round, even in winter when warm air masses are scarce in the high desert. Attempts to locate methane gas leaks in the area have been fruitless and phosphorous minerals are not found in the Chihuahuan Desert. Absent a clear explanation for the phenomenon, a bewildering variety of different paranormal theories have emerged to explain the phenomenon.

Ghosts, evil spirits, witches, and pixies have all been offered as supernatural explanations for ghost lights throughout history. Ghost hunters are likely to argue that they are the souls of the deceased who are caught in limbo between two worlds. Perhaps the most popular explanation for the Marfa lights is that they are ghosts of conquistadors, condemned to wander the desert for eternity. One particularly spooky theory provided to me by a middle-aged woman on my second night at the center is that the lights are alien atmosphere probes. The aliens are sampling our atmosphere for air quality, chemical composition, the presence of viruses, and so forth—all a prelude to an invasion. They test all the time, but we can only see them at night. Even cryptozoologists have an opinion: intelligent nocturnal flying creatures, in fact, living dinosaurs; pterosaurs to be specific.[7] I am personally rooting for the pterosaurs explanation.

Our Paranormal Culture

What Marfa, Texas, the *Queen Mary*, and Roswell, New Mexico, demonstrate is that the paranormal has become yet another source of entertainment available in the vast consumerist marketplace. Ideas that

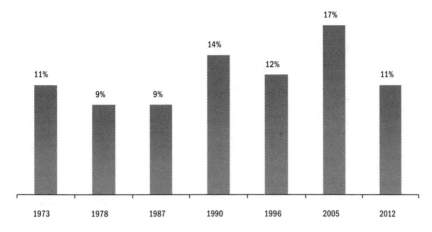

Figure 1.2. Percentage of U.S. Citizens Claiming UFO Experiences over Time (1973–2012) (1973 to 1990: Schuessler 2000; 1996: Newport 1997; 2005: Baylor Religion Survey 2005; 2012: National Geographic 2012)

used to be hidden away from view have now become part of American popular culture.[8]

While popular culture certainly points to a rise in paranormal belief, it can be difficult to document those changes with survey data, as different news polls and surveys have asked about paranormal subjects in many different ways over the years. It is possible that apparent differences are merely due to variation in sampling techniques, question wording, and interpretation. What we can state with confidence is that the paranormal is not going away any time soon. Since the 1970s the Gallup Organization and other polling firms have intermittently asked Americans if they have experienced a UFO sighting (see figure 1.2). In 2005, the Baylor Religion Survey asked respondents if they have "ever witnessed an object in the sky you could not identify," with 17% percent responding in the affirmative. More recently, a 2012 National Geographic Channel survey—conducted by Kelton Research—found that about 11% of Americans claimed a UFO sighting. We should not read too much into spikes and dips in the percent of respondents answering in the affirmative, as exact question wordings among these polls differ and they have different margins of error. Nevertheless, we can conclude that over the last forty years at least 10% of Americans claim to have had a UFO sighting at any given time.

Who Are They?

The seeming fascination the American public has for the paranormal is tempered by negative attitudes about the people who experience it. When friends, family, co-workers, or students learn that we have been on a Bigfoot hunt or have spent the night with ghost hunters in a haunted house, the two questions they generally ask are (1) Did you see a ghost/Bigfoot/UFO/etc.?, followed by some variant of (2) Who are these people anyway?

The second question is usually asked with a smirk or a giggle, but sometimes with concern. People wonder if we ever felt in danger when spending time with Bigfoot hunters in the woods or if we were afraid of UFO abductees because they might be "crazy." Such questions are asked because in our culture there are a number of prevailing attitudes about people who believe in or experience the paranormal. It seems that Americans want to explore the paranormal but also feel the need to reassure themselves and others that they maintain a healthy distance from it. Are people who claim UFO sightings uneducated, rural folks who do not know the difference between a satellite and a flying saucer? Are people who study astrology or visit psychics a bunch of overprivileged, silly "New Agers" from California?[9] Paranormal believers are often perceived as a little bit "nutty," if not completely out of their minds. Ohio congressman Dennis Kucinich learned as much after admitting to a UFO sighting during a 2007 presidential debate in Philadelphia. Publicly reporting a paranormal experience or belief invites scorn and concern for one's mental health.[10]

Unfortunately, media coverage of the paranormal generally does not allow viewers to either confirm or deny the validity of such stereotypes. When the local news covers a nearby UFO sighting or haunted house, the reporters often pick the strangest people they can find to interview— because they offer the most interesting sound bites. The local anchors wink and smirk at one another after the story, before wishing their viewers a good night. Certainly such stories are interesting, but with the exception of the most cursory of demographics, we learn little to nothing about the typical paranormal believer or experiencer.

The goal of this book is to answer simple questions that have never been adequately dealt with: Who are these people anyway? Does holding an unconventional belief, such as in the existence of Bigfoot, mean that one is unconventional in other attitudes and behaviors? Do those who claim UFO experiences fit the popular stereotypes? Does religion provide a set of beliefs and practices that prevent experimentation with the paranormal? Or does being religious mean that one has a general supernatural orientation to the world, leading to greater paranormal belief? How do people who attend paranormal conferences or purchase related books differ from those who simply hold a belief? Do people who believe in many paranormal things differ from those who are more selective? We have spent the last decade trying to answer these and many other questions about paranormal believers.

Chasing the Paranormal

The paranormal is frustratingly elusive. More than sixty-five years of reported UFO encounters have still not produced conclusive evidence of extraterrestrials.[11] Purported films, hair samples, photos, footprint casts, and eyewitness reports have failed to convince scientists that the woods are home to a giant ape.[12] Ghosts remain as mysterious as ever, despite tales older than the written word. Thankfully, *people* are the focus of our inquiry—and people are not as hard to find as ghosts or aliens. Consequently, we undertook two related investigations: survey research and qualitative field research.

First, we conducted several national surveys of the American public. In 2005, 2007, 2010, and 2014 we added a host of items about the paranormal to the Baylor Religion Survey (BRS); rather than the 2007 data, we largely use the data from the next wave, conducted in 2010 and published in 2011. The BRS is based on mixed-mode (combination telephone and mail) national random samples collected by the Gallup Organization. In 2014 and 2015 we also added items on paranormal beliefs to the annual Chapman University Survey of American Fears (CSAF).[13] Together these surveys contain the most thorough battery of questions concerning the paranormal ever administered to national samples of Americans.

Past research on the paranormal is informative, but such efforts are hampered by geography,[14] generalizability issues,[15] or a lack of recent data.[16] Our surveys asked respondents if they believe in the reality of things such as psychic phenomena, astrology, strange creatures, UFOs, haunted houses, fortune-telling, prophetic dreams, and the ability to talk to the dead. We also asked people if they have ever read a book on the paranormal, visited a New Age bookstore or website, or otherwise researched a host of topics ranging from "UFO sightings, abductions, or conspiracies," to "the prophecies of Nostradamus." Further, we determined the extent to which Americans actually experience the paranormal by finding out if respondents consulted their horoscopes, called a psychic hotline, met in person with a psychic or palm reader, visited or lived in a home they believe to be haunted, used a Ouija board, or witnessed a UFO.

With a few exceptions, the phenomena we have discussed so far are reported outside of established religions. As of yet we do not have a church of Bigfoot. Scientology notwithstanding, churches developed around UFO tales and psychic phenomena are relatively rare.[17] However, Americans do claim experiences with unexplained supernatural forces inside established religious settings as well. Some Americans claim to have been granted access to a special language from God that allows a more direct line of communication with the Almighty, a phenomenon known as "speaking in tongues," or "glossolalia." Others report guardian angels saving them from harm, experiencing a miraculous physical healing, or even hearing the voice of God speaking to them. Previous studies have been unable to resolve how such experiences are related to the "paranormal." In order to examine this connection, we also asked our survey respondents many general questions about religion, including extensive series about religious beliefs and experiences. All told, our respondents answered dozens of questions that provide a deeper understanding of their encounters and beliefs about the world beyond. With data from nearly six thousand Americans across these five surveys, we can carefully examine different views of the paranormal, as well as the social, moral, religious, political, and cultural differences that accompany these beliefs.

However, it is far too easy as academics to remain behind our desks and draw conclusions solely based on statistics and survey research. Paranormal experiences are highly personal, and often ephemeral and abstract in nature. We therefore felt it necessary to supplement our national survey data with field research, and throughout this book we relate these experiences and observations.

We hunt for the disruptive specter of Smith Hall and visit the Big Cypress Coffee House in Jefferson, Texas, which is purportedly haunted by 150 angry spirits, watching as a psychic collapsed to the ground, over-powered by the "presence of evil." We follow the North American Wood Ape Conservancy into the woods of east Texas one bitterly cold evening on a search for the elusive Sasquatch. Purported Bigfoot screams echo through the woods as NAWAC members attempt to lure the creature with their call blaster, and we huddle in the bushes wondering if we made a wise choice. We observe a support group for people who claim to have been abducted by aliens. Psychics warn us of future peril, palm readings trace our life lines, and astrologers read our stars at psychic fairs in Dallas and Orange County, California. We also explore extraor-dinary religious experiences, such as speaking in tongues or being pro-tected from harm by a guardian angel in churches in rural Texas and southern Appalachia.

By combining information from our national surveys with extensive fieldwork, we aim to provide balanced and in-depth information from which we can speak confidently and empirically about the paranormal in American culture.

Our Perspective on the Paranormal

Everybody has an angle. This is one of the primary reasons why experts in various fields may interpret the same occurrence in vastly different ways. For instance, in the case of a shooting in a public area, a psycholo-gist, a ballistics expert, a criminologist, a bystander, a victim, and an offender could all offer knowledge of the event—but each from a differ-ent vantage point. The ballistics expert will provide a detailed report on the direction from which bullets were fired based on the victim's wounds and damage to the physical surroundings. The psychologist will report on the trauma of the victim after the event and perhaps the inner tur-moil that spawned the gunman's actions. The criminologist will report on trends in gun violence and how these reflect changes in neighbor-hood composition, policing strategies, and poverty rates. The offender may apologize for, attempt to excuse, or even deny his actions, while the bystanders will provide differing accounts depending upon their proximity to the events (and perhaps their relationships to the victim or offender). With the exception of flagrant lies one might tell, none of these "experts" is incorrect. They simply have different concerns and areas of expertise, so their accounts of the same event differ.

In a similar vein, it is important that readers understand our perspective on the paranormal. Most books about Bigfoot, psychic phenomena, and other paranormal topics are focused upon presenting evidence for (and in rarer cases against) the reality of the phenomena in question. Bigfoot books often analyze the famous Patterson-Gimlin film, catalog sightings, or present the results of forensic tests of hair samples. UFO books recount sightings from pilots, police officers, and other figures believed to be credible witnesses.

Incredible though it may seem, to us the question of the factual, objective existence of paranormal phenomena is irrelevant to the purposes of studying belief in and experiences of the paranormal. An analogy can be drawn between the sociological study of the paranormal and the social scientific view of religion. When studying religion, it is relevant to ask how religious beliefs affect the lives of believers. Do these beliefs affect other attitudes and motivate specific patterns of action? What types of groups organize around specific beliefs, and how do these groups operate? How are beliefs maintained and reinforced? The literature in the sociology of religion is replete with studies addressing such questions. The question of the validity of religious beliefs is, however, a matter that simply cannot be addressed with social scientific methods.[18] No survey we administer or interview we conduct will prove God's existence or nonexistence. No amount of fieldwork will grant us a picture of heaven. We can only address the effects that believing in God and heaven have upon believers. We use this same approach with regard to the paranormal.

This is not a book about evidence for or against the paranormal. We are not ghost hunters, Bigfoot experts, parapsychologists, or UFO field investigators. We are sociologists. Our research perspective guides our fieldwork in a number of ways. It means we are not seeking or evaluating evidence about the existence of the paranormal. Even though we participate in many activities surrounding the paranormal, our primary interest is in the believers, how their beliefs are perceived by others, and how these beliefs influence the lives of those holding them. During our Bigfoot hunt in east Texas, NAWAC members found a strange imprint in a creek bed, which they believed to be the track of a Bigfoot. We are not animal track experts and cannot assess whether the track is evidence of an undiscovered ape. Rather, we monitored how members reacted to the find and what it meant to them. We remain outside of debates regarding the existence of the paranormal, and we recognize that regardless of what exists "out there" in the world, paranormal beliefs show remarkable staying power. It is the formation and maintenance of such beliefs and their consequences we are interested in.

The Plan of the Book

This book attempts to answer the question: Who believes in and experiences the paranormal? To address such a broad question, we examine the paranormal in several different ways. Specifically we assess survey data, draw on fieldwork observing and talking to participants in various aspects of the paranormal, and examine the narratives told and retold within various paranormal subcultures. Groups of people cannot be properly understood on a cultural level without examining the stories they tell.

People use an astounding array of terms to refer to beliefs about UFOs, astrology, psychic phenomena, ghosts, and the like. Some people refer to such beliefs as "New Age." Others prefer the term we frequently fall back on, "paranormal," or one of many others such as "occult," "mysticism," or "the supernatural." In chapter 2 we tackle the difficult issue of defining the paranormal. We visit two psychic fairs, where one can sample a wide array of the "products" of the paranormal in one easy shopping experience. By noting what is *not* present at the psychic fairs, we can better differentiate between religion and the paranormal.

We also find that there are two distinct types of beliefs that fall under the broader rubric of the paranormal. First, there are beliefs and experiences focused on *enlightenment*: personal, internal, spiritual growth. The clients of psychics, intuitives, fortune-tellers, astrologers, and the like seek to become better people either by learning something about the future, understanding the past, or perhaps by gaining supernatural insight into the present. Such people are often unconcerned with unequivocally proving the "reality" of their experience; so long as something works for them they are happy.

Second, others become involved in the paranormal as a form of *discovery*; they hope to find compelling evidence for the existence of a phenomena not currently recognized by institutional science. In recent years the media has latched on to this form of paranormal interest (witness the spate of television reality shows); ghost-hunting clubs, UFO spotting groups, and Bigfoot research organizations have sprung up around the country to fulfill the desire for paranormal discovery. Some people have already had a personal experience with Bigfoot or a UFO, and they seek concrete proof of its existence to prove to others that what they saw was real. Others dream of having their first experience with a giant, undiscovered ape by joining an expedition. Some seek discoveries because they hope to prove a new reality to science, while others are just out for an adventure. Many quest for both. Regardless of the specific subject in question, the importance of paranormal experiences for creating strong believers and subcultures is clear.

Armed with a basic understanding of American paranormal beliefs, we move to examining the characteristics of believers. In chapter 3 we address the common stereotypes about people who believe in the paranormal or claim related experiences. Unfortunately, information about the people who believe in or claim to have experienced the paranormal rarely goes beyond the anecdotal. To aid in our understanding of the paranormal we explore an example in depth, that of beliefs about UFOs and how they have evolved over time into tales of abduction, drawing on several years observing the activities of a support group for people who believe they have been abducted by evil alien beings and subjected to medical experiments onboard flying saucers. Are UFO abductees just sick? Are they strange, marginalized people who have nothing left to lose by claiming a bizarre experience or ascribing to a stigmatized belief system?

In chapter 4 we focus on ghost beliefs and experiences, returning to the scene of the interrupted lecture with a group of celebrity ghost hunters who attempt to investigate the occurrence. We also pay a visit to the Big Cypress Coffee House, run by Duane, a self-identified warlock who told us at dinner on the evening of our stay in the haunted location, "You will never be the same once the ghosts touch you." Once we were scratched, pushed, prodded, or spoken to by the ghosts, our lives would be changed, echoed the psychics present. We could have no more doubts, no more comfortable skepticism. A key benefit of field research is its ability to reveal important features of events and people that statistical techniques simply cannot capture by providing access to situational, experiential, and interactive factors of events as they occur. In this house of 150 ghosts we learned the importance of interpretation in paranormal experiences. According to the psychics present, we were under continual assault by spirits as the evening progressed. What we saw was quite enlightening.

In chapter 5 we explore the connection between supernatural beliefs available in organized religion and those of the paranormal. Social scientists have long speculated about the importance of the paranormal to mainstream religion in the United States.[19] The commonly used term "New Age" suggests a change in the way people practice religion, and scholars have documented an increasing shift from mainstream to unconventional forms of religious belief.[20] The true significance of the paranormal may depend upon who believes in those topics. If paranormal beliefs, and the consumption of related materials and services, are primarily confined to those already outside of the religious mainstream, then their effect on dominant religious traditions may be minimal. However, if, as part of a general cultural trend, members of all American religious groups are increasingly drawn to paranormal beliefs, goods, and services, then the movement may gradually draw people away from the mainstream. If the appeal of such "outside" materials depends upon the type of religious group in question,[21] then certain religious groups or traditions may see more of their members gravitate toward astrologers, psychics, and seers.

The paranormal consists of sets of ideas and experiences that have not yet been adopted, at least wholly, by the dominant religions in a given society. Paranormalism generally lacks the stability and organization that characterize successful religious groups, operating on the periphery of American religion, spreading through conferences, the media, and the Internet rather than through sermons and encyclicals. And yet the paranormal comprises a pool of concepts from which new religions can draw sets of ideas that may prove to be the content of future religions, something evident in religious histories.[22]

Many new forms of religion have sprouted from the fertile cultural soil of the paranormal, as in the 1950s when several self-styled prophets built new religions around claims that they could channel extraterrestrials.[23] A short-order cook and self-proclaimed philosopher by the name of George Adamski was one of the first to report contact with extraterrestrial beings. On November 20, 1952, Adamski claimed an extended meeting with a "man from space" near Desert Center, California. The humanoid alien indicated that he was part of a friendly landing party from Venus that had come to Earth to teach humans to be more peaceful.[24] Adamski's tales, outlined in a series of popular books with titles such as *Inside the Spaceships* and *Flying Saucers Farewell*, combined UFO tales with Christian themes. The Venusians, for example, told Adamski that Jesus was also Venusian. Other hopeful prophets soon followed suit. The Englishman George King built a new religion, the Aetherius Society, around his claim of having met Jesus aboard a flying saucer. Ruth and Ernest Norman went a step farther, claiming to be advanced space beings themselves and the reincarnations of key religious figures of Earth history, such as Mary Magdalene and Confucius. So many people were claiming to be in friendly communication with aliens during the 1950s and 1960s that they were given their own specific name—UFO contactees.

But can a religious movement succeed by combining paranormal ideas with concepts from conventional religion? There are reasons for skepticism. Many paranormal beliefs are in conflict with the teachings of established churches, an effort to force parishioners to choose between the two spheres.[25] For example, there is a rhetoric of "spiritual warfare" that pervades certain strands of Christianity. Some religious figures such as Billy Graham have cast the paranormal as Satan's work:

The [paranormal] is, in fact, another storm warning indicating man's search for "transcendence" without regard for righteousness. Whether it's Dianetics, est, Unity, Gaea, Transcendental Meditation, Taoism, ufology, crystalology, goddess worship, reincarnation, harmonics, numerology, astrology, holistic healing, positive thinking, or any of a hundred "conscious raising" techniques of our day, the modern age is on a search for some mystical "divine unity."[26]

On the other hand, it is possible that holding any supernatural belief will make people more likely to hold another, no matter what its origin. As we noted, we cannot "prove" or "disprove" the existence of God. The same is true of UFOs, and in a certain sense neither is more plausible than the other. Each requires faith and the willingness to suspend disbelief, and perhaps acceptance of one belief opens a person up to the other.[27] For example, is the Virgin Mary a "small step" from Sasquatch? Using surveys and building upon previous research,[28] we determine which religious traditions and groups in the United States are the most and the least receptive to paranormal ideas. A careful, nuanced approach is necessary to understand the relationship between conventional religious and paranormal beliefs and experiences. Specifically, there may be different connections between these spheres depending on the type of beliefs (both religious and paranormal) in question.[29] Who expresses greater belief in the paranormal, Jehovah's Witnesses or Unitarians? Who is most hostile to ideas outside of the Christian mainstream, Southern Baptists or Episcopalians? Do people who frequently attend church also see UFOs? Does having a literal view of the Bible preclude one from believing in Atlantis and ghosts? This chapter solves the riddle of how conventional religious beliefs and experiences interact with the paranormal.

In chapter 6 we begin to delve into people deeply interested in the various mysteries of the paranormal. For most the paranormal is a relatively small part of life—stories come up at family gatherings and parties as conversation starters or as sources of amusement. A person might watch the occasional episode of *Ghost Hunters*, go out to see the latest UFO invasion movie, or perhaps recall fondly an aunt who claims prophetic dreams. For others a paranormal topic (if not the paranormal in general) becomes an intense interest, a hobby, and for some even an obsession. Here we examine the world of people who devote themselves to paranormal "quests."

We engaged in extensive fieldwork observing the North American Wood Ape Conservancy, a nonprofit organization dedicated to finding the elusive primate. Unlike the popular image of Bigfoot hunters, many members of the NAWAC are highly educated people working in professional fields. We joined business professionals and a doctor for a weekend excursion to search for Sasquatch in the woods of southeast Texas. Despite their enthusiasm for the subject, members manage their Bigfoot beliefs carefully. The doctor is very cautious about revealing his activities to certain people. We asked if his colleagues knew what he did on the occasional weekend. He was emphatic that they not find out, as it could potentially cause some serious problems for him in the workplace. Such instances speak to the fact that while prevalent in popular culture, paranormal beliefs are still stigmatized by many Americans. Are people who research the paranormal, purchase its goods and services, or enter the field in the hunt for Bigfoot or ghosts really that "different" from those who do not?

In chapter 7 we address the issue of involvement in the paranormal from a different perspective. Individuals and specific groups can vary widely in approaches to the paranormal, even on the same subject. For instance, within the community of people interested in Sasquatch there is considerable speculation, on message boards, blogs, and in books, connecting Bigfoot to other paranormal mysteries. There are stories of Bigfoot creatures emerging from landed flying saucers. Some speculate that the outstanding elusiveness of the creature may be due to its ability to jump between dimensions, or perhaps it has psychic powers that it can use to confuse its pursuers. Paranormal author Nick Redfern has speculated that Sasquatch, the Loch Ness Monster, Mothman, and other mysterious creatures may be demonic entities that manifest to frighten people and leech their emotional energy.[30] Similarly, when we interviewed the late paranormal enthusiast Jon-Erik Beckjord, he argued that creatures such as Bigfoot were interdimensional entities.

Such claims are infuriating to the NAWAC. Most members we spoke to were singular in their interest: they care about Bigfoot and Bigfoot only. To them Sasquatch is merely an undiscovered ape. Indeed, the NAWAC's entire approach is based upon this understanding. Members place camera traps near rivers, natural pathways, and other animal "highways," hoping to catch a clear photo of the beast as it goes about its daily business. They play primate sounds in the woods because other monkeys and apes are known to respond to such calls. They leave pheromone chips high in trees to entice the creature to investigate the presence of a possible mate because this works for bears.

One member, David, did not hesitate to call things like UFOs, ghosts, and other psychic phenomena "stupid" flights of fancy. He stated that every time someone makes the Bigfoot subject look "kooky" by connecting it to UFOs or other strange things, their work becomes that much harder. Scientists will refuse to listen to them if they think the NAWAC are just a bunch of paranormal enthusiasts. Besides, why place camera traps if Bigfoot can elude such cameras with its psychic abilities? Why would an alien care about pheromone chips? And how will they ever bring a specimen to the doors of the Smithsonian if it can slip into another dimension at will?

In our travels and research we have encountered many who are the exact opposite of David and the NAWAC, people who are interested in exploring the paranormal in all of its varied forms. Laura, who claims to have frequented an alien mothership hovering above Earth is one such person. She is a UFO contactee and abductee who has been on alien craft numerous times. But that is not all she is. She also considers herself a Buddhist and occasionally attends a Roman Catholic Mass. She likes to read about Bigfoot and talk to witnesses, believes she may have had past lives, and routinely visits a Native American shaman. Laura is as experimental and diverse with her beliefs as David is singular and focused. People such as Laura are truly treating religion and the paranormal as a great spiritual cafeteria, piling onto their trays any and all beliefs that appeal to them.[31]

Robert Short, a UFO contactee and founder of the alien-based Blue Rose Ministry, claims to be able to "channel" messages from extraterrestrials. When he wishes to receive a communiqué, he sits in a chair, relaxes his body, and "opens himself up." Before long, his head rocks back and forth, his shoulders tense, and a deep voice emerges from his body, punctuated by occasional, bizarre noises. Short's experience is strikingly similar to a phenomenon that occurs in some Christian churches. Visit any particular Pentecostal church on Sunday, and you will witness members writhe, twist, and ultimately begin speaking in strange tongues, whispers, squeals, and other noises. They are not channeling messages from Venus. Speaking in tongues for these practitioners is a sign of deep devotion, and those who engage in "glossolalia" believe that God has gifted them with a special language, a direct line of communication with the Almighty. The difference lies in where those who have these experiences attribute the source—and how others view the validity of this source.

Chapter 8 again explores the contested ground between religion and the paranormal, such as beliefs and experiences that are closely connected to Christianity yet not fully accepted in many Christian settings. In addition to including thorough sets of questions on the paranormal, we asked extensive questions about perceptions of supernatural religious evil. Who believes Satan and demons are active forces on Earth? Who believes that humans can be possessed by the devil? Who fears an upcoming Armageddon? Sometimes such beliefs about evil coalesce into widespread panics, as occurred in the 1980s when the FBI began to receive reports from therapists across the country that their patients had "recovered" memories of hideous abuse perpetrated by secretive, underground Satanic cults.[32] The victims claimed to have witnessed animal and human sacrifices. Some reportedly were forced to kill their own children after being impregnated by cult members, and victims often alleged that high-ranking members of society, such as doctors, lawyers, and judges, were cult members. Around the same time, reports surfaced of Satanic cults using daycare centers as a source for children to abuse in their rituals.[33] A chorus of sociologists, psychologists, and some critical journalists exposed the claims as the latest outbreak of Satanic panic.[34] They noted the suggestive techniques used by therapists and a complete lack of physical evidence.[35] But before the hysteria died down, several accused Satanists were forced to endure long and costly trials to defend themselves. Obviously one did not have to believe in the reality of Satanic conspiracies to be impacted by them. Similar Satanic panics have emerged at periodic intervals in U.S. history, and in each case many innocent people have been significantly affected before the panics eventually quieted.[36] Chapter 8 profiles a man who was himself accused and criminally convicted of being the ringleader of a secretive, underground Satanic cult.

Reemerging from the darkness of Satanism tales, we explore religious experiences, showing that Pentecostals are among the least accepting of paranormal beliefs and experiences, and yet they are the most likely to claim other supernatural experiences—healings, glossolalia, and so forth—that outsiders would consider equally strange; however, for those not strongly tied to institutional religion through high levels of practice, claiming religious experiences and believing in the power of supernatural evil does indeed lead to higher levels of paranormal experiences. Chapter 8 provides an entrée into this normalized version of the paranormal—those supernatural experiences that are associated with the dominant religious traditions in American culture. We find out how many Americans claim such experiences, what they are like, and whether people who speak in tongues also report UFO sightings.

In the course of exploring the paranormal, we cover who believes in the paranormal, who has paranormal experiences, how the paranormal relates to mainstream religion, how paranormal beliefs vary by status subgroups, and the impact that such beliefs have upon individuals and society. Chapter 9 summarizes our findings and attempts to answer the question: What will happen to paranormal beliefs and experiences in the future? Our statistical data provides us with a key tool in this regard; we know who currently believes in the paranormal. By analyzing data on which societal groups are growing and receding, and which religious groups are facing growth or decline, we can predict whether paranormalism will increase or decrease in popularity in coming decades.

Our journey begins in the realm of all things psychic.

2

The Truth Is Within

Sometimes it is easier to recognize something than it is to define it. So it is with the loose association of beliefs, ideas, phenomena, and experiences variously labeled as "New Age," "paranormal," "supernatural," "occult," "unexplained phenomena," "metaphysics," "pseudoscience," "mysticism," and a host of other terms. Depending upon one's personal definition, crystal balls, Bigfoot, ghosts, and palm reading are similar things; by other definitions they are vastly different. Adding to the confusion, researchers and retailers often label the same phenomena using different terms than do the general public. For example, scholars of religion often use the term "New Age" to refer to a social movement that started in the 1960s, which focused on the development of personal enlightenment and freedom from conventional thinking and religion.[1] To the bookstores, New Age is simply a section in which employees shelve books on ghosts, the Loch Ness Monster, UFOs, psychic powers, Atlantis, and the like.

We do not wish to add to such confusion here by coming up with new terminologies, but we hesitate to use a term such as "New Age." First of all, the term refers to a specific movement that emerged at a particular time. Further, it suggests that our phenomenon of interest is something "new." This is hardly the case.

Consider the following tales:

Auxerre, France

Germanus and a few of his friends decided to have a little adventure, traveling the region around his town on foot so he could get to know the landscape and people better. Perhaps unwisely, they chose to begin their travels in the dead of winter and found themselves in a rural area with no place to stay on a bitterly cold evening. Running out of options, they entered a dilapidated building on the side of the road, which locals believed to be haunted. The building's fearsome reputation did not bother Germanus, and he quickly drifted off to sleep. One of his fellow travelers was reading when he shouted an alarm. A specter was slowly rising up through the floor. At the same time, the walls were pelted by a shower of pebbles. The assailant was nowhere in sight. The alarmed traveler begged Germanus to protect him from the ghost. A deeply religious man, Germanus invoked the name of Jesus and commanded the spirit to provide its name and purpose. It told Germanus that he and a friend had been chained together and killed as punishment for some unrevealed crime, their bodies denied proper burial. The next day the men dug at a spot identified by the spirit and found two bodies tied together with chains. Germanus arranged for a proper burial, and the haunting ceased.

New York City

John was a charming and successful man, widely known as a person of great achievement, calm temperament, and careful reasoning. After the death of his wife, he became "withdrawn from general society; I was laboring under the great depression of spirits."[2] In his grief, he began reading about death and the afterlife, and sought the council of mediums. He soon began attempting to contact spirits himself, experiencing and meticulously documenting anomalous events such as the following:

> During the last illness of my revered old friend Isaac T. Hopper, I was a good deal with him, and on the day when he died I was with him from noon till about seven o'clock in the evening. I then supposed he would live yet for several days, and at that hour I left to attend my circle, proposing to call again on my way home. About ten o'clock in the evening, while attending the circle, I asked if I might put a mental question. I did so, and I knew that no person present could know what it was, or to what subject even it referred. My question related to Mr. Hopper, and I received for answer through the rappings, as from himself, that he was dead! I hastened immediately to his house, and found it was so. That could not have been by any one present, for they did not know of his death, they did not know my question, nor did they understand the answer I received. It could not

have been the reflex of my own mind, for I had left him alive, and thought he would live several days. And what it was but what it purported to be, I can not imagine.[3]

Seattle, Washington

Sara and her husband moved into a rental house near the University of Washington, sharing with an old friend, Jason, to save money. Sara fell in love with a room on the main floor; Jason happily took one of two rooms on the upper floor. About a month after they moved in, strange things started to happen. Sara was the first to get up in the mornings. Oftentimes while getting ready for work, she would hear the unmistakable sounds of someone walking down the stairs. The footsteps ceased at the landing, but no one was ever there. Sara learned to ignore the sounds, becoming flustered only when her two cats would on occasion stare and hiss at the stairs. She even put up with the lights in her bedroom, which sometimes switched on and off by themselves. The experiences were irritating but never menacing.

Jason was not so lucky. He worked a swing shift at a warehouse pulling orders for grocery stores. One evening he arrived home at around 11 p.m. and went up to bed. He had just turned off his light when he felt a weight at the end of the bed. In the darkness a hazy form slowly took shape near Jason's feet. What looked like an old man with a hunched back was facing away from Jason, its head in its hands, seemingly distressed. As if it could feel Jason's eyes upon its back, the "man" turned and looked directly at him. Jason shrieked upon seeing the wrinkled, balding visage with completely black eyes, and he flipped on the light. The spirit faded away, but an impression remained for several minutes where it had been sitting on the bed. Jason slept with a light on after that.

Although ghosts have been reported for at least three thousand years, the basic elements of such stories often remain the same, reflecting seemingly timeless human concerns.[4] The belief that a ghost may result from a violent death or improper burial, or that the spirit of a relative might appear to warn of impending danger were favorites of medieval times and are still with us today. Indeed, the tale of Germanus occurred in 488 CE and the Germanus in question was bishop of Auxerre at the time, and is now a Roman Catholic saint. His traveling companions consisted of clerics under his command.[5] Barring such details (and the anachronistic name), this story could easily pass for one that would be breathlessly reported on the latest television installment of *Ghost Hunters*.[6]

Meanwhile, the second story, concerning John W. Edmonds, highlights some noteworthy aspects of the religious movement that came to be known as "Spiritualism" in the United States. Edmonds was an accomplished lawyer and politician, elected to both the state house and senate, and later appointed to serve on the New York Supreme Court. Yet, after the death of his spouse and numerous spiritual encounters, he was forced from public service because he became an advocate for Spiritualism, for which he received considerable public condemnation—but also support from others—reiterating the simultaneously loved and loathed position of paranormalism in American culture. The above story is one of many experiences Edmonds recounts in his book making the case for the reality of spiritual phenomena and supporting the burgeoning movement sparked by the infamous "rappings" during the séances of the Fox sisters.[7] Edmonds was a socially respectable firsthand witness, convert, and proselytizer for the movement.

Drawing on and then contributing to traditions of mesmerism, Swedenborgianism, Theosophy, transcendentalism, and New Thought, the Spiritualist movement popularized two enduring aspects of paranormalism: séances and professional mediums.[8] Edmonds was one of the most respected evangelists of the Spiritualist movement, which was at the height of its popularity in antebellum America.[9] Yet even a person of Edmonds's standing was not above the penalties for publicly expressing belief in what would today be called the paranormal. The judge's publication of *Spiritualism* (1853) led his own party to ostracize him from the judiciary, choosing not to renominate him for the state supreme court later that year, as he made plain in a letter to the *New York Times*, arguing it was a case of religious persecution:

> I have your note in allusion to my position as a candidate before the Nominating Convention, in which you apprise me that while it was freely and fully admitted that my ability, integrity and judgment were beyond

dispute, and that my judicial reputation was unimpaired, the prejudice against my spiritualism, alone, was noticed as a reason for declining to nominate me. I am not at all surprised at this. I am fully aware of the strong prejudice there is in the public mind against spiritualism in all its aspects. The manner in which my religious faith has been . . . assailed in the press, in the pulpit, and in private conversation, has left me no room to be ignorant of the state of public feeling on the subject. . . . I have not for a moment been unaware that I was thereby hazarding my position on the bench.[10]

Despite the condemnation and derision Judge Edmonds received in response to his advocacy for Spiritualism, upon his death in 1874, the *Times* noted in his obituary that "[t]he procession that followed the remains to the grave was one of the largest ever seen in this city."[11] Although Spiritualism as a formal movement lost steam with failed attempts by parapsychology to bring spiritual contact into the mainstream of twentieth-century science, the ideas championed by Spiritualists still haunt American culture.

It is very likely that you have heard stories like these before. Most people have a ghost story, if not more than one: an aunt, uncle, parent, grandparent, or other relative who claims a ghost sighting as a child, or a best friend who insists his home was haunted. Some of us have seen a ghost ourselves. As testament to the ubiquity of such tales, the last story above is from the first author of this book, when Christopher and his wife, Sara, shared a home with their friend Jason near the University of Washington in 1990.[12]

The Paranormal

Ghosts may be ever-present, but they are anything but new. Nor is astrology, or the belief in psychic phenomena, or even belief in the possibility of humanoid beings living in the woods. Many such beliefs stubbornly persist on the edges of society, believed in by many but never fully accepted. These beliefs often violate our taken-for-granted understanding of the "nuts and bolts" working of the world and mundane experience. They are not normal, but *paranormal*.

But what is paranormal? This question is remarkably difficult to answer, not least of all because the subject matter is often inherently ambiguous. Take ghosts, which exist somewhere between life and death, present and absent, material and ethereal, present and past, human and inhuman, and so on. Further complicating matters is the fact that, properly (in our view) defined, the "paranormal" is a cultural category that can shift across time and place, rather than being a fixed property of particular beliefs and experiences. Academics studying the paranormal have tended to focus on the rejection of the paranormal from institutional science.[13] This is an important aspect of the paranormal to be sure, but also omits a critical feature of what becomes classified as "paranormal" by overlooking the role of institutional religions in defining what counts (in their view) as legitimate or illegitimate supernatural beliefs and experiences.

We can take some cues on this front from the man most responsible for creating the category of the paranormal as we know it today: Charles Fort. Fort was a voracious reader of newspapers and scientific journals, and he scoured publications from all over the world in search of anomalies. His first book centrally uses the religious metaphor of damnation to describe the realm of culture that would come to be known as the paranormal. *The Book of the Damned* amalgamates a variety of anomalies, which share the characteristics of rejection (damnation) by institutional science.[14] Fort opens the text with: "A procession of the damned. By the damned, I mean the excluded. . . . The power that has said to all these things that they are damned, is Dogmatic Science."[15] The capitalization and designation of "Dogmatic Science" reveals Fort's view that institutional science shares far more with religion than its advocates would care to admit. Or, more succinctly, "Positivism is Puritanism."[16] All of it merely accumulated acts of "Scientific Priestcraft."[17] Better yet, in his inimitable, contrarian style, Fort told readers: "I shut the front door upon Christ and Einstein, and at the back door hold out a welcoming hand to little frogs [falling from the sky] and periwinkles."[18]

In short, "what Fort invented was our modern view of the paranormal . . . he tore down the hallowed traditions of religion and science."[19] In defining this realm of inquiry, Fort makes a remarkably sociological observation:

That anything that tries to establish itself as a real, or positive, or absolute system, government, organization, self, soul, entity, individuality, can so attempt only by drawing a line about itself, or about the inclusions that constitute itself, and damning or excluding, or breaking away from, all other "things."[20]

Fort is unmistakably correct. In essence, institutional science, as the cultural arbiter of material reality, defines what is "natural," and therefore within its investigative jurisdiction, and also by contrast what is "supernatural."[21]

In addition, institutional science demarcates what topics and methods are considered legitimate within its boundaries by marking unwelcome practices, beliefs, and ideas that claim to be scientific as "pseudoscience," which has been defined as "any cognitive field that, though nonscientific, is advertised as scientific."[22] Rooted in the Popperian tradition of the philosophy of science, a central feature of what institutional science advocates define as pseudoscience is non-falsifiability.[23] Thus, there are two ways that institutional science plays a role in creating the category of the paranormal: first by defining what is "natural," but also by damning beliefs and practices that claim to be scientific, such as creationism or cryptozoology, as beyond the pale of what is officially considered science. The examples of creationism and cryptozoology are instructive, showing that what gets banished from science can be taken up by advocates as either religion or the paranormal, depending on whether the rejected cultural domain falls within the bounds of organized religion or not.[24]

This leads to the second, typically overlooked dimension of how the paranormal gets defined as a cultural category. Despite academics' focus on the importance of the role of science in defining the paranormal, there are two social institutions doing boundary work damning the paranormal. For topics designated as supernatural, organized religions hold (and compete for) cultural legitimacy. Social movements based on supernatural beliefs and (someone's) intensive physiological and cognitive experiences, particularly trances, visions, and voices, must determine and adjudicate which supernatural beliefs and intensive experiences are to be considered "true," and by contrast, which are to be considered, at best "false," and at worst "the work of the devil."[25]

An area where religion and the paranormal continually collide is in the realm of mysticism and extraordinary sensory experiences. In effect, science and "mainline" religions demarcate contemporary automatisms and "enthusiastic" experiences as supernatural and false; that is, not truly of supernatural origin. As scholar of religious experiences Ann Taves notes, "*Supernaturalists*, who could be secularizers when it came to false religion, understood true religion as particular, exclusivist, and revealed."[26] Meanwhile, sectarian and new religious movements attempt to harness the power of intensive physiological and psychological experiences, choosing particular varieties justified as true and condemning experiences other than those validated by the group as "of the devil."[27] Because higher-tension religious groups—those that impose stricter behavioral and ideological restrictions on their members—apply theological frames to the problem of what counts as "true religion," sectarian groups demonize such experiences occurring outside their tradition. For instance, in 2007, roughly one out of five Americans agreed with the statement: "Certain paranormal phenomena (such as UFOs and Ouija boards) are the work of the devil." As a result, demonology often becomes a cultural borderland between religion and the paranormal. Thus, where "supernatural" (or "superstition") and "pseudoscience" are damnable categories for science, the "occult" and analogous terms are damnable categories for religion.[28]

In contrast to defining religious and paranormal phenomena as the same, as many scientists do, or denying the similarities between "paranormal" and religious experiences, as many religious groups do, we instead advocate a *bounded affinity* theory of the paranormal that incorporates both the similarities between religious and paranormal beliefs and experiences, along with the cultural distinctions drawn by organized religious groups. The social processes demarcating experiences as natural or supernatural in origin, as well as those subsequent within religious subcultures designating such phenomena as true or false (or "of the devil") mark a trail to what gets considered paranormal. From this perspective it is clear that the "paranormal" can be most usefully defined by accounting for its relations to both institutional science and religion.[29]

Despite our jest about bookstores earlier, the analogy works well here.[30] If a prospective book buyer wants to read about a phenomenon that is at least partially understood and recognized by science, she should visit its respective section of the bookstore. The health and medicine section will have books on heart health, chemotherapy, and other topics "owned" by modern medicine. For information on investing, taxes, market conditions, or retirement, one must wander to the economics or business shelves. But if our shopper wants to read about a topic not currently recognized by scientists, she must hunt the fiction aisles for horror, fantasy, or science fiction, or browse the bookstore's New Age and religion stacks. If the topic of interest is the resurrection of Jesus, healing through prayer, being "saved," or another concept closely associated with Christianity or another world religion, the religion stacks are the best bet. Those scientifically dubious topics that are not tightly connected to mainstream religion, such as crystal balls, ghosts, and UFOs, fill the New Age shelves.[31] Here one also finds books that might belong in another section were their topics to someday become accepted by science.[32] Books on the healing power of crystals are consigned to the New Age section, waiting for a scientific discovery to facilitate a call-up to the legitimacy big leagues in the medicine section. Volumes that promote the power of positive thinking in acquiring fame and fortune sit here also, rather than in the business stacks.

Following what retailers already know, we group together a wide assortment of beliefs and experiences under a single banner labeled "paranormal." Such beliefs and experiences are dually rejected—not accepted by science *and* not typically associated with mainstream religion in the United States.[33] Thus, the belief that a crystal ball can foretell the future would be paranormal in nature, as would be the belief that an unidentified ape roams the Northwest woods.[34] Both of these beliefs refer to unexplained phenomena and neither is associated with mainstream religion in the United States.[35] Belief that Jesus Christ was resurrected from the dead would not qualify as part of the paranormal per this definition, since Jesus is associated with the majority religion in the United States—Christianity. The distinction is important, but we do not make it for theological reasons. Previous research and theory by sociologists, as well as our own research, indicate that believers *themselves* make this distinction. We realize that some people may combine elements from organized religion and paranormalism, but overall the

Paranormal Phenomena	Beliefs, practices, and experiences that are not recognized by science and *not* associated with mainstream religion
	Examples: *Extrasensory perception, ghosts and spirit phenomena, astrology, crystal therapy, belief that extraterrestrials have visited earth, Bigfoot*
Religious Phenomena	Beliefs, practices, and experiences that are not recognized by science but associated with mainstream religion
	Examples: *Belief in the divinity of Jesus, belief in the power of prayer, faith healing, Satan and demons*

Figure 2.1. Definitions of the Paranormal and Religious Phenomena

distinction remains relevant. Figure 2.1 summarizes the categories of religious and paranormal phenomena.

As we will show, this definition of the paranormal makes sense of the empirical relationships between religiosity and paranormalism, and explains why different aspects of religion can hold negative, positive, or curvilinear relationships to paranormalism, depending on the cultural and empirical contexts under examination. This approach also recognizes and highlights the importance of the "paranormal" for disciplines engaged in studies of religion by locating each in relation to the intensive physical and psychical experiences that lie at the heart of both. Put simply, in contemporary Western societies, science delineates natural and supernatural, then religious groups divide religion from the paranormal.

Unfortunately, definitions are never perfect, and the paranormal rests on ever-shifting sands. Does a book on aromatherapy belong in the "self help" section or is it part of the paranormal? It depends on whom you ask. Does a book about visions of the Virgin Mary end up in the paranormal section or religion section? It often depends upon who published it or the perspective taken toward the material. A book from a Christian publisher that uses the Marian visions at Lourdes as a testimonial will be filed with the religion books. An author who discusses visions of the Virgin Mary as another manifestation of the same phenomena that produces faeries and ghosts, or that deemphasizes the Christian aspects of the Marian visions, may find her book filed under the paranormal.[36] Indeed, books about angels are routinely found in *both* the religion and paranormal sections.[37] It is also worth noting that advocates from some paranormal subcultures will be more closely connected to science or religion by virtue of how they frame their beliefs and practices. Many of the Bigfoot hunters we spent time with saw their pursuits as squarely scientific, while some the psychics or mediums we shadowed saw their practices and experiences as more akin to religion.[38]

We must also be clear that labeling of a belief, practice, or experience as "paranormal" is not meant here as judgmental or pejorative, at least on our part. It is possible that extrasensory perception (ESP) is a legitimate phenomenon that science is simply too stubborn to recognize.[39] It is also possible that the many dedicated Bigfoot hunters will one day capture the beast, moving it from paranormal status to nature status in one fell swoop. But until and unless such things occur, Bigfoot and ESP will continue to inhabit the fringes. To express belief in such phenomena in certain circles may prompt scorn or concern about one's judgment and even mental health.

I (Chris) took a tentative step into the world of the paranormal on a Saturday afternoon in December, to experience its dizzying array of beliefs and practices.

December: Anaheim, California

The Learning Light Foundation might best be described as a New Age learning center. The organization was founded in 1962 by a former Methodist minister named Walter Tipton. Disillusioned by organized religion, Tipton began seeking out "like-minded individuals" to gather for philosophical discussions about the meaning of life. At first, Walter and his wife, Lola, hosted groups at their home in Orange, California. The meetings quickly grew too large for their home and the group began gathering in a rented house. Membership continued to grow. In 1972, the group moved into a former Church of the Nazarene in Anaheim.[40] The group's mission is "[t]o provide quality education, training, and research for individuals to develop their fullest potential on all levels."[41]

One of the educational opportunities provided by Learning Light is its biweekly Holistic Health & Spiritual Fair. The fair provides the opportunity for the general public to attend free classes, purchase items from vendors, book a healing session with an "energy worker," or purchase a fifteen-minute session with one of the "readers" in attendance.

A Spiritual Cafeteria

Readers at the Holistic Health & Spiritual Fair claimed to provide services of great value, such as knowledge about one's place in life, information about what the future holds, guidance for personal transformation, and spiritual meaning. Clearly, these are some of the same benefits offered by religious denominations, even if they might be referred to in different terms. Yet access to the benefits provided by a religious denomination often requires membership in the organization or at least some commitment to its beliefs. The paranormal, on the other hand, has a strong focus upon personal spiritual transformation over devotion to a particular belief or practice.[42] Personal fulfillment and exploration trumps singular commitment.[43] Those interested in the psychic realm can freely select from a variety of "tools" in their hunt for transformative experiences and may explore their interests via the media, by attending conferences, lectures, and fairs, or by developing relationships with psychics.[44] It is as if some of those involved in the paranormal are walking the line at a spiritual cafeteria and piling on those beliefs and practices that most interest them at the moment.

An astounding buffet of products and services were available at the fair. I walked in the side door of the converted church, paid my $2 entry fee and wandered into the Learning Light Bookstore. Along one wall rested dozens of books about crystals, various forms of healing, angels, the mystical powers of dolphins, channeling, and how-to guides for developing psychic gifts. In the center of the room was a small table displaying crystals of differing sizes and price points. The strong smell of incense wafted through the building. Exiting the bookstore, I entered the sanctuary of the former church. Light shone into the room from a stained glass window of an angel high on the wall. Arrayed around the edges of the room were vendors selling various forms of incense and oils, more books and crystals, and various CDs and books on psychic powers and healing.

In the center of the room was a grid of sixteen tables. Some were empty, others occupied by the readers present at the event (see figure 2.2). Some sat alone, patiently awaiting their next clients. Others were in the midst of readings—some with their eyes closed, some shuffling

Angelic/Higher Guide Readings	The reader claims to communicate with angels or other spiritual beings that are attached to or protecting the client.
Animal Communication	A reader who specializes in psychic communication with animals. Clients may bring a photo of their current pet and ask for help in understanding its moods or behavior. Or they may ask the reader to communicate with a beloved dead pet.
Astrology	Astrology assumes that the position of stars and planets at the point of one's birth will have effects throughout life. The reader provides insight into one's personality and information on how the current position of stars and planets will impact the near future.
Aura Readings	An aura is purportedly an energy field surrounding a person that can be viewed by psychics. It is believed that the colors of the aura will reveal characteristics of the individual.
Channeling	A channeler claims to receive or "channel" messages from discarnate entities, such as spirits, angels or elementals. Some channelers will claim to speak in the voice of the entity, others will simply relay any messages received.
Clairaudience	A reader who claims to be able to "hear" voices, music, or other messages from the spirit world. A clairaudient may claim to hear the voice of a dead relative when conducting a reading.
Clairvoyance	The reader claims to receive psychic knowledge about the past, present, and future through touch or feeling.
Oracle Card Readings	Unlike tarot card decks (see below) which follow a set structure, oracle card decks are idiosyncratic, with varying numbers of cards and differing themes. For example, the reader may utilize an oracle deck that consists of images of different angels. The reader intuits the meaning of each card as it is drawn.
Past Life Readings	A past-life reader claims to be able to intuit previous incarnations of the client. It is thought that difficulties in previous lives may cause problems or "imbalances" in this one.
Psychic/Medium	The reader who claims to receive information about the client's past, present, and/or future through supernatural means, generally without the use of tarot cards, crystal balls, or other accessories.
Psychometry	The reader relays psychic impressions received from an object, such as a family heirloom. The reader may, for example, provide details about the meaning of the object to a deceased person.
Reiki	A massage/relaxation technique in which the masseuse alternates between physically massaging the client and manipulating the client's "energy."
Runes	The reader uses stone "runes" to intuit the client's past, present, and/or future. The client may draw a single stone from a bag or the reader may throw the runes and interpret the resulting pattern.
Tarot	The reader uses a set of cards with stylized characters such as "The Fool" and "Death." The client or reader shuffles the deck and lays out a number of cards in a spread (numbers vary). The reader interprets the meaning and layout of the cards.

Figure 2.2. The New Age Cafeteria: Services Available at the Holistic Health & Spiritual Fair in Anaheim, California (December 2015)

through decks of cards, an older woman in the back grasping her client's hands and loudly speaking in a strange voice. Many readers uti-
lized objects to facilitate their readings including tarot cards, runes,
astrological charts, and oracle cards (similar to tarot decks but without
suits). Others retrieved information about their client's past, present,
or future by channeling discarnate entities, contacting the individual's
"spirit guide" and/or guardian angels, communicating with dead relatives, reading one's aura, or, in two cases, even psychically contacting
the client's pet(s).

I immediately sat down in front of an unoccupied reader, who kindly
informed me that readings were booked by buying tickets in another
room. In the ticket room, a bulletin board displayed details about each
of the readers. I booked readings with Shelley, whose skills were listed
as "psychic/medium, intuitive Tarot, pet psychic"; Gera, who offered
"angel readings, pet readings, mediumship"; and Dee, listed simply as a
"medium-channel." I paid $25 each for readings with Shelley and Gera.
Dee, the channel, was a little more expensive, at $40 for a fifteen-minute
reading. The cashier provided a ticket for each, with a sticker affixed to
it listing the appointment time.

Ichabod the Spirit Guide and a Dog Named Fritz

Having experienced psychic readings before, I knew that the readers
would ask me what topics I wanted to discuss. I decided to come armed
with two. First, despite years of experience participating in paranormal
excursions of various types, I have never had an unexplained experience.
Do ghosts not like me? Have I shut myself off to UFOs and Bigfoot? I
planned to go straight to the "source" and find out why the paranormal
and I cannot get along.

For my second topic I decided to ask about the family dog. Three
years previous, we had adopted a German shepherd from a local rescue
organization. The dog did not have a name or a history. He had been
found in a local wooded area without a collar and with burns on his legs
and ears. The organization's best guess was that he was about two years
old at the time of the adoption. We named the dog "Bennett" and he
instantly bonded with myself, my wife, and our two sons. Unfortunately,
we are the only four people Bennett bonded with—should anyone else

enter the home, he will sneak behind that person and bite him or her on the back of the leg. He also seems to intensely dislike both small dogs and cats. Two of my readers, Gera and Shelley, offered "animal communication" services. I decided to ask about our mysterious dog and its troublesome habits.

Shelley, a woman of about sixty with short, auburn-colored hair and a slightly nervous disposition, was my first appointment. I sat down and introduced myself. She turned a small egg timer to fifteen minutes and asked me what I wanted to talk about. I decided to start by talking about Bennett. She asked me what was my concern and I told her that he was biting people outside of his inner circle and had an unknown past. "Do you have a photo?" she asked next. I pulled out my phone and scrolled to a photo of Bennett. She held it in her hands for a few moments and then began making a series of observations.

It seems that Bennett previously belonged to a "man who drank" who did not provide him with a collar. The man did not abuse Bennett, but did frequently leave him in the yard alone. The dog eventually tired of this neglect and ran away from the man, which is why he was found in the park. Bennett is really grateful to our family, she said, and wants to make sure that we are protected, which is why he tries to drive others from the house.

Shelley had not intuited that Bennet had been in a fire, nor that he had a problem with small animals. I decided to ask her about those issues. "Ahh . . . ," she said and thought for a moment. Bennett had been in a wildfire after he had escaped, which explains his burns. He does not like small dogs because a poodle used to live next door to him and "teased him mercilessly." We might want to "use an animal specialist to try and get him some help," she continued, and "make sure to have a long talk with him before any visitors enter the house to tell him that person is OK."

Shelley appeared to bore of talking about Bennett and handed me a deck of tarot cards. I shuffled the deck and handed it back to her. There was a long pause, followed by a line of questioning about my family. She began to lay the cards out on the table, face up in rows of six. Shelley would turn over a card, ask a question and turn over another. Once she completed one row, she began another on top of the previous.

"So do you have two or three kids?"

"I have two."

"Is the youngest one a girl?"

"No."

"So he's a boy then?"

"Yes."

"And the older one?"

"He's a boy."

"OK. I see that the younger one is really into sports?"

"Not really."

"Well he will have some interest in Little League next year."

The egg timer sounded and I moved on to my second appointment.

Dee a short, thin, blonde woman in her sixties is a medium-channel whom I had noticed throughout the morning as she drifted into trances before her clients. Dee told me that she planned to channel an ascended master to discuss any issues I wanted to raise. I decided to ask Dee about my inability to have paranormal experiences. Is there anything the "other side" could tell me about why?

Dee smiled and informed me that she was going to start "channeling her guides." "I am going to close my eyes," she said, "and pretty soon it will no longer be me that is speaking." The transition from "Dee" to whomever she claimed to channel was not abrupt or pronounced. Her eyes drifted shut, her mouth took on a slight grin, and she began speaking in a voice and cadence indistinguishable from her own. Once I figured out that I was speaking to the ascended master and had exchanged a few pleasantries, she began to discuss my paranormal "problem."

"You do have a block," she said, "but the reason is very, very far-fetched. You are going to find this interesting. What is going on is that you have simultaneous lives going on. In your dream state you actually do a lot of your work. So when you are trying to do it here, it is too easy. Your brain sets up this block as a challenge. You want to challenge yourself."[45] Surprisingly, Dee/the ascended master immediately followed this revelation with: "But this could all be hogwash. Take it with a grain of salt. If it doesn't resonate, find something else."

Our time nearly up, Dee/the ascended master told me that I would, indeed, experience the paranormal some day (in my waking life). Soon

I will become aware of my own personal spirit guide. He is a powerful wizard who will lead me on this journey, she finished.

For my final reading of the day with Gera, a pet psychic and angelic reader, I split my time between the two issues I had elected to raise with the psychics. We started by talking about the family dog, Bennett. I told her I had a dog with some problematic behaviors and an unknown past. She asked for Bennett's name, the type of dog he is, and what he looks like. Armed with this information Gera closed her eyes and "tuned in" to Bennett.

"Oh . . . he's already talking to me. He just said hi to me. German shepherds are so smart."[46]

Gera giggled and exchanged a few pleasantries with Bennett. Finally, she asked what Bennett was doing that made us unhappy. I told her about his tendency to nip extended family members.

"Yeah. So . . . So . . . territory is important to him. Do you have any other dogs?"

"No."

"No. All right. All right. He's so grateful to your family for rescuing him that he feel like you are his pack. All right. So he's protecting you. So now I need to tell him that its all right. . . . 'Bennett . . . it's all right to relax your protection for Chris' family . . .'"

Eyes still closed, Gera giggled again.

"Oh . . . got it. . . . OK. . . . He says. 'You're not in charge. You need to be the alpha male.' I'm tellin' him that . . . that Chris is now in charge, that you're the alpha male. He's in charge of protection of the territory of the pack . . . of the family . . ."

A long pause.

"Oh my God. . . . You're gonna laugh. He says, 'Well if he's in charge then he should mark.' So if you can you go out in the yard and do that . . . at night . . . when nobody's lookin'? Because he needs some boundaries and he needs to know that if you're in charge you need to mark your scent. . . . OK, take this seriously. You're the alpha male. He's pretty literal about it."

As Gera continued her psychic conversation with Bennett, she filled in his back story. Bennett is a very "staunch" and "serious" dog with a "totally German energy" who demands to be treated with respect. He lived with another family before ours but ran away when that family "would not take him seriously." He feels respected by our family, Gera reported, except for his name:

> "He just wants some staunch German name. Bennett is more English than German. He wants to be called . . . Fritz."

In addition to a name change, she said, Bennett/Fritz also wants "more treats . . . lots more treats," and a thicker cushion on his bed. Via Gera's psychic gift, Bennett and I made a deal—he could have a thicker cushion, but must keep the name "Bennett." Bennett agreed.

Nearly out of time at this point, I raised the other topic of the day—my inability to have paranormal experiences. Gera contacted one of her angelic guides and asked them this question. After a short pause and nod, she told me that a traumatic experience in a past life (or this one) has made me decide to shut down my "crown chakra."[47] I would need to learn how to open up the chakra to enable paranormal experiences.

> "Your spirit guide can help you with this process," she continued. "Let me ask the angels who your spirit guide is. . . . What do you do for a living?"
> "I am a professor."
> "That's funny! Your spirit guide is also a professor."
> "Really? Does he have a name?"
> "Ichabod."

Gera's alarm rang, indicating our time was up. Learning more about Ichabod would have to wait.

American Belief in Psychic Powers

As I completed appointments with different readers, I could see the appeal of such phenomena. One could not help but impart some meaning to the possible futures and current insights produced by the readers. Earlier in the day, I sat in on a free, half-hour class on angelic reading provided by Gera. Shassa, a woman of about forty with a thick Russian accent, told Gera that she has always "felt like a stranger here," and knows that she "has a home somewhere out there. Somewhere white." Gera contacted the angels and told Shassa that she had lived on the planet Vega in a previous life and someday will return. Shassa left the room beaming. Another woman, Jill, told us that she had "always felt I had more to give the world than just being an administrative assistant." Gera's angels informed Jill that she has a spirit guide named Master Chen, who will soon guide her down a path to healing others. Tears rolled down Jill's face. The need to learn something that would provide meaning or hope in one's life was palpable in the room. Perhaps my need would have been more pronounced should I have come seeking guidance on more serious issues than an unfriendly dog and an inability to see ghosts.

While the appeal was obvious, skepticism was warranted. From two different readers I heard two different back stories for the family dog. Bennett was either kept by a solitary alcoholic that he ran away from due to neglect, or fled from a family that did not afford him proper respect. Shelley did not say anything about the fact that Bennett had been in a fire until asked. The topic never came up with Gera, and Bennett never mentioned anything about such a traumatic experience during their psychic conversation. According to Dee, I will soon discover a powerful wizard as my spirit guide who will lead me to paranormal experiences. Per Gera, however, Ichabod the professor is already waiting to guide me, should I open up my chakras.

Americans express similar concern when asked about such topics. Fully 18% of Americans believe that astrologers, palm readers, fortune-tellers, and others who claim psychic abilities can see the future (see figure 2.3). But this also tells us that the majority of Americans (82%) remain skeptical about the ability to foresee the future (at least as far as these types of readers are concerned).

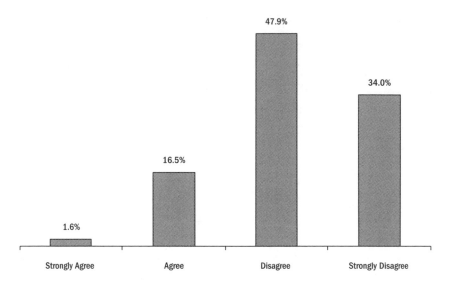

Figure 2.3. Astrologers, Palm Readers, Fortune-Tellers, and Psychics Can Foresee the Future (Chapman University Survey of American Fears 2014, n=1573)

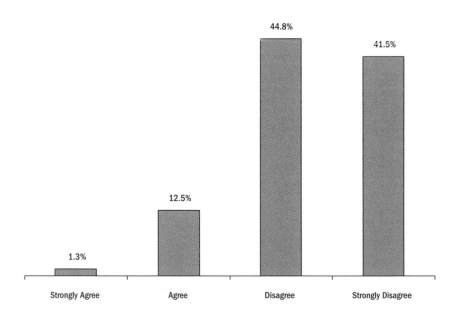

Figure 2.4. Astrology Impacts My Life and Personality (Chapman University Survey of American Fears 2014, n=1573)

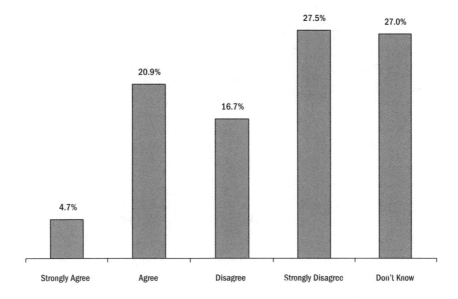

Figure 2.5. The Living and Dead Can Communicate with Each Other (Chapman University Survey of American Fears 2015, n=1541)

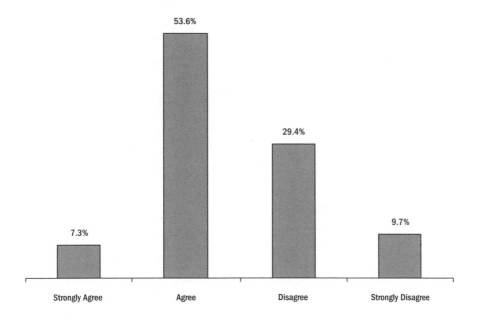

Figure 2.6. Dreams Sometimes Foretell the Future (Chapman University Survey of American Fears 2014, n=1573)

We find a similar pattern when we ask Americans more specifically about astrology (see figure 2.4). Americans are slightly more open to the idea of communication with the dead (see figure 2.5). On the other hand, most are convinced that dreams can foretell the future (see figure 2.6).

There are reasons for the mixed feelings Americans seem to have about the paranormal. To visit a psychic is to experience some "hits" surrounded by much incorrect information. Temple University mathematician John Allen Paulos recognized this phenomenon and labeled it the "Jeane Dixon effect."[48] When presented with a large amount of information, some true and some false, we are naturally more interested in the true statements. People tend to forget statements that are clearly false, leading them to overestimate the accuracy of psychics. Skeptics argue that psychics use the Jeane Dixon effect to their advantage. Readers pummel their clients with predictions, counting on the few hits to be recalled with reverence and the many misses to be forgotten. We can attest to this phenomenon. One cannot help to feel a slight thrill whenever an accurate statement is presented. The inaccurate statement immediately previous is much less interesting.

Skeptics have noted other processes at work in such readings. Readers often make vague statements that have a high probability of success, such as "I see that you have suffered a great loss in the last year." One who has recently lost a parent to illness will connect with this statement, as will someone who recently had to put their beloved pet to sleep, suffered great losses in the stock market, or recently broke up with a boyfriend, and so on. Such vague statements are often coupled with observations that the client *wants to be true*. I certainly *wish* I was being followed by the ghost of a former professor. I *want* to believe that our dog Bennett is happy with our family, even if we refuse to rename him Fritz.

We could continue by discussing the possibility that many psychics are master "cold readers," but to do so would be missing the point.[49] Neither the readers nor the clients were at the fair in the hopes of proving the reality of paranormal phenomena to a skeptical public. People attend because they desire help and guidance and have not found the answers they seek through other means. Behind the use of crystal balls, palm reading, aura photography, attempts to contact dead relatives, psychics and clairvoyants, crystals, aromatherapy, past-life regression, handwriting analysis, and so on is the desire to better oneself. Clients hope to learn more about themselves by determining the color of their aura or gain supernatural insight into their future through the use of tarot cards or by communicating with dead relatives.

As the sociologist Jeremy Northcote notes, many paranormal believers "privilege experiential knowledge over empirical validity and the power of the imagination over the authority of physical reality."[50] That the methods being used at psychic fairs to elicit change or improvement remain unaccepted by science appeared of little concern to those involved. Personal enlightenment trumps scientific proof.

Enlightenment vs. Discovery

Wandering the Holistic Health & Spiritual Fair, I noted the absence of materials on several popular aspects of the paranormal. Bigfoot was in hiding, ghosts and UFOs largely absent.[51] Judging by the prevalence of television shows, movies, books, and web pages devoted to such subjects, it might at first seem surprising that Sasquatch and aliens did not have a prominent place at such an event. Yet in our exploration of the paranormal, we have found that there are two distinct spheres within it, which we call—as described in chapter 1—*enlightenment* and *discovery*. These different approaches tend to align with different subjects.

For those that view the paranormal as a source of personal *enlightenment*, the "truth" is ephemeral and within: they seek to better themselves or learn about their fate by traveling in the realms of astrology, psychic powers, and similar practices. So long as psychic readings of one sort or another help them to come to grips with their strengths and weaknesses, they are satisfied. Since *enlightenment* pursuits highlight mystical experiences and magic, they share much in common with religion and rest closer to the boundary between it and the paranormal. The difference between the paranormal and religion is *not* ontological, at least from the perspective of science, for both psychic phenomena and religious phenomena share a focus upon the supernatural and are resistant to scientific confirmation. Further, religion and the paranormal are often not phenomenologically distinguishable either, as intensive religious and paranormal experiences can be very similar in their experiential features. The boundary is, rather, culturally defined, with organized religious groups deciding which types of mystical experiences are "authentically religious," leaving those not included or demonized as "paranormal." [52]

Paranormal subcultures centered around enlightenment may attempt to transition into organized religions, but the road to cultural acceptance is treacherous and littered with the failed efforts of many a new religious movement. True to form though, the paranormal allows such efforts to avoid cultural death. As a result, the paranormal becomes a repository of supernaturalism that has not made the cultural "leap" into religion—a pool of ideas that new religions or other cultural movements may pull from (perhaps at their own peril).[53] The paranormal can also become a repository for older religious ideas and traditions that have lost the benefit of conventionality, as is evident in the extensive borrowing from Eastern and esoteric traditions in New Age movements.

In contrast to enlightenment, others are interested in the paranormal because they hope to take part in, whether personally or by proxy, a major *discovery* for the world at large. People interested in Bigfoot and mysterious creatures in general, UFOs, and ghosts often appear more concerned with trying to prove to themselves and others that their subject is indeed "real." They want to find the truth—a truth that anyone will accept. They want to find out if UFOs are real, or they know UFOs are real and want to convince others of that fact. Some of the most serious Bigfoot hunters hope to drop a Sasquatch carcass on the doorstep of the Smithsonian one day. They study materials on websites and in books, and debate the best evidence on blogs and at conferences. Others watch television shows such as *Ghost Hunters* with great interest, hoping the hosts will finally capture undisputed video of a restless spirit.

Consequently, *discovery* inhabits the borderlands between the paranormal and science, with professional scientists making distinctions between accepted knowledge and "amateur" or "pseudo" science.[54] Meanwhile, the border between religion and science involved supernaturalism, but also the goal of the practices prescribed by each. Put another way, it is the ultimate goal toward which ascetic practices are directed that distinguishes religious asceticism (enactment of religious order) from scientific practice (systematic generation of knowledge

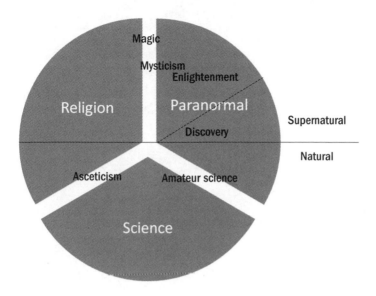

Figure 2.7. The Paranormal, Religion, and Science

about the physical world).[55] Figure 2.7 outlines this cultural landscape of the paranormal in relation to religion and science.

The appeal of *enlightenment* is to learn about oneself, to maybe become a better person. The appeal of *discovery* is to share in an adventure, to feel the thrill of searching for the unknown, and perhaps to be the one who finally brings in the "proof." Clearly, some subcultures blend aspects of enlightenment and discovery paranormalism, such as when UFO abductees emphasize spiritual themes or when ghost hunters utilize both mediumship and technological tools; but one need only to participate in each type of pursuit to feel their stark contrast.[56]

3

The Truth Is Out There

Paranormal Beliefs and Experiences

People have seen strange objects in the sky seemingly for as long as
we have had records. The Old Testament prophet Ezekiel reported the
sighting of a "whirlwind from the north." Apparently based on a passage in a book by Washington Irving, UFO books and websites claim
that Christopher Columbus reported a "light glimmering at a great distance" in his ship's log two days before first landing in the New World.[1]
In the 1800s the United States experienced a rash of sightings of flying,
cigar-shaped objects similar to dirigibles, which sometimes disgorged
humanlike pilots.[2] Since the late 1800s, mysterious "ghost lights" have
been sighted dancing across the Chihuahuan Desert in Marfa, Texas.
During World War II some Allied pilots reported sightings of small
disks or globes of light that followed their planes, which were ultimately
nicknamed "foo fighters."[3]

What *has* changed quite a bit over time is the interpretation of such
objects. Ezekiel believed his whirlwind was a sign from God. The air-
ships of the late 1800s were widely assumed to be the work of "secret
inventors." The Marfa lights were dismissed as the lanterns of lost pros-
pectors wandering the desert, or cattle rustlers absconding with their
booty at night. The U.S. military thought the foo fighters were weapons
of the Japanese or Germans. As technology changes, so do our mysterious aerial objects, always staying one step ahead of us. Nowadays some
UFO enthusiasts assume Ezekiel's experience is evidence that extraterrestrials were visiting Earth in biblical times; therefore Ezekiel's interpretation is assumed to be the wrong one.[4]

The widespread interpretation of mysterious objects in the sky as
extraterrestrial in origin is often traced to the June 24, 1947, sighting
by Kenneth Arnold, a fire-equipment salesman. An experienced civil-
ian pilot, Arnold was flying his private plane from Chehalis to Yakima,

Washington, when he took a brief detour over Mount Rainier to search for the wreckage of a recently crashed plane. Arnold was startled by a bright flash while making a turn high over the town of Mineral. He spotted nine peculiar craft approximately one hundred miles away, soaring at a bearing that would bring them in front of his plane. At first Arnold thought the objects were jets until they drew closer; he could see wings but no tails. One of the objects was almost crescent-shaped, with a small dome midway between the wingtips. The others were flat "like a pie pan," with a reflective surface.[5] The craft wove around the mountaintops allowing Arnold to clock their speed at roughly sixteen hundred miles per hour, nearly three times faster than conventional aircraft of the 1940s.

Recounting the sighting to reporters, Arnold described the objects' flight as "like saucers skipped over water." In the flurry of news coverage that followed, writers began using terms such as "flying disks" or "flying saucers" to describe the objects, although the exact provenance of the term is unclear. Clearer was the new interpretation of strange flying objects. Arnold's report, if true, was of intelligently controlled objects clearly beyond the capabilities of the time, so the possibility that such "flying saucers" were of extraterrestrial origin became firmly cemented in popular culture.[6] In later years, the preferred term for mysterious objects of assumed extraterrestrial origin became "UFO"—unidentified flying object.[7]

Of course, the term "UFO" simply refers to an object seen in the sky that has not yet been conclusively identified. The object need not be extraterrestrial. However, many Americans assume that aliens have visited our world. As of 2015, nearly one-fifth of Americans (18%) agreed or strongly agreed that "aliens have come to Earth in modern times." Nearly another 40% remain uncertain on the matter (see figure 3.1).

For some, the belief in extraterrestrials extends to our very origins as a species, much to the dismay of mainstream archeologists. Proponents of the so-called ancient astronauts thesis contend that aliens created mankind or at least accelerated human development via the granting of wisdom and technology. This idea dates back, in some form or another, to the late-nineteenth-century works of the Russian mystic/theosophist Helena Petrovna Blavatsky, but the Swiss author Erich von Däniken is responsible for its most influential iteration, in books such as *Chariots of the Gods* (1968), *In Search of Ancient Gods* (1973), *Miracles of the Gods* (1974), and many others.[8] His books were so popular that Däniken be-

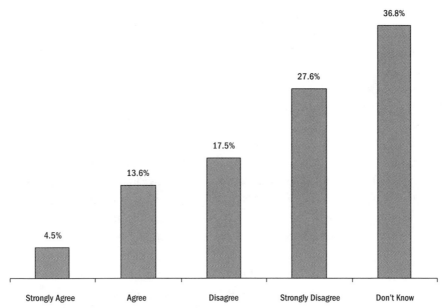

Figure 3.1. Aliens Have Come to Earth in Modern Times (Chapman University Survey of American Fears 2015, n=1541)

came a minor celebrity. His theories were the subject of countless television documentaries and the inspiration behind his own Swedish theme park, Mystery Park (unfortunately, it folded in 2006). Zecharia Sitchin, who also believes that extraterrestrials played a role in human history, Däniken, and others marshal an assortment of archaeological evidence to support the theory of ancient astronauts.[9]

Perhaps the most common claim among ancient astronaut enthusiasts is that impressive feats of ancient engineering—the pyramids of Egypt, the statues on Easter Island, the great temples of South America—were simply beyond the capacity of their associated societies. Däniken speculates openly about the builders of the great monuments of Egypt:

How on Earth did the Ancient Egyptians build these edifices without twentieth-century technology? . . . [H]ow were the statues of Memnon near Thebes that weighed 600 tons transported, or the stone blocks of the terrace at Baalbek, some of which are over 60 feet long and weigh 2,000 tons? And now the sixty-four thousand dollar question: Who nowadays can still accept the "serious" archaeological explanation that these stone blocks were moved up inclined planes using wooden rollers? . . . I get no answers to questions like that. So could it be true that extraterrestrial space travelers helped with their highly developed technology?[10]

Däniken uses this rhetorical technique throughout his work. He outlines the incredible effort that would have been required of ancient peoples to construct a particular monument, raises concerns about their ability to do so, and finally speculates that it all would have been much easier with help from the stars. Since the entire exercise is framed in the form of questions, it allows Däniken to make astonishing allegations with the benefit of distance; he is not making unreasonable claims, simply asking questions. The ancient astronaut literature leaves the reader with the distinct impression that ancient peoples could not accomplish much on their own.

The books of Däniken and others provide a complete, alternative reading of the historical record and the meanings of religious doctrine, myth, and legend. God figures in elaborate headdresses depicted in ancient artwork become literal astronauts in their space helmets.[11] References to strange celestial objects or godlike figures in holy texts are reinterpreted as historical accounts of visitations by extraterrestrials. Landscape features such as the admittedly mysterious Nazca Lines of Peru, a collection of lines scraped into the soil that reveal themselves to be enormous representations of birds, monkeys, and other figures when viewed from a great height, are frequently mentioned by ancient astronaut theorists. Archaeologists disagree as to whether the Peruvian artists meant this amazing achievement in landscape art to function as an irrigation system, an astronomical calendar, or, just maybe, simply as art. To ancient astronaut proponents the purpose is obvious—the lines are runways for ancient spacecraft, or perhaps artwork meant to be pleasing to extraterrestrials hovering high above Earth. Of course, such claims have been the focus of intense criticism,[12] but they have maintained a foothold in paranormal subcultures. These ideas are even relatively prevalent among college students taking archeology classes, with over one-third believing in ancient aliens,[13] and have certainly captured the attention of the American public, with over one-fifth believing that "aliens visited Earth in our ancient past" (see figure 3.2).

Further confusing popular understanding of mankind's history is a persistent belief in ancient, advanced civilizations such as Atlantis, Lem-

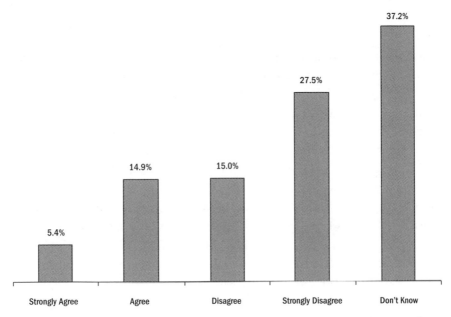

Figure 3.2. Aliens Visited Earth in Our Ancient Past (Chapman University Survey of American Fears 2015, n=1541)

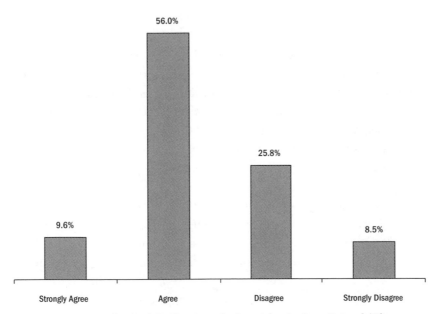

Figure 3.3. Ancient Advanced Civilizations, Such as Atlantis, Once Existed (Chapman University Survey of American Fears 2014, n=1573)

uria, and Mu.[14] Plato's dialogues provide the first reference to Atlantis, a powerful nation that supposedly sank under the waves during a natural disaster. Ever since, those with an interest in Atlantis have fretted over whether Plato's reference is meant as a parable on hubris (even the most powerful can fall to forces beyond their control), or a recounting of historical fact. Ignatius Donnelly took up the case in his 1882 work *Atlantis: The Antediluvian World,* in which he forcefully argued that archeological data, legends, and historical records point to a real Atlantis.[15] As the legend passed through the hands of Helena P. Blavatsky, Lewis Spence, Edgar Cayce, and others, the nature of Atlantis changed. What Plato described as a society advanced for its time was transformed into an amazing civilization far beyond current understanding and with ties to extraterrestrials. Its reported destruction by natural disaster morphed into death by technological malfeasance.[16]

While we cannot assess the extent to which Americans believe in alien intervention in early history specifically, we do know how they feel about Atlantis. Over 60% of Americans agree or strongly agree that ancient advanced civilizations like Atlantis once existed (see figure 3.3).

Aren't They Just Nuts?

Telling someone that you are writing a book on such subjects as UFOs, ancient astronauts, and astrology solicits some very interesting, often colorful remarks. When this project first began, one of the authors was telling his family doctor about it during a routine medical appointment. The doctor listened patiently to the description of the project, and his first reaction was: "Why study these people? Aren't they just nuts?" Even though a large number of people in the United States believe in UFOs and other paranormal phenomena, the popular stereotype is that those who lend credence to such topics are very strange indeed, or "just nuts." But is this true?

A big problem in answering such questions had been a lack of good information on the believers themselves. A number of researchers have explored the social correlates of the paranormal, but failed to produce consistent findings. For example, a number of scholars found that people with higher education levels and younger people were more prone to report paranormal experiences.[17] Yet other studies failed to find such relationships.[18]

Data problems plagued the field for many years and many reasons. Some surveys that asked Americans about their paranormal beliefs and experiences were geographically limited, while others were limited to subsections of the population. Historically, much of the available information on paranormal beliefs was collected from college students, as getting captive audiences in classes to fill out surveys is quick and cost effective.[19]

In 2005 we launched what, at the time, was the most comprehensive panel of questions on paranormal beliefs, practices, and experiences in a national probability sample: the Baylor Religion Survey.[20] That sample, with its demographic, paranormal, religious, and lifestyle questions, allowed us to develop a sense of average, general paranormal believers in America. In 2014 and 2015 we collected new data to update many of these measures, allowing us to reexamine the relationships we documented previously.[21]

On the Margins

One of the most consistent stereotypes about the supernatural is that such beliefs are the realm of those who live on society's margins—the poor and powerless. Though they are more reserved in their terminology, some influential social theorists argued that those who held supernatural beliefs were, indeed, nuts. Karl Marx made one of the most famous statements in this regard. He argued that, in so many words, the rich and powerful are able to get what they need out of this world by conventional means, and the world is set up to reward them. Religious beliefs perform the vital social function of providing comfort to the less powerful, and those who are currently suffering. Without the belief that they would be compensated for current suffering with magnificent rewards in the afterlife, the working class would revolt and undermine the capitalist system. As such, per Marx, belief in an unseen world is merely a coping mechanism to deal with life on the margins of society, the "sigh of the oppressed creature."[22]

In a similar vein, many theorists wonder if the desire to experience the supernatural, whether in the organized form of religion or via the paranormal, is simply a reaction to uncertainty. Those with a higher level of social achievement such as a good education, a high-paying, "respectable" occupation, and a stable family life are apt to feel more in control of their lives.[23] The decisions they have made and the actions they have taken have produced highly valued achievements. As a result, they have greater confidence in their own abilities to exert influence over circumstances.[24] Those who have fewer socioeconomic resources, or who are marginalized from society, are more apt to feel as if they have lost control over their very futures. They seem to be at the mercy of unseen forces rather than in control of them because they are burdened by heavy hardships. Social scientists call the sense that one controls one's own fate an *internal locus of control*. Women, the poor, those with low levels of education, and racial/ethnic minorities have been found to have less perceived control over their lives.[25]

Humans generally do not like uncertainty and try to reduce it. This is a fundamental assumption about human action that underpins much social science research in sociology and economics.[26] We humans collect information and attempt to make the best decisions about our futures from our own current perspective. We try to find ways to take control of our lives. Some religion scholars believe that those who lack the ability to change their circumstances themselves may ultimately seek divine assistance in the task. In other words, perhaps we seek the supernatural's help when we cannot help ourselves.[27] Marx's work and the concept of a locus of control led to a widespread belief among early sociologists that all forms of religious and paranormal beliefs and experiences would be most prevalent in the poor and oppressed. Life, however, is rarely as simple as theorists would like it to be.

There are many reasons why religious beliefs should appeal to both rich and poor, those with great power and those without it. Religion's primary "products" provide answers to the big questions in life (such as whether our existence has a purpose) and usually offer a means by which to achieve life after death. These are things that cannot be bought with money or earned with a higher social status, so they should hypothetically be equally attractive to rich and poor alike, the mainstream and the marginalized. Indeed, we find that both rich and poor tend to be religious in some form in the United States. People of higher socioeconomic status are more likely to be involved in organized religious activities such as attending services at a temple, mosque, or other house of worship regularly. People of lower socioeconomic status attend religious service less, but are more likely to believe strongly in supernatural precepts, engage in private acts of piety such as personal prayer, and have intensive, sensory religious experiences.[28] Still others have an entirely personal or idiosyncratic religiosity that is more focused on privatized spirituality or other contacts with the supernatural, an expression which is contingent on both social class and ethnicity.[29] In sum, what varies more than attraction to religion is *how* different socioeconomic groups manifest their religiosity.

In addition to promises of eternal salvation, religious congregations offer many rewards that can be obtained on Earth, such as leadership positions and access to influential financial and personal networks. The powerful (i.e., those from higher socioeconomic groups) tend to monopolize these material yet religious rewards just as they do in many other aspects of life. In the United States, religious groups are strictly voluntary associations; therefore, they must depend upon the resources, both monetary and human, of their members. People who are powerful in the local community are likely to be the powerful members within conventional religious groups as well.

So what does this have to do with paranormal beliefs, practices, and experiences? Like most people, the socially marginal are seeking rewards from religion, but they are not reaping those direct, concrete rewards from religious life that have been usurped by the more powerful members. The failure to secure empirical rewards may lead to disappointment, alienation, and estrangement from conventional society. Such individuals may reject the beliefs of the mainstream without giving up on the desire for some sort of relationship with the supernatural realm. This can lead to experimentation with alternative beliefs or experiences.

Some of the disaffected are able to fulfill their desires within a religious framework. They become more open to intense and unconventional religious experiences not typically associated with upper- and middle-class religious practices. For instance, using BRS data, there is a significant decrease in the odds of claiming a variety of intensive, sensory religious experiences for each increase on a scale of income, even after controlling for sociodemographics, religious tradition, frequency of religious service attendance, frequency of prayer, and biblical literalism. This is particularly the case for claiming miraculous physical healing, speaking in tongues, and having religious visions.[30] Religious sects, which tend toward more charismatic experiences, draw more heavily from those of lower socioeconomic status.[31]

Those with a weaker connection to religious beliefs or who have grown disenchanted with conventional religion experiences may experiment with more esoteric beliefs such as psychic phenomena, astrology, or UFOs.[32] Finding an intense or unique supernatural experience that the upper classes do not share can be empowering to socially marginal people.[33] Unique beliefs or experiences can make one *feel* unique, worthy, and valuable. To the extent that such a belief is an organized activity, it can even confer a certain social status among fellow seekers. In some cases alternative beliefs give the marginalized a sense of control over their lives that they cannot find elsewhere. All of this suggests that groups with lesser power, however defined, may experiment more with the paranormal.

One way to determine if there is indeed greater paranormal belief among the marginalized is to examine patterns of belief by gender and race. Despite the 2008 election, and 2012 reelection, of an African American president, white males continue to hold power disproportionately

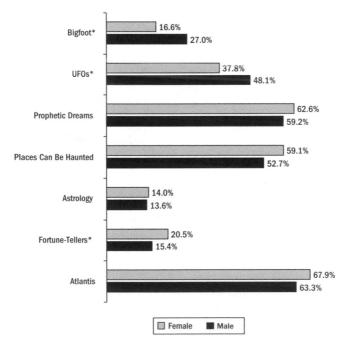

Figure 3.4. Paranormal Beliefs by Gender (Chapman University Survey of American Fears 2014, n=1501). * = Statistically significant difference.

in the United States.[34] If marginalized people drift toward marginalized beliefs, should we then expect women to express more belief in such topics than men, and nonwhites to show more interest than whites?

With respect to gender, we do find gender differences (see figure 3.4). Women are more likely to believe in the ability of some people to foretell the future and that places can be haunted. And while an effect for astrology does not appear in this simple analysis, women are more likely than men to believe in astrology, once we control for other demographic and religious characteristics (see the appendix).[35] Men, on the other hand, are more likely to believe in two items we would characterize as *discovery*-based forms of the paranormal—UFOs and Bigfoot.

At first glance, paranormal beliefs do, indeed, appear to be powerfully related to race (see figure 3.5). Here we compare white respondents, African American respondents, and Hispanic respondents.[36] African Americans demonstrate significantly higher levels of belief in Atlantis,

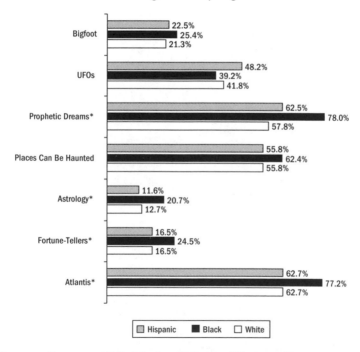

Figure 3.5. Paranormal Beliefs by Race/Ethnicity (Chapman University Survey of American Fears 2014, n=1573). * = Statistically significant difference. Each bar represents the percentage of respondents that agree or strongly agree with statements about the reality of each phenomena.

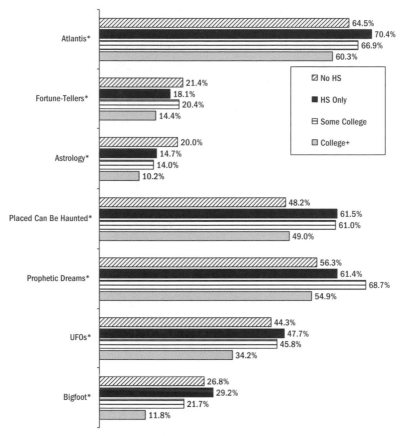

Figure 3.6. Paranormal Beliefs by Educational Attainment (Chapman University Survey of American Fears 2014, n=1573). * = Statistically significant difference. Each bar represents the percentage of respondents that agree or strongly agree with statements about the reality of each phenomenon.

the ability of some people to foretell the future, astrology, and prophetic dreams. However, many of these simple, bivariate effects are masking more complex relationships. Once we control for income, education, religion, and other personal characteristics (see the appendix), most racial effects disappear, with only the higher belief in Atlantis amongst African Americans remaining statistically significant in the presence of such controls. These findings suggest that racial effects on the paranormal likely have more to do with the correlation between socioeconomic characteristics and race/ethnicity than with race itself.

Those who have less education tend to have less success in earthly affairs and may be presumed to seek comfort in the paranormal. Or perhaps, those with less education attempt to exert control over their lives
via the supernatural. At least these are less offensive explanations than the
popular argument that people with lower levels of education are simply
more gullible than others. Nonetheless, there is indeed some evidence that
education is associated with paranormal beliefs. Consider the relationship
between schooling and paranormal beliefs presented in figure 3.6.

Here it is clear that obtaining a college degree has a dampening effect on paranormal belief. Those who have college degrees are significantly less likely to believe in Atlantis, fortune-tellers, astrology, haunted
places, prophetic dreams, UFOs, and Bigfoot. In more complex analyses presented in the appendix in which we control for a host of other
demographic and religious characteristics, these effects remain for all
but UFOs and Atlantis, indicating that the effect of education on paranormal belief is powerful and quite consistent. So it does seem that the
paranormal may occasionally serve the function of bringing "power" to
the powerless, of giving people on the margins a way to exert control.

The figures presented so far in this chapter show that paranormal beliefs vary by core demographic measures, particularly gender and education. In figure 3.7 we present a complete profile of paranormal belief
by analyzing the impact of demographic characteristics simultaneously.
This allows us to identify more definitively which items matter most.
Is it gender, education, or income that matters, or do all three matter
equally? In some cases, demographics exhibit a powerful relationship
to paranormal beliefs, allowing for a composite profile of the typical believer. For example, a younger female with a lower level of education and
income who happens to be either married, divorced or separated, or cohabitating is the most likely person to believe that places can be haunted.
In other cases, we can tell very little. When it comes to UFOs, males are
more likely to believe than females, but a UFO believer could be a male
of any age group, marital status, racial group, and may have a higher or
lower level of education and income. Further, some characteristics matter more than others across paranormal beliefs. Marital status is quite a
powerful predictor of paranormal belief, being significantly related to
all beliefs but UFOs (more on this in chapter 6). Income, education,
and gender also have fairly consistent effects. Lower levels of education

	Atlantis	Fortune-Tellers	Astrology	Places Can Be Haunted	Prophetic Dreams	UFOs	Bigfoot
Gender	--	Female	Female	Female	--	Male	Male
Age	--	--	--	Younger	Younger	--	--
Race	African American	--	--	--	--	--	--
Marital Status	Cohabitating	Cohabitating	Not Married	Married, Divorced/ Separated, Cohabitating	Widowed, Divorced/ Separated	--	Cohabitating
Income	--	Lower	Lower	Lower	--	--	Lower
Education	--	Lower	Lower	Lower	Lower	--	Lower

Figure 3.7. Profiles of Paranormal Beliefs in the United States (Chapman University Survey of American Fears 2014, n=1573)

are associated with all beliefs except Atlantis and UFOs. Lower levels of income increase paranormal belief as well, with the exceptions of, again, Atlantis and UFOs, but also fail to tell us much about prophetic dreams.

These data partially support a marginalization thesis of why people believe in the paranormal. In no cases are society's most privileged demographic, highly educated, high-income white males, the predominant believer in a paranormal phenomenon. But is also clear that marginalization hypotheses are not a complete explanation for paranormal beliefs. Race tells us virtually nothing about paranormal belief and men are more likely to believe in some paranormal topics than are women.

Armed with this information we can provide a preliminary answer to the doctor's question. People who believe in the paranormal *are* different in some ways. We can predict someone's level of belief in the paranormal if we know certain things about them. Groups with less societal power, such as women and those with lower levels of education or income are somewhat more paranormal in orientation. Those with a college degree are least likely to believe in *any* of the paranormal items.

Of course, it is one thing to be open to the possibility that aliens exist and quite another to *know* that they exist because you have seen one or even been aboard a UFO (if you are lucky or unlucky, depending on the scenario). Perhaps these are the truly marginalized—people so distanced from society that they live within the realms of the strange and unreal. A detour into the subculture of UFO abductions allows us to consider this possibility. We also consider an alternative hypothesis— maybe belief in UFOs, Bigfoot, and other paranormal topics can be the luxury of the privileged, as opposed to the cry of the oppressed.

The Paranormal Experience: Alien Abductions in the United States

On September 19, 1961, Betty Hill, a New Hampshire social worker, and her husband, Barney, a postal worker, were driving home from a vacation in Canada when they spotted a "white star" in the sky. The Hills ignored the object until they became convinced it was tailing their car. A "chase" ensued during which they became extremely frightened. At one point Barney pulled to the side of the road to gaze at the object through binoculars. The object tilted downward in response and began a descent. Barney panicked as a row of windows came into focus, behind which stood figures in shiny black uniforms and matching caps. Fearing the creatures were going to capture him, Barney jumped back into the couple's car to escape. And then . . .

The couple was suddenly closer to home, with no memory of how they got there. Puzzled, they wearily completed their journey. The next day Betty called Pease Air Force Base in Portsmouth, New Hampshire, to report the encounter.[37] Unable to forget the incident and plagued by nightmares, Betty became fascinated with UFOs. She checked out books from the library and contacted Donald Keyhoe, a well-known UFO investigator and author. Another UFO investigator, Walter Webb, interviewed the couple, who were frustrated by fragmented memories of being aboard the witnessed saucer. In reconstructing their terrifying evening with still other investigators, the Hills realized that the usual four-hour drive from Canada to New Hampshire had taken them seven hours. Where had they been during this "missing time"? The couple believed there was more about their experience to be uncovered. They tried to find the exact site of their encounter, but this did not help spur memories. Meanwhile Betty continued to dream about beings with strange faces performing medical experiments upon her.

By December 1963 the couple had contacted the Boston psychiatrist Benjamin Simon. The Hills hoped that hypnotic regression might help them to recover a more complete account of their UFO encounter, and Simon was experienced with the technique. The skeptical therapist agreed to help the Hills, though he believed their stresses had a more earthly than extraterrestrial explanation.[38] From January to June 1964 the Hills had occasional meetings with Simon, during which he hypnotized one or both. A fantastic tale emerged from these sessions, supposedly filling in the blanks of their memories.

It seems that the object that tailed the couple several years previous had landed near their car. Several strange creatures then emerged and escorted the dazed Hills into their craft. Barney described the odd creatures in a hypnosis session with Simon. At first he likened them to a "red-headed Irishman" and then a "German Nazi" before ultimately settling upon a description more familiar to modern-day UFO enthusiasts:[39]

[They] had rather odd-shaped heads, with a large cranium, diminishing in size as it got towards the chin. And the eyes continued around to the sides of the head, so it appeared that they could see several degrees beyond the lateral extent of our vision. . . . The texture of the skin . . . was grayish, almost metallic looking. . . . I didn't notice any hair . . . [and] there just seemed to be two slits that represented nostrils.[40]

The beings subjected the couple to a series of medical examinations. They placed Barney on a table that was too short for his body and poked and prodded him with an assortment of tools. They expressed great curiosity about his false teeth and pulled them out, bewildered as to why Betty's teeth could not also be removed. Betty endured skin scrapings, nail clippings, a "pregnancy test" in which a long needle was inserted into her abdomen, and some type of full-body scan with a strange device. During her examination, Betty conversed with an alien who appeared to be the leader of the crew. When she asked where he was from, the leader produced a "star map" that Betty later drew from memory.[41] Eventually, the creatures escorted the Hills from the ship, during which time an argument broke out between the leader and crew members. The leader had given Betty a book full of strange symbols that she planned to use as proof of the encounter. Other crew members protested. Not only did they not want Betty to have physical evidence of the encounter, they did not want the couple to remember the events at all. The leader relented, took the book, and somehow "erased" the couple's memories of the encounter. During their sessions with Simon the couple were adamant that their memories had been "immediately wiped out after they left the [UFO]" and that hypnosis had not created their memories, but *recovered* them.[42]

John G. Fuller's recounting of the Hill tale, *The Interrupted Journey: Two Lost Hours "Aboard a Flying Saucer,"* became a best-seller in 1966. It was serialized in *Look,* a popular magazine of the time, and was the subject of a 1975 television movie starring James Earl Jones as Barney and Estelle Parsons as Betty. Unfortunately, Barney enjoyed little of the resultant fame; he died of a cerebral hemorrhage in 1969. Betty, on the other hand, became a celebrity in UFO circles and the subject of frequent interviews and documentaries until her death in 2004.

The publication of the Hill story arguably created the new phenomenon of UFO abductions.[43] Although abduction narratives have evolved over time, they share certain features. The abduction is usually at the hands of diminutive, gray-skinned beings with large black eyes and oversized craniums, similar to those in the Hill story. So ubiquitous is this little creature in modern accounts that it has been nicknamed the "Gray" in the UFO subculture. Unlike the earlier contactee tales, the first abduction accounts were generally unpleasant and nonconsensual. Abductees often view themselves as victims, not the chosen messengers of extraterrestrials, and report various forms of mental or physical abuse on the part of the aliens, whether it be forced medical examinations or even rape and impregnation. Most abductees also report a period of "missing time" that hides the details of their encounter. Memories erased by the aliens must be recalled in some way, generally through hypnotic regression as pioneered by Benjamin Simon and the Hills. Throughout the 1970s and into the 1980s, dozens of books appeared recounting UFO abduction experiences with these key elements.

Budd Hopkins and the Abductees

In the 1980s the UFO abduction subculture blossomed. Up until this time the ranks of abductees were relatively small. Those few people who reported their tales often became minor celebrities like the Hills. For example, Travis Walton, an Arizona logger who claimed to have been zapped and kidnapped by an alien craft, only to be returned with limited memory days later, was the subject of books, tabloid reports, and, ultimately, a movie called *Fire in the Sky*. But something happened wherein the count of abductees dramatically increased. We were no longer faced with a few celebrities but a mass of anonymous victims.

Skeptics and believers disagree on what happened. True believers think that people have recognized a previously hidden problem—we are finally *aware* of alien abduction after ignoring it for years, similar to problems like child and spousal abuse. Skeptics believe that abductions are simply a new panic or mania that spread culturally with the benefit of mass media and tabloid attention. Whatever the perspective, it is clear that a New York artist named Budd Hopkins is largely responsible for the UFO abduction movement.

Born in 1931, Hopkins received an education at Oberlin College in Ohio before moving to New York City in 1953. His interest in UFOs stems from an August 1964 sighting of a large object he could not identify in the skies above Cape Cod. He began to read books about UFOs and followed the Hill case with much interest. By the mid-1970s, Hopkins was an active UFO investigator, focusing upon those cases that involved elements of "missing time." To uncover what he thought might be hidden memories of abductions, Hopkins began to hypnotize potential abductees, sometimes by himself and sometimes with the help of mental health professionals. The first book related to his investigations, *Missing Time*, appeared in 1981.

A key revelation contained in Hopkins's book is that it is not necessary to have a UFO sighting to claim a potential abduction. Recall that Betty and Barney Hill claimed to have memories all along of seeing a strange object in the sky tailing their car and then watching that object speed away. They simply filled the gaps in between. One of Hopkins's first cases convinced him that a person could have been abducted by aliens without having *any* prior suspicions. It seems that a young man with the pseudonym "Steve Kilburn" informed Hopkins that he was deathly afraid of a stretch of road between his home and that of his girlfriend. Hopkins thought this "an almost ridiculously flimsy pretext for entering into the costly and time-consuming process of hypnotic regression," but ultimately relented.[44]

In 1978, the therapist Girard Franklin hypnotized Kilburn, who recounted a by-then familiar narrative. While en route to his girlfriend's house on an evening, a strange force had pulled Kilburn's car to the side of the road. Beings forced him aboard a hovering craft, subjected the terrified man to physical examinations, and then released him—memory erased but with a floating, subconscious fear intact. Armed with these findings, Hopkins embraced the idea that the world might be filled with abductees who have no memories of their abuse save for a feeling of uneasiness or anxiety about a place or a piece of time that could not be accounted for. These feelings might, just might, be evidence of hidden memories of alien abduction ready to boil to the surface with proper therapy.

The second key observation in *Missing Time* concerns the reported experiences of "Virginia Horton." She underwent hypnosis with Hopkins and produced memories of encountering gray aliens as a child in the 1950s. But in a later session, she recovered a memory of a different abduction experience that occurred during a family picnic years later. To Hopkins the two distinct memories suggested that extraterrestrials had been tracking Horton throughout her life as part of an ongoing experiment of some kind. This was a virtually unheard-of notion at the time, as other early abductees (such as the Hills and Travis Walton) were assumed to be just unlucky.[45] Walton had been at the wrong place at the wrong time when the aliens appeared. Someone else could easily have gone in his stead. Horton's experience presented an entirely different scenario. Surely it was not chance alone that led this girl to have been abducted (at least) twice? The aliens must be up to something more nefarious. Horton was somehow special to the aliens.

Noting that Horton had reported suffering from a bloody nose after aliens inserted a probe into her nostril (along with similar cases from his files), Hopkins concluded that the majority of abductees show evidence of having multiple abduction experiences going back to childhood. Aliens are using an "implant" or tracking device, usually inserted through a nostril, to keep track of these subjects over time. Clearly the "extraterrestrials need something from humans—possibly a certain kind of genetic structure," Hopkins concluded.[46] By his second book in 1987, *Intruders,* Hopkins had developed a complete cosmology, drawing upon further revelations from his clients to outline an alien breeding experiment to create half-human/half-alien beings:

> I want to describe the general pattern of these accounts. An individual, male or female, is first abducted as a child, at a time possibly as early as the third year. During that experience a small incision is made in the child's body, apparently for sample-taking purposes, and then the child is given some kind of physical examination. There will often follow a series of contacts or abductions extended through the years of puberty. In some cases sperm samples will be taken from young males . . . and ova samples taken from young females. . . . In the cases in which artificial insemination is attempted, the women are apparently re-abducted after two or three months of pregnancy, and the fetus is removed from the uterus.[47]

Hopkins's theories changed the nature of the abduction phenomenon and opened the door for UFO-related support groups to emerge—the first of which met in his New York apartment. Hopkins's informal group eventually morphed into the Intruder Foundation, which along with the Program for Extraordinary Experience Research (PEER) and the International Center for Abduction Research fostered the development of support groups across the country and referred potential abductees to local therapists.[48]

Hopkins spurred such interest in alien abductions that in 1992 a truly astonishing event took place—a dreadfully serious conference on the subject at MIT. A discussion of UFO abductions as mass delusion would not have been surprising in such an august academic setting, but that MIT hosted dozens of talks on subjects ranging from the specific procedures reported by abductees once aboard alien spacecraft to speculation about the biological characteristics of alien/human hybrids was unprecedented.[49]

Hopkins passed in 2011. David Jacobs, a retired Temple University history professor, has since taken up leadership of the UFO abduction movement. Books such as *Secret Life* (1993), *The Threat* (1999), and *Walking among Us* (2015) outline an evolving eschatology regarding extraterrestrials that the first author watched him present to the December 2015 public meeting of the Mutual UFO Network in Costa Mesa, California.

In a talk titled "The Workforce in the Abduction Phenomenon," Jacobs told the assembled UFO enthusiasts about the goals and methods of alien abductors. Jacobs has been informed of a complex hierarchy of extraterrestrial beings by UFO abductees he hypnotizes in therapy sessions that goes far beyond the "Grays" that were the focus of earlier abduction research. At the top of the alien pecking order are the "Insectalins," beings that look similar to giant praying mantises. The Insectalins do not engage in abductions themselves. Such work is left to the Grays, which come in tall and shorter varieties. Underneath the Grays in this hierarchy are the Reptalins, bipedal, reptile-like creatures who are uncommon, but occasionally take part in alien abductions. Grays and Reptalins engage in abductions in order to gather the genetic material necessary to engineer hybrids. Over the years the aliens have become sufficiently adept at creating half-human/half-alien creatures that Jacobs has started calling the latest models "Hubrids."

Resting at the bottom of the alien hierarchy are the abductees themselves, said Jacobs. In addition to providing the genetic materials required by the alien hybrid program, abductees are often tasked with teaching the Hubrids about life on Earth, so that they can more easily pass as human. Hubrids are now "moving into apartments in groups of two, three, and four" said Jacobs, indicating that the aliens' goal to reseed Earth with half-alien/half-human creatures is well underway.

Alien Life Support

Aileen Bringle was in a deep sleep in the passenger seat of her car when her husband shook her awake. The couple was on their way to Stanfield, Oregon, passing through an expanse of wheat fields. She was shocked to find that, as far she could see, the land was "encompassed in a brilliant green light between kelly and chartreuse . . . everything, myself and my husband included, was green."[50] The terrified couple could never find the origin of the intense light that finally faded when they rounded a bend in the road, but it forever changed Aileen's life. She devoured books, magazines, and videos, looking for answers to her own experience, and she became fascinated with those of others. She was ultimately drawn to the tales of people who had been contacted or abducted by aliens and feared they lacked the necessary support to deal with the resultant trauma and ridicule. Determined to help, Aileen founded the UFO Contact Center International in 1981. She publicized the new group through advertisements and by leaving brochures at New Age fairs. Its mission:

> The UFOCCI (UFO Contact Center International) was started with the purpose of helping people to examine their bizarre experiences as a result of being abducted by strange beings and being taken aboard what we know of as flying discs, commonly called UFOs. After gathering the information, which has come from all parts of the globe, piecing together parts of the puzzle, the serious investigation began.
>
> Of immediate attention and concern, this organization has focused on the humanoids from our universe. We have been watched and monitored since WWII, perhaps being programmed for their use in a future take-over. Many abductees report that they have had something inserted into their nostrils, implanted into the brain at the base of their heads![51]

Although it is now defunct, the organization spread quickly during its heyday. The first UFOCCI center opened in Federal Way, Washington, a bedroom community of Seattle, and quickly expanded to sixty-five affiliate centers around the United States and into Canada. These centers were largely autonomous, holding meetings when and where they wanted, but Aileen had become a certified hypnotist in order to help the members recover abduction memories, and she encouraged affiliates to

provide the same service. The UFOCCI even produced its own magazine for a time, *Missing Link*, which contained tips on how to conduct
abduction therapy and record personal abduction accounts, as well as
news and announcements.

The first author (Chris) observed the monthly meetings of the Federal
Way UFOCCI on an intermittent basis between 1989 and 1997, hoping to
gain insight into the lives of people who claim dramatic paranormal experiences, and the group graciously allowed someone with no claimed UFO
encounters to observe. Meetings followed a standard format. They opened
with an overview of recent news, recited by Aileen, from the UFO community. Participants would then discuss whatever UFO story or sighting
had captured their interest, often followed by a guest speaker—an author
of a UFO book or a self-proclaimed channeler of aliens. In a certain sense,
all of this was setup for the main event—the sharing of abduction tales.
Once other activities died down, Aileen would ask those present to share
any newly recalled encounters that emerged from recent abduction therapy
sessions. Aileen conducted most of these therapies herself. Any member
who felt that she had experienced "missing time" could contact her for help
in recalling details of possible abduction events. Some of the memories
shared at the monthly meetings were, indeed, very fresh, having been recovered in hypnosis sessions with Aileen mere days or hours before.

Budd Hopkins popularized the notion that the abducting aliens are,
if not evil and selfish, at least indifferent to human suffering and expressed outrage at the "physical rape of the abductees by a group of
aliens apparently interested . . . in replenishing their own failing genetic
stock."[52] David Jacobs has only continued to promote the idea that alien
abductions are part of an evil extraterrestrial plan. Yet, despite this tendency toward the negative among some of the UFO subculture's leading
figures, other researchers argue that pessimistic views of "abduction"
experiences are based on fear, paranoia, and misunderstanding.[53] It is
possible that the aliens have our best interests at heart and that the experiences only *seem* terrifying because we do not understand their full
purpose. Positive abduction researchers such as Richard Boylan argue
that "[f]or most of us, the ETs who have contacted us have become interesting acquaintances and, in some cases, friends. After getting over
our initial fright and upset, we have come to share a deep respect for
them."[54] As the ranks of abductees with a less negative spin on their ex-

periences grew, they developed a new term, "experiencers," to describe themselves, devoid of the negative baggage attached to "abductee."

The personal stories of UFOCCI members definitely did not fit into tidy categorical boxes. During the same December 1996 meeting, one member recalled a harrowing account of abduction and humiliating medical experiments at the hands of aliens, while another told of a friendly invitation to board a spacecraft for a tour of the universe.

"Clay" even told of a UFO abduction in a previous life. He has hazy memories of working as a pilot in the 1930s. During a routine flight he experienced engine troubles, and while assessing his situation, a saucer-shaped object moved into position in the sky alongside him. The shock of witnessing the craft and the several "small, gray-skinned creatures" that appeared at its windows caused Clay to lose concentration and crash to the ground. Suddenly, he found himself viewing the wreckage of his plane from above, the mysterious saucer hovering above him. The ship somehow pulled his "spirit" aboard, flew away, and docked with an "enormous mothership." Once aboard the ship Clay noticed that he had a new body. His skin had become extremely white, and he was wearing a silver jumpsuit. Two small "Grays" introduced him to the crew, which featured humanlike aliens who were working in concert with the Grays. Three beings led Clay into a small room, seated him in a recliner, and showed him a movie of his just-ended life. They then ushered him into another small saucer, flew past the moon to a blue-green planet, and brought him to a room filled with glass coffins. An alien helped him into one of the coffins, and he immediately passed out. His next memory is as an infant, sitting in a crib looking up at a happy Gray alien floating near the ceiling. The aliens helped Clay to reincarnate in his current form, he believes. It is now incumbent upon Clay to discover the "higher purpose" behind these extraterrestrial manipulations.

As the end of the day's UFOCCI meeting neared, the conversation between Aileen and other members turned to scars. Alien experimentation on humans, it seemed, could leave scars on one's body. The presence of such scarring without an explanation was a sign of a hidden alien encounter. Aileen asked if I had any scars on my hands. Pointing to a long, ridgelike scar on my right pinkie finger, I admitted that I did not know how it occurred. Aileen chuckled to herself and winked at the others. "Don't worry," she said, "you'll find out."

Province of the Elites?

In spending time with people who claim to have experienced the paranormal, we have been continually struck by how poorly they seem to fit a marginal person model. For instance, while searching for Bigfoot with members of the North American Wood Ape Conservancy (see chapter 5), we found ourselves sharing the woods with three men who were intelligent and capable, rather than marginalized and disenfranchised. Two of the three men claim to have had visual encounters with the creature. Clearly, then, not all aspects of paranormal belief and experience fit most people's preconceived notions.

To find out what UFO abductees are like I asked the UFOCCI for permission to conduct a national survey of the organization.[55] The UFO subculture is very conspiracy-minded, so at first some members were concerned that I might be a government agent who would pass their personal information on to intelligence agencies. But after spending time with the group and assuring them that survey information would be kept anonymous, they finally gave permission to submit surveys to UFOCCI affiliates around the country in 1989. Ultimately I was able to gather detailed demographic information on fifty-five people who claim to have been abducted or contacted by extraterrestrials, the most extensive survey of its kind.

Nearly all of the UFO abductees (89%) reported their race as white, with the remaining respondents describing themselves as Native American. Despite the fact that one of the first abductees, Barney Hill, was an African American, alien abductions appear to be the province of whites. More striking were the findings for income and education. In 1990 fewer than half of Americans surveyed (46%) had attended college, compared to the majority of UFO abductees (68%).[56] On the other end of the education spectrum, only about 12% of UFO abductees did not have a high school diploma, compared to almost a fourth of Americans (22%). More than half of the abductees held well-paying, white-collar jobs; they were electronics technicians, professors, therapists, and marketing representatives. Unless we choose to define someone as a fringe member of society simply because they claim to have been abducted by aliens or are chasing Bigfoot (which might be a reasonable definition to some), abductees are *not* marginal people. Many of the people we have met would be better described as elites.

One way to understand why elites might be attracted to the paranormal is to think of paranormal beliefs and experiences as something that is "cutting edge." Whenever a new technology enters the market there are people who immediately embrace it, people who are excited by new things and ready to take risks. Marketers call such people "early adopters." Then there are the rest of us, who want to wait until a new idea or technology is fully proven before we jump onboard. Early adopters tend to be those that have more education, more income, and expansive social networks. They are people who have been continually exposed to new ideas throughout their lives via higher education and contacts with other educated people. They also have the resources to try new things. It is hard to imagine people doubting the staying power of the television, but when TV first became available it was the more educated, higher-income people who purchased the first sets.[57] Of course, people with higher levels of income could both afford the new sets (new technologies are always more expensive when they first appear) and ignore the risk if TV did not take off. The latest smartphone is a less risky purchase for someone making $100,000 a year than for someone scraping by on $10,000.

If we conceive of the totality of religion in America as a marketplace of supernatural ideas, then the paranormal represents fringe and often relatively new "products."[58] A number of religion scholars have suggested that a similar rule applies as to the consumption of other new products; early adopters of new religious ideas would be elites. Those with higher educations will have been exposed to a wider variety of new ideas and even a variety of religions they may not have experienced otherwise. In addition, rapid social and technological change can create existential crises, a deep questioning of basic beliefs about the meaning and purpose of life. Younger and better-educated individuals are more likely to be acutely aware of rapid change, more likely to suffer such crises, and more open to new explanations.[59] Elites are religious innovators, seekers, and adapters.[60] Thus we might expect elites to be more likely to create new supernatural products and more likely to adopt those products once they appear.[61]

In fact, the histories of many religious movements have shown exactly this. For example, the early Mormons drew their first members from the more prosperous, educated areas of New York State.[62] Then there was the New Thought movement, which billed itself as a bringer of universal brotherhood, decried racism and sexism, and sought stronger links between science and religion. It was nurtured by the highly educated urban elite culture of Boston and Harvard University during the second half of the nineteenth century,[63] and counted among its practitioners and supporters Ralph Waldo Emerson and the inventor Phineas Quimby.[64] The Human Potential Movement of the 1960s developed a bohemian village (Esalen Institute) for those who were seeking to uncover the life force of the universe and use its power to transform mankind. It was co-founded by Stanford graduates Richard Price and Michael Murphy, and the noted scholar Aldous Huxley was an early advisor.[65] Scientology has become noted for its ability to attract wealthy and powerful members such as Tom Cruise and John Travolta. Even members of witch covens tend to be in professional and white-collar occupations.[66]

But lest we think that the paranormal is a safe playground for the creative elite, we must also consider its inherent risks. To delve into unconventional beliefs and practices is to run the risk of being labeled strange or deviant.[67] For people who are already socially marginal, being labeled a deviant is of lesser importance. Those with a lot of resources are somewhat protected from the consequences of risky behaviors, but at the same time they have more to lose. Engaging in deviant behavior can have a detrimental effect on one's social standing for members of higher socioeconomic classes. Just as it is important to belong to the right clubs, drive the right cars, live in the right neighborhood, and make the right friends to maintain one's social standing, it is also important to maintain the "right" religious practices.

When it was revealed that former first lady Nancy Reagan was consulting an astrologer about White House business, she became the object of scorn and ridicule—it was not the type of thing that someone of her standing should be doing. In fact, on November 7, 2008, then president-elect Barack Obama made an off-handed remark in a news conference about Reagan's paranormal practices, for which he later apologized.[68] Interestingly, not much was made of George W. Bush's persistent practice of opening cabinet meetings with prayer.[69] One is a conventional practice, the other is not.

A former vice-mayor of Phoenix, Arizona, by the name of Frances Emma Barwood, learned a similar lesson about the dangers of embracing the paranormal. On March 13, 1997, hundreds of persons reported lights in a flying V-shaped formation above the city, an incident known as the "Phoenix Lights." Those who witnessed the lights were not pleased with the government's official explanation of flares set off by the Maryland Air National Guard on special maneuvers over the Arizona desert. At a Phoenix City Council meeting, Barwood asked her colleagues to help investigate the light sightings, seeking a more convincing explanation. She was met with both silence and ridicule. Her situation was not improved by a spoof press conference called by then governor Fyfe Symington, featuring his chief of staff wearing a Gray alien costume. Ms. Barwood later described the humiliation:

> I remember Mayor Rimsza handing out business cards with my name on it, saying, Frances Emma Barwood from the planet Xenon. Talk into the aluminum foil and she'll hear you. Or something like that. And he was handing them out to people like that. I wonder why they were so intent upon ridiculing me, other than to just shut me up. He was even on television, doing a speech before National Guard pilots, and he ridiculed me about trying to find out about things flying over Phoenix.[70]

Barwood's career suffered. She tried to run for secretary of state, but her opponent garnered 76% of the vote. Ironically, ten years after the event, the same former governor, Symington, admitted to having seen the Phoenix Lights himself. He had refused to acknowledge this in 1997, knowing what it would mean for *his* career.

There are some signs that the public costs of expressing some interest in UFOs may be diminishing. Speaking in New Hampshire in January 2016, Democratic presidential candidate and former first lady, senator, and secretary of state Hillary Clinton responded to a reporter's questions about Area 51 and UFOs. Candidate Clinton vowed to "get to the bottom" of the extraterrestrial issue. She, and her husband, former president Bill Clinton, are both on record as being open to the possibility that Earth may have been visited by aliens.[71] Surprisingly, in a highly contested presidential campaign, this story received very little attention in the national news cycle. Perhaps those in power are becoming less afraid of admitting to paranormal beliefs?

Paranormal Experiences in the United States

Do the wealthy flock to the paranormal as a creative outlet or avoid UFOs and the paranormal for fear of embarrassment and lost country club memberships? Paranormal experiences are, in fact, surprisingly common in the United States (see figure 3.8). The most common is having a dream that came true (41%), followed by consulting a horoscope (27.5%). Nearly 12% of Americans have taken the trouble to personally consult a psychic, medium, or fortune-teller for information about their future or to understand current circumstances, 13.7% report having lived in a haunted house as an adult, and 15.9% of Americans have witnessed a craft in the sky that they could not identify.

Academics love to be able to tell a clear, straightforward story with their data. Unfortunately, the paranormal simply refuses to behave. When we break down paranormal experiences by key demographic characteristics, such as gender, age, race, marital status, income, and education, we find a complicated tale (see figure 3.9). By running a series of analyses we can determine which factors predict the likelihood of claiming a series of paranormal experiences. For example, whites are

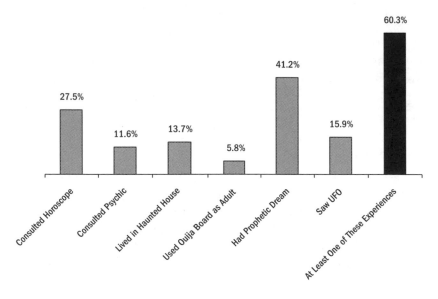

Figure 3.8. Paranormal Experiences in the United States (Chapman University Survey of American Fears 2014, n=1573)

most likely to report having lived in a haunted place. The likelihood of claiming a haunting is increased if a person has lower levels of education and income. Marital status is also related to hauntings—people who are married, divorced or separated, or cohabitating are more likely to report hauntings than are people who are either widowed or single. However, hauntings are equally reported by those of all ages and of both genders.

Gender is related to several paranormal experiences, with women most likely to claim them. Women are more likely to report having consulted a horoscope, visited a psychic, and to have had a prophetic dream. We can say that, in general, women are more paranormally oriented than men. But from here the story gets more complicated, as simplistic notions of who has specific paranormal experiences are incorrect.

If paranormal experiences are the province of the marginalized, we should find a powerful relationship with education, income, and race. Yet income and education are only related to one paranormal experience—living in a haunted place. People of all levels of income and education are equally likely to report consulting horoscopes, visiting psychics, having prophetic dreams, or a UFO sighting. Race is also related to paranormal experiences in an inconsistent manner. African Americans are more likely to report prophetic dreams than others. However, whites are more likely to claim hauntings and whites, African Americans, *and* Hispanics are more likely to consult horoscopes than those of other races and ethnicities.

People who join and form new religious movements tend to be from the upper classes, but we do not find conclusive evidence that paranormal experiences are primarily a creative outlet for the privileged few.[72]

Perhaps our most important finding is that we cannot use simplistic, broad-brushed explanations to understand the paranormal. Nevertheless, we can dismiss one stereotype conclusively—people who believe in and experience the paranormal are not simply "nuts." We find no evidence that paranormal beliefs or experiences are the exclusive realm of hyper-marginalized people, as we should expect if they have mental problems.[73] More than half of Americans (figure 3.8) claim at least one of the following paranormal experiences: consulting a horoscope, visiting a psychic, living in a haunted house, had a prophetic dream, using a Ouija board, or witnessing a UFO. To attribute these beliefs and expe-

	Consulted Horoscope	Consulted Psychic	Lived in Haunted Place	Had Prophetic Dream	UFO Sighting
Gender	Female	Female	---	Female	---
Age	Older	Older	---	---	Older
Race	White, African American, Hispanic	---	White	African American	---
Marital Status	NOT Married or Widowed	Not Widowed	Married, Divorced/Separated, Cohabitating	Divorced/Separated	Cohabitating, NOT Widowed
Income	---	---	Lower	---	---
Education	---	---	Lower	---	---

Figure 3.9. Profiles of Paranormal Experiences in the United States (Chapman University Survey of American Fears 2014, n=1573). Demographics were not significantly related to using a Ouija board.

riences to being "crazy," we would have to believe that over half of the adult population of the United States is "crazy," a frightening prospect to be sure.

Oftentimes we search for simple answers to phenomena we do not understand. For example, "brainwashing" is frequently trotted out to explain why people join strange religious groups even though sociologists have been outlining the complicated reasons people do so for years.[74] In a similar vein, it is much easier to flippantly label someone as nuts if they have seen a UFO than it is to delve into the complex sociological, psychological, and idiosyncratic reasons why someone might interpret a light in the sky as extraterrestrial in origin. The media relies on such demonization and simplicity far too often. Complex stories make poor copy.

4

The Thrill of the Haunt

Ghosts, by their very ephemeral nature, cross boundaries and confound attempts at definition. They often ignore our tidy distinctions between *enlightenment* and *discovery* and appear in cultures across time and space, a fact noted by social anthropologists, both classical and contemporary.[1] This results from the natural tendency of the human brain to perceive the spirit or "soul" (or some synonymous construct) and body as distinct, and also to posit anthropomorphic supernatural agents. Put another way, our tendency to imagine consciousness as distinct from the body allows spirits to exist or persist without bodily presence.[2]

By definition, ghosts violate a number of binaries held as central tenets of human, and especially Western, thought. Primary examples include body/soul, life/death, past/present, presence/absence, and human/inhuman. This violation of fundamental categories of thought, this "in-between-ness," lends spirits a potentially powerful cultural position, onto which varying narratives can be projected.[3] In other words, ghost stories are powerful because they violate some of our basic categories of thought, but the content and meaning given to experiences of and beliefs about spirits is highly flexible, and thus moldable into diverse, culturally specific expressions.

In the recent proliferation of paranormal-themed media, the most frequent and successful subject of paranormal television programming has proven to be ghosts, with dozens of examples spread across the networks, including *Ghost Hunters*, *Ghost Adventures*, *Ghost Stories*, *Celebrity Ghost Stories*, *Haunted Collector*, *The Dead Files*, and *Haunted Encounters*.[4] Accompanying this media expansion, public opinion polls indicate increasing belief in ghosts as institutional religious participation wanes.[5] The trend in the Western world toward the privatization and deinstitutionalization of religion has opened up more space for paranormal spiritualism.

To get a better understanding of both the commonalities and differences between people dedicated to ghost hunting, we spent time with multiple groups that offer ghost tours and services in different locations across America: California, Texas, and southern Appalachia.

Orange, California

Ernie Alonzo, forty-four, of Orange, California has a long-term interest in the paranormal dating back to the age of seven. In the late 1970s his great aunt moved into a house in a historic neighborhood in Orange, which she shared with her brother. During occasional overnight visits with his elderly aunt and uncle, Ernie always slept in his aunt's room. He found the house creepy. Those feelings were confirmed by the experiences of other family members. Ernie's uncle, who used the front parlor as a bedroom, often screamed at an entity that would appear at the end of his bed, irritating his sister. A cousin was sitting in this same parlor one day when he felt a presence in the room. After spotting a large, dark shape behind him, he fled the house. Another relative reported a disembodied, floating head.

Although Alonzo never had a personal experience in his aunt's home, the family stories remained with him. For many years he worked as a realtor, but always looked up local ghost tours and events while on business trips around the country. In 2009 Alonzo founded Haunted Orange County (www.hauntedoc.com) as a way of pursuing his interest in the paranormal. Haunted Orange County has since joined the burgeoning ranks of organizations providing "ghost tours" in most major metropolitan areas in the United States and many of its smaller towns.[6] Alzono's ghost tours of Orange and Santa Ana, California, allow customers to hear about the spirits of the Howe-Waffle House, Chapman Antique Mall, and other locations. Located just south of Los Angeles and Hollywood, in close proximity to the stars of many paranormal reality shows, Alonzo recruited celebrities to join the ranks of Haunted Orange County for occasional special events.

In the fall of 2015, Alonzo reached out to me (Chris). Haunted Orange County hoped to shoot publicity materials of a ghost investigation for an upcoming event and viewed Chapman University as a possible location. Upon hearing about the recent tale of a professor's interrupted lecture that opened this book, along with other ghost stories from the Waltmar

Theater on campus, Alonzo agreed to round up a team of "celebrity investigators" to examine the claims.

I followed Alonzo's group on an overnight investigation of Smith Hall and the Waltmar Theater. Joining us was Ben Hansen, former host of the SyFy channel's paranormal show *Fact or Fake,* singer-songwriter and paranormal enthusiast Ryan Adams, Susan Slaughter of *Ghost Hunters International* (SyFy), Kristen Luman of *Ghost Mine* (SyFy), Chad Lindberg of *Ghost Stalkers* (Destination America), psychic/sensitive Don Staggs, Frank Argueta and Genevieve Federhen of the paranormal podcast *West of the Rockies,* and Christiane Elin and Ernie Alonzo of Haunted Orange County.

At about 9 p.m., the group gathered on campus for introductions, to hear the claims about spirits at Chapman University, and to prepare their equipment for the investigation. It was immediately apparent how excited the group was to be able to use their ghost-hunting equipment, some of it recently purchased. Susan Slaughter produced a large, hard case and opened it up on a table, carefully removing a series of devices from layers of molded foam as Chad did the same next to her. The table quickly filled with flashlights and batteries, alongside equipment more specific to ghost hunting.

Each had an EMF meter, a small handheld device which detects fluctuations in electromagnetic energy that ghost hunters believe may indicate the presence of spirits. Both had GoPro cameras, specially modified to see into the UV and IR spectrums by removing some of the camera's lens filters. The result is called a "full-spectrum camera," believed to capture images that may be invisible to the naked eye. Each carried a small, handheld recorder that would be used to attempt to capture spirit voices or EVPs (electronic voice phenomena). Chad showed off his "spirit box," a device that continually sweeps through the AM/FM radio spectrum, stopping on each station for a brief moment before moving to the next. Ghost hunters ask questions of a spirit and hope that it will use the device to cobble together a message composed of words from different radio stations.[7] Susan inserted batteries into a REM-Pod, a proximity sensor that would light up should it detect a change in static electricity in the atmosphere.

Certainly the most unique of the investigatory tools produced by Susan and Chad was a teddy bear. The teddy bear was a new purchase for Chad and he was excited to test it out. He told me it was a "trigger object." Trigger objects are items that ghost hunters believe might attract the attention of spirits. For example, in places that are purportedly haunted by the ghosts of children, ghost hunters might bring along a ball, hoping that spirits will push the ball during their investigation. Should a ghost be reported to be angered by the sight of a picture of the deceased or by the smell of cigar smoke, the ghost hunters might set such a photo on a table or smoke a cigar in the haunted building. Although there was no reason to suspect that the spirit of Smith Hall or the Waltmar Theater might be a child or otherwise attracted to teddy bears, Chad brought it anyway, to test it out. Unlike other trigger objects that are everyday items, Chad's teddy bear came specially equipped. Encased in its body were motion detectors and colored bulbs that enable the bear to light up if it senses movement. Embedded heat sensors detect any changes in room temperature, with especially cold temperatures indicating the possible presence of a ghost.

Trumping these features was the inclusion of a voice synthesizer in the bear. Should it become cold or feel movement around it, the bear would announce in a cartoonish voice that it had detected a presence. At random intervals, the bear would speak on its own, saying phrases such as "play with me," in the hopes of enticing interaction with a reluctant spirit.

Once this bevy of equipment had been prepared and stowed away in pockets and bags, the team of investigators split into two. I followed half of the investigators to the Waltmar Theater, while the other half traveled to Smith Hall.

A Face in the Window?

The ghost of Smith Hall has no purported identity to date, but the disturbances at the Waltmar Theater are rumored to be the activity of a former professor who suffered a heart attack in the 1980s the day before the opening of a new show. Theater technicians claim to have seen a dark figure walking along the catwalk and lights turning on and off in offices. Our group moved up to the catwalk immediately upon entering the theater, turned out the lights, and prepared for an EVP session. Ben Hansen turned on his tape recorder and warned the group to announce

Figure 4.1. Ben Hansen shows the author a strange object filmed on a thermal camera

loudly any accidental noises, such as coughs and footsteps, to ensure that incidental noises were not mistaken for sounds made by a spirit.

Ben proceeded to ask a series of questions, pausing between each to allow time for the spirit to imprint its answer on the tape: "Are you a faculty member here?" "Do you walk along this catwalk?" "We are here to tell your story. We may not be able to come back here again. Here is your chance to tell us . . . who are you?" "Can you make a noise for us?" At several points during this exercise, Ben and others reported hearing creaks and noises coming from the stage below us and another that sounded as if someone sat down in one of the audience seats.

Failing to generate any further responses, the group moved to the stage. Ben decided to observe the space with a thermal camera, which is designed to pick up differences in temperature, registered as different colors on the display. Before long, Ben became excited by images captured on his camera and called me over to view a recording (see figure 4.1). As the video played, I could see the shape of the window in the grainy shades of red and green produced by the camera. A small white dot appeared in the center of the window and moved across it, occasionally dipping out of view and then ascending again. To Ben and some of the other investigators looking on, the dot appeared to be a head, as if someone was walking back and forth in front of the window, playfully ducking out of view and reappearing. Unfortunately, the potential specter was quickly brought down to Earth when members of the team realized that the "dot" was actually a reflection of the camera lens on the window. The group accepted this explanation, despite their initial exuberance.

A Knock at the Door and a Ghost in the Closet

Having failed to document any ghostly activity in the Waltmar Theater, our group reunited with the investigators in Smith Hall. Unfortunately, I had been at the wrong place at the wrong time. The group from Smith Hall excitedly briefed us on an abundance of ghostly activity.[8]

Psychic Don Staggs had been running the investigation and assembled the group in Smith Hall 211, the scene of the ghostly footsteps that had interrupted a professor's lecture. Don stood near the front of the room. Singer Ryan Adams and actor/ghost investigator Chad Lindberg were also near the front of the room, sitting on the floor with their backs

Figure 4.2. Chad Lindberg and Ryan Adams in Smith Hall 211 (Chapman University)

leaning against the whiteboard (see figure 4.2). The remainder of the team sat in tables at the back of the room.

Don almost immediately felt a "cold spot" in the room, which moved from near his location to underneath a nearby table.[9] This prompted Don to ask a series of questions as others in the group swept the room with EMF detectors and thermal cameras: "Do you have a name?" "Are you a boy or a girl?" He set a small flashlight on the corner of a table and told the ghost, "Go ahead and knock this over." The flashlight did not move, but Ryan Adams soon announced that he could "feel cold over here." Don moved his hands near Ryan and confirmed that the cold spot had moved.

Meanwhile, Susan Slaughter had moved toward the front of the room, near the door. Soon after, she announced: "Whoa! Did you hear that knock?" Both Chad Lindberg and Don Staggs confirmed hearing a light knock at the door. Lindberg quickly opened the door but did not see anyone outside. Chad closed the door and Don implored of the ghost, "If you are here, please knock on the door again."

At that point, according to those present, a loud, audible knock came from the door. Lindberg immediately threw open the door but found no one outside. Several in the group raced in to the hallway and looked down the stairwell, but could find nobody that could have produced the knock and escaped quickly enough to be out of sight. As Don Staggs reported to me: "Something actually knocked on that door. At the time that it did it, I didn't pick up on anything. We opened the door and there was nobody there and nobody could have run away fast enough."

This concluded the reported activity for the evening, but Don was able to add several psychic "impressions" of the possible spirit. First of all, the ghost was male and "worked here" sometime in the past. At the time of his death, the ghost was in his "late thirties" and had dark hair. Don did not pick up any impressions about the cause of the ghost's demise, but did sense that his name was "Henry or Hank."

And Henry liked to hide in a storage closet down the hall. "There is something in that locked storage room," he had told the group earlier in the evening. Later he confirmed that sometimes spirits will "hide somewhere they don't think you will go." When asked what would be the purpose of a spirit hiding, Don noted that some spirits know that people such as him can facilitate them "crossing over to the other side," but some ghosts might be afraid to do so, because they fear what might happen to them when they are judged in the afterlife. "Perhaps the spirit was an adulterer," he speculated, "and grew up believing that adultery could cause him to go to hell. He may be afraid of the 'light' and what will happen if he goes into it."

Don was able to provide some comfort to the employees, students, and faculty that work in Smith Hall. Whoever "Henry" or "Hank" is, he reported, "he is not something bad or demonic." Demonic spirits will "try to do things like pinch, push, and scratch. . . . Nothing like that is going on here."

Jefferson, Texas

In contrast to the supposedly harmless ghosts encountered at Chapman, all three of the authors accompanied ghost hunters in Texas who were tracking purportedly demonic entities. Situated on Big Cypress Bayou in the piney woods of northeast Texas lies the city of Jefferson, a haven for ghost hunters. Before the railroads moved into the northern part of the state, Texans were dependent upon boat traffic to receive goods and supplies. Jefferson was founded in 1840 at the perfect location for a port. Boats traveled up the Mississippi River to the Red River, which fed into nearby Caddo Lake. Even large stern wheelers could paddle through the lake to its eventual meet-up with Big Cypress Bayou.

By default the town held a monopoly on shipping for hundreds of miles around. Cotton moved through by the ton. During the Civil War, the Confederacy depended upon the Jefferson port to provide Texas troops with supplies. Stores, hotels, shipping companies, and other signs of a bustling economy competed for downtown real estate with taverns, cathouses, pool halls, and other necessary vices of a nineteenth-century boomtown. Indeed, the good and the bad appeared in equal measure during Jefferson's heyday. The population swelled to nearly eight thousand by 1872. Grand homes appeared on the hills. At the same time, fights at the local bars were frequent, with an especially dangerous area near the river earning the nickname "Murder Alley."

As the railroad came and reliance on river traffic eroded, so did Jefferson's fragile economy.[10] Shipping companies folded; the population dwindled over the years to about two thousand citizens; houses sat empty and the taverns closed; a bayou formerly alive with the sounds of steamboats and dock workers became silent. It's a familiar story of the American frontier: a boomtown gone bust. Today Jefferson is bucking that trend. Its cobblestone streets are lined with quaint, locally owned shops, hotels, and bed-and-breakfasts, and on weekends the town center buzzes with activity. Even midweek a surprising number of people stroll around the antique stores, restaurants, and gift shops.

Jefferson's resurgence is due—at least in part—to the ghosts of its sometimes violent past. Rumored to be one of the most haunted locales in Texas, nearly every major downtown building and many of the surrounding homes claim spirit manifestations. Guests at the historic Jefferson Hotel, dating to 1851, report mysterious footsteps at night, faucets that turn on and off by themselves, and the laughter of unseen children. Visitors frequently request the most haunted rooms. Nearby is the Excelsior Hotel, where the filmmaker Steven Spielberg is said to have been frightened away by a ghostly child.[11] A "Ghost Train" operates from the depot during the tourist season. The Grove, a historic home, provides tours on Sunday mornings for those hoping to spot its several resident ghosts, which include a woman and priest in the house, as well as a sinister smiling man who roams the gardens. With few exceptions, the town has accepted its ghostly reputation.

Jodi Breckenridge, a local resident, is one of the biggest beneficiaries of Jefferson's ghosts. For several years she has led a nighttime walking ghost tour. On a busy weekend sixty people (more during the Halloween season) follow the affable Jodi through the city streets and into the surrounding residential areas. Christopher joined an excited group of about thirty on a November Saturday evening. Jodi led us past a two-story brick building with an iron balcony, where she reported that previous tours had captured pictures of a Confederate soldier and had heard sounds of a little boy singing. From there we wandered past the Excelsior and Jefferson hotels, hearing tales about the most haunted rooms. A brisk walk uphill on darkened streets brought us to another historic mansion where the figure of a ghostly lady reportedly glides about the yard. From there we meandered to The Grove and learned about the spectral priest and his friends.

Surprisingly, Jodi readily admits that she is quite afraid of ghosts. It is part of her charm, and she reports several frightening encounters during tours. She claims she watched as a brash skeptic was hit in the back of the legs by a mysterious opening door. Ghostly voices and invisible hands on her back have led her to flee buildings at various times. One place frightened Jodi more than any other—a former tavern turned coffee bar by the name of Big Cypress Coffee House. "On a scale of one to ten this place is an eleven," she told our group, as she nervously led us into the building. We were warned against using the bathrooms, where people report being grabbed by unseen presences and trapped by a door that sometimes refuses to let patrons exit. Upstairs, however, is where most of the action occurs. The tour previously included a visit to the second floor, before people reported being pushed by spirits on the stairs. Others heard voices ordering them to "get out!" and Jodi once felt something pull her hair. A visiting psychic declared the building home to 150 restless, sometimes angry spirits. These days, Jodi prefers to stay downstairs near the exit as she relates these tales.

The House of 150 Ghosts

The now defunct Big Cypress Coffee House became notorious for its tales of angry ghosts that push, prod, and otherwise harass those who dare to visit. Part of the building's fearsome reputation was directly due to its owner Duane's self-described status as a Wiccan.[12] Although Wiccans worship Earth in a personified form, typically referred to as "Gaia," the strong philosophical differences between Wicca and Satanism were lost in Jefferson's rumor mill. Locals said Duane was a warlock.

Warlock or not, he proved an accommodating host, as he agreed to let us, along with a group of graduate students, spend the night in the upper floor of the coffee house. Concerned that we might not have the complete "ghost-hunting experience" if left to our own devices, Duane invited three others to accompany us on our overnight stay in his ghost-infested shop. He introduced us to "Lee," a short, blond, thirty-something professional medium who lived in a smaller town nearby. On weekends Lee used to linger at the coffee shop, providing psychic readings for $30. Also in attendance was "Gloria," who prefers the label "clairvoyant" to medium. Also in her thirties, Gloria is a colorful character, as evidenced by her bright red hair, sporting a prominent white streak. When not at her day job at a cartography company, the

Figure 4.3. Gloria uses an EMF meter to look for ghosts

recently divorced Gloria provides psychic readings and uses her skills to aid ghost hunters. Accompanying Gloria was her friend Victoria, a thirty-two-year-old bank employee. Making no claim to psychic powers, Victoria considers herself an amateur ghost hunter. Throughout the evening she generously allowed us to borrow her ghost-hunting equipment.

At the coffee house, the psychics immediately sensed the presence of ghosts. Lee held a brief conversation with an elderly male spirit standing behind us. The spirit was not particularly pleased by our presence, she stated in a somber voice. Victoria took us on a tour of the downstairs. A narrow hallway to the left of the coffee bar led to a bathroom and storage room at the back of the building. Only the bravest would dare set foot in the bathroom, Duane warned us, a sly grin on his face, since the spirits especially enjoy poking, prodding, and speaking to people using the facilities.

Victoria told us of a dramatic encounter she had during a previous investigation at the coffee house. Her group heard a mysterious buzzing sound coming from a storage area behind the coffee bar. There they saw a dark red streak of light ascend through the ceiling with a loud pop. Ghost hunters believe that spirits can manifest themselves as orbs or streaks of light, which often appear in photographs and sometimes are seen with the naked eye.[13] "The color of orbs is important," Victoria told me, "because it tells you the nature of the entity involved." Unfortunately for us, she continued, "red energy indicates evil."

The downstairs bathroom aside, the majority of ghostly activity is reported from a room on the second floor of the coffee house. As Victoria and our psychic guides chatted with Duane around a table, we decided to finally see the upstairs for ourselves. We cautiously ascended the staircase as it wound around two landings, wary because the ghosts have a propensity for pushing and pulling people climbing the stairs. It was with a small measure of relief that we entered the haunted upper floor without incident. The staircase ended at a hallway. To the left was a small alcove packed with a ladder, buckets of paint or plaster, and assorted tools. Duane told us this was equipment left behind by workers frightened away by the angry spirits. Turning to the right we entered the room where we would spend the night. And what a room it was.

Dusty, wood-paneled floors creaked, groaned, and otherwise protested as we walked back and forth in a space about the size of a small café. Evidence of a Wiccan Halloween party recently hosted by Duane was strewn about the room: large rubber spiders hung from the ceiling, rubber rats peered from behind furniture and between books on a shelf, a large witch doll sat on a chair, and a big fake skull rested on an end table. Near the doorway were two thronelike chairs on a riser (see figure 4.4). According to Duane, the "thrones" remain from a time when the space was used by local Freemasons. A nearby table had been used as their altar, he said. He warned us about sitting on the thrones, as people claim to have been physically ejected from them by unseen hands.

A queen-sized bed on an iron frame was in the back half of the room. "I used to sleep there," Duane told us later, until the night he heard growling that sounded like a large dog and footsteps going around his bed. He now slept in a different part of the building, though the bed remained. "I decided they didn't want people staying in here."

A set of curtains hanging from flimsy rods blocked off the back third of the room. Behind them was another random assortment of ladders,

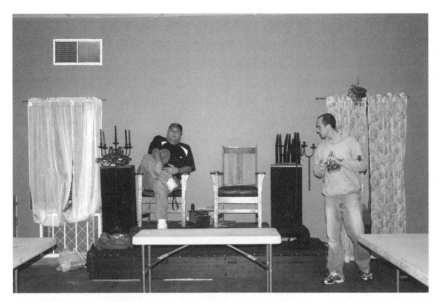

Figure 4.4. The upper floor of the Big Cypress Coffee House

a table saw, boxes, and more buckets of paint and plaster. As we were about to step into this area to explore further, Gloria, Lee, and Victoria entered the room, looking quite concerned. In an emotion-filled voice, Gloria said, "I don't like this room!" Gesturing at the curtains, she continued, "The evil is strongest back there. The spirits come from here." Duane later confirmed for us that most of the "activity" in the room originates from behind the curtains. He claimed that a man had been found hanged in the far left corner. Police ruled it a suicide, but the man's hands had been tied behind his back. He went on to tell us that a woman had jumped out a nearby window, and another woman had been raped in the alley outside. We did not attempt to confirm these claims.

Victoria waved an EMF meter behind the curtains. It emitted a dramatic squeal, signaling the presence of strong energy. She then pulled out her camera and pushed her arm through the curtain to take photos and scanned the resultant pictures for orbs. Gloria, in the meantime, was becoming progressively more upset. She told us that she could feel the negative energies of the Ku Klux Klan. Upon questioning, however, she could not clarify what this meant. Were there ghosts of dead KKK

Figure 4.5. Gloria overcome by spirits

members present in the room? Were angry victims of KKK activities looking for vengeance? As she became progressively more distraught, Gloria whispered, "I . . . just . . . don't like the KKK or what they stand for," before collapsing to the floor (see figure 4.5).

For several minutes Gloria mumbled unintelligibly as Victoria tended to her. "She is so hot!" exclaimed Victoria. Indeed, Gloria's forehead was quite warm to the touch. After some rest and a drink of water, Gloria sat up. "The spirits are angry we are here. Several rushed me at once," she said. The influx of spiritual energy had overwhelmed Gloria, as if "a hundred voices were speaking at once."

Gloria, Lee, and Victoria conferred in hushed voices. It would be impossible for us to stay the night absent some form of protection from the spirits, they decided. Springing into action, they carefully rearranged items in the room. Gloria pulled the drapes as closely together as possible. Victoria roamed the room and removed some of the Halloween decorations. Finally, Gloria and Lee arranged four tall candleholders in a large circle around Duane's abandoned bed.

Gloria fetched a ritual dagger from her car and began a protection spell. She murmured softly to herself as she slowly circled the candle-holders, occasionally raising the dagger above her head with both hands. The ritual would create a "magic protective circle" within the area cordoned off by the candles, Victoria told us. Spirits in the room would be allowed to communicate with those within the confines of the circle if so desired, but the ritual would ensure that evil entities could cause no harm. With a final flourish, Gloria lit each candle, completing the ritual. Feeling spent by the ritual, Gloria fell back upon the bed and closed her eyes. For the next couple of hours, she would intermittently awaken, mumble, and fall back into a semi-stupor. Lee was concerned that she might have been possessed by a spirit. But other than seeming exhausted, Gloria suffered no ill effects that we could perceive.

For the next several hours we roamed the building. On occasion we would borrow an EMF meter to search for spirit energy. We shot pictures from various angles, looking for orbs. We took turns sitting in the haunted thrones. Finally tiring of the hunt, we rolled out our sleeping bags on the floor and laid down to sleep. Christopher and Carson slept inside the "protective circle"; Joseph slept outside of it, offering his services as the "control group," but the night passed without incident. We awoke in the early morning and packed up for our return home.

Naturally, family and friends who knew of our adventure wanted to know what had happened during the night. We imagine our recounting of the night's events differs substantially from the psychics'. For Gloria, Lee, and Victoria, the evening was one of continual and dramatic events. Victoria saw orbs of evil energy in her photographs. Gloria was overwhelmed by dozens of ghosts rushing her at once. They talked to ghosts that were standing behind us and conducted rituals to keep us safe. Gloria swooned, gasped, and collapsed at the behest of the pushy spirits. We were able to spend the night, in their view, only through their direct intervention to stave off evil forces.

Greenville, Tennessee

One late summer day in a rural southern town, I (Joseph) am in a large suite located inside a hotel that was originally constructed in the late 1800s. Gruesome stories about the tavern that previously existed on the site from the late 1700s through the Civil War still circulate locally. There is a well-known spirit that supposedly steals spoons from the restaurant in the hotel that everyone calls "Green Room Grace." The room I am standing in is dimly lit and ornately decorated with antique furniture. In my hands are dowsing rods, tools traditionally used to locate water or oil; however I am seeking neither—instead I am attempting to use them to communicate with spirits that haunt the historic building. My efforts to communicate with these ghosts are part of the instruction I am receiving in a "ghostology" class that trains would-be ghost hunters. I signed up for the class to get firsthand experience with dowsing as a form of spirit communication, which is not a widely used method by ghost hunters. I wanted to spend some time with believers in dowsing and get a sense of how they understood the practice.

Ghostology 101

Before officially beginning the course, the instructor regaled the class with multiple stories of deathlore (folklore about death) about the hotel, and the specific room where we held class, which he claimed was the most haunted room in the hotel.[14] The instructor formally began the class with a traditional Christian prayer, and then provided a brief overview of the group's view about what ghosts are, how to track them, and how to communicate with them. He talked about quantum mechanics and stated that scientific theories were beginning to come around to the inclusion of life after death and the soul. He also stated that "what we believe about the world determines reality" and that "we would get out of the process what we put in," meaning that if we did not believe in ghosts we would not be able to see the evidence of their presence. He then went through a list of ways investigators can determine if a location is haunted, ranging from disappearing objects to results from photography and EVP sessions, as well as changes to electromagnetic fields and temperature.

After instructions on how to identify the presence of spirits, the students began to take photos throughout the room in an effort to capture "ghost orbs," especially those with "Kirlian emanations." We were told to take multiple pictures of the same spot in order to have "control pictures." Once a "hot spot" of ghost activity had been located by successfully capturing orbs in multiple photos, we moved on to efforts to try and communicate with the spirits in the room through the use of question and answer, with dowsing rods acting as the medium for spirits to communicate with us.

The dowsing rods are used to receive yes or no answers from spirits responding to voiced questions. The instructor told us that if the rods crossed in front of us the answer to an asked question was "yes," and if they opened out the answer was "no." In addition, the rods could be used to locate spirit activity by virtue of pointing toward haunted locations in a space, then crossing when one actually encountered the presence of a spirit. As instructed, I entered a meditative state of mind, holding the rods loosely between my thumbs and index fingers, and walked in the direction the rods pointed. When the rods crossed the teacher instructed me to stop and attempt to communicate with the spirit apparently haunting the suite. I asked the ghost, "Are you a female?" The rods crossed, indicating an answer of yes. I then asked, "Were you more than fifty when you died?" Again the rods crossed rather than opening out, indicating another yes.

Eventually my classmates would also take turns attempting to communicate with the spirits in the suite. We each went one by one, while everyone else except the instructor waited outside. The goal was to have multiple students talk to the same spirit to corroborate and triangulate the information obtained, but it turned out that the responses we received were somewhat conflicting. As a result, our instructor had to "settle the score" by communicating with the spirit, as we novices were unable to successfully tap the lines of contact, at least with the same spirit. The instructor reported that the spirit was a woman who was between thirty and forty years old when she died, and also that he had spoken with her before while dowsing in the lobby of the hotel on previous occasions.

The all-day class ended with the instructor showing us archives of what he considered to be the best visual (orbs) and aural (EVP) evidence his group had collected. Reflecting on the course, I marvel at how talk of science, religion, and the paranormal, the use of contemporary technology and divination, and quests for enlightenment and discovery all blended together in the experience of using metal rods to talk to spirits.

Themes of Ghost Hunting

Ghosts in the Machines

In our time doing comparative field work with ghost hunters, we have noticed some common themes among such groups.

First, the use of various forms of technology is ubiquitous. Even among people who claim to be "sensitive" or mediums, the use of technology to track the purported movement of spirits was present among all groups. Serious ghost hunting in the contemporary West requires digital thermostats, electromagnetic field meters, AM radio scanners, night vision technology, and photography—moving and still—of all manner of imputations (e.g., radiographic, digital, film). Figure 4.6 provides a summary of some of the common language and subcultural argot used by ghost hunters.

Ghost hunters utilize a dizzying variety of highly sensitive and technical equipment in their investigations. One might expect that such technology would serve to clarify empirical reality. In fact, the wash of ambiguous sensory input produced by such equipment blurs perception, substituting the uncanny for the everyday and firing the imagination. These various forms of technology allow participants to take measurements, set up quasi-experimental scenarios (often combined with mediumship), and make interpretations of the data generated. The ability to derive meanings from ambiguous sensory information serves to enhance mediums' powers while simultaneously affirming shared and preexisting beliefs, especially as individuals review evidence and come to an agreement about meaning.

Syncretism and Magical Rites

Within religion or philosophy, syncretism refers to the combination of different beliefs and practices into a singular belief system. We have found ghost belief to be inherently syncretic in nature. Although the belief in ghosts is often considered beyond the bounds of exclusive, organized religious institutions, ghost believers themselves rarely consider their beliefs to be isolated from conventional religious beliefs (especially angels and demons) or New Age belief systems (especially astrology and psychic powers). There are many people for whom conventional religious beliefs

Term	Definition
Cold Spot	Ghost hunters believe that ghosts may absorb the heat or "energy" in an area in order to manifest, leaving a spot in the room that is colder than the surrounding area. When ghost hunters either feel a cold spot or use a thermometer to detect one, they believe that a ghost is present.
Electronic Voice Phenomena (EVP)	The purported voice of a ghost captured on tape. Ghost hunters frequently use handheld recording devices during their investigations. They will ask questions of the ghost and allow the tape to run. In most cases, the "voice" is not heard during the taping and only discovered upon playback and manipulation of the recording.
EMF (Electromagnetic Field) Meter	An EMF meter is a device that detects electronic and magnetic fields. Ghost hunters believe that ghosts produce magnetic energy that they can detect with the device.
Ghost/Spirit	A ghost is generally believed to be a manifestation of a deceased person. Sometimes witnesses will claim to see a ghost. At other times they will believe a ghost is present due to hearing strange noises or voices, witnessing or noting the movement of household objects without an obvious explanation, or detecting unexplained odors. Generally the ghost is believed to be present because it has become "trapped" on the earthly plane or has some form of unfinished business on Earth. At times, ghost hunters may determine through their investigation that the ghost is actually a "residual haunting" or "inhuman entity" (see below).
Haunting	The claim that a particular area receives regular visitations from a ghost.
Medium/Psychic/ Sensitive	A person who claims to be able to communicate with spirits. Mediums may claim the ability to see or communicate with ghosts that are not visible to others, to psychically witness the past events that produced the ghost, and/or to enter a trance state in which the ghost speaks through them.
Nonhuman/Inhuman Spirit/Demon	At times ghost hunters will claim that a ghost is not the result of a human person that once lived on Earth. Nonhuman spirits are often believed to desire to harass, harm, or even possess the people they are "haunting."
Orbs/Ghost Orbs/Spirit Orbs	Some ghost hunters believe that ghosts may manifest as small orbs of light. Sometimes these "orbs" will be visible to the naked eye. At other times, ghost hunters will only find the orbs after examining photographs taken at the haunted location.
REM-Pod	A small, electronic device with multicolored lights. The device detects changes in electromagnetic fields using sounds and lights to alert ghost hunters of any changes in these fields.
Residual Haunting	Ghost hunters believe that ghosts and nonhuman spirits possess intelligence, making it possible to communicate with them. In certain cases, it is believed that, by some unknown means, a home or other location has "recorded" past events and replays them on a regular basis. For example, if the owners of a "haunted" home claim to witness a young girl walk down a hallway at a particular time, ghost hunters may conclude that the home has a residual haunting and that it is not possible to communicate with the ghost.

Figure 4.6. The Language of Ghost Hunting (*Continues on next page.*)

Term	Definition
Spirit Box	An electronic device that continually scans the AM/FM radio spectrum for stations, stopping briefly at each. Some ghost hunters believe that spirits will use the device to cobble together a message consisting of words taken from multiple stations.
Thermal Camera	A camera that captures different levels of heat, displaying them on the camera monitor and in any films taken in shades of blue and red.
Trigger Object	An object that is used to entice a purported spirit into interaction. For example, a ball might be placed in a room in the hopes that a nearby spirit might cause it to roll across the floor.

Figure 4.6. (*Continued.*)

are their exclusive interest in the supernatural, but ghost believers tended to hold a plethora of other supernatural beliefs.[15] Each of the groups we studied also used some form of magical rites—typically involving incantations and ritual objects such as sage, holy water, or daggers—to communicate with, protect people from, or cleanse locations of spirits.

Different groups fused ghost beliefs with varying other forms of supernaturalism. For instance, for the group in Jefferson, this syncretism was expressed with reference to a wide array of New Age beliefs and ritual practices. Astrology, Wicca, and psychic powers were prominent features. Three members of this group maintained at least semi-regular professional activity in New Age circles through their roles as a medium, a psychic, and the entrepreneur of a small café that functioned as a meeting house for locals interested in New Age themes and services. In this group, there was virtually no discussion of traditional religious versions of supernaturalism, while there was an extensive integration of ideas from tarot, neo-paganism, and the occult. New Age elements were used to explain hauntings, and also as a means of communicating with apparitions.

In contrast, the group in southern Appalachia fused ghost beliefs with other aspects of paranormalism such as UFOs and Sasquatch, but also with deinstitutionalized versions of Christian supernaturalism, as revealed in interesting phrases such as "Jesus was the greatest metaphysician who ever lived." Meanwhile, another group I did field work with in southern Appalachia blended ghost belief strictly with Christian demonology, identifying New Age beliefs and practices as being "of the devil."[16] The content of the syncretic beliefs and practices fused with ghost hunting varies from group to group, but generally spirit belief is fused with some type of deinstitutionalized supernaturalism from other traditions.

While the contents of the belief systems for each of the groups were distinct from one another, they all used rituals for cleansing or protection. These rites had the character of magic, where practitioners attempt to control or appease spirits through prescribed bodily movements, sacred recitations, use of ritual objects, and direct commands to the spirits. The goal is one of performing the rite in order to produce a this-worldly result. These rites serve as a means of perceived agency, as practitioners attempt to control the hauntings in a given location.

Centrality of Narrative Experience

A final theme we noticed among ghost hunters is the fundamental importance of personal narratives to maintaining ghost-related subcultures. Personal stories, often layered with a veneer of semi-skepticism, are used to neutralize preemptive or potentially skeptical objections from a "rationalist" point of view.[17] Narratives in the settings we observed took three primary forms: *historical framing via deathlore*, vicarious haunting *experiences* (shared interpretations of empirical or narrative information), and *experiential recollection*.

In each of the groups we observed, historical deathlore was used to set the mood of a haunted location, explain perceived anomalies detected via technology and experienced in such locations, and retrospectively to reconstruct experiences; in short, before, during, and after ghost encounters. Put another way, it is vital that haunted places have a "story." If that story is not readily provided by local folklore or known tragic events that occurred at or near the location, ghost hunters will take an active part in constructing the ghostly narrative of a location, often relying upon psychics and sensitives to fill in absent details about the presumed identity and motivation of the spirit or spirits.

Concerning vicarious hauntings, such experiences occur in a number of ways. Some people experience hauntings indirectly via the consumption of ghost-themed media, individual or collective assessment of information generated via technologically mediated reality, and affirmation of the personal narratives of ghost experiences of others. Consumption of ghost-themed media includes viewing movies, television shows, and websites centered on ghosts, as well as reading about ghosts. This form of vicarious experience tends to be the most privatized, although it can clearly be shared as well. The assessment of data generated by technology occurs almost incessantly in the process of a ghost hunt, and also typically well after the event through analysis of the gathered information, such as listening for EVPs and inspecting photographic and video footage after the fact. While this process may begin individually (e.g., a person gets a spike on a Gauss meter while walking around a haunted space or hears a voice in a playback), it moves quickly to collective assessment as others are called in to confirm the evidence. Accordingly, evidence gathered through technology is often consumed in a collective setting where believers affirm each other's views that the information is evidence of spiritual activity. This usually involves a process whereby those who may initially be skeptical or oblivious to the evidence presented are persuaded of the data's validity through verbal cues.

Consumption of others' personal narratives of spectral experience is the most powerful form of vicarious experience. This type of vicarious experience is so powerful that it can become a primary fount of belief. Many people believe in hauntings primarily on the strength of the experiential testimony of trusted others.[18] For example, when we were following the group in Jefferson, Victoria assisted Gloria the entire night, vicariously experiencing apparitions through the commands and utterances of the medium. She told us she "had no special gifts" like the medium and considered herself "an amateur ghost hunter at best." Nonetheless she believed in the medium's power, which she fed on (and supplied credence to) by shadowing her in order to experience hauntings second-hand. As this example shows, in many cases the line between vicarious and direct spectral encounters is not absolute.

Experiential recollection of first-hand haunting experiences is the bedrock of ghost belief. For believers, direct experience of apparitions is one of the most powerful and dramatic events that can occur to the still living. Among individuals in all of the groups we studied, recollections of spectral encounters formed the core of what makes ghosts compellingly real and cognitively intriguing. Whether it was Duane's experience of awaking in the night to a howling, malevolent apparition at the foot of his bed or one of the Appalachian group's primary investigator's recounting of a ritual cleansing in which light bulbs splintered into shards, personal stories of ghost encounters are the primary form of evidence believers present for the reality of apparitions. Indeed, although ghost-hunting groups regularly present a wide range of technologically mediated information as evidence, personal narratives consistently hold the most sway over audiences. Skeptical audience members may question the authenticity, veracity, or interpretation of mediated evidence, but are much less likely to question the legitimacy of personal encounter narratives. After all, how can one disprove someone else's past personal experience? To attempt to do so would be tantamount to calling the narrator a liar. This "just so" characteristic lends the personal narrative a central place in ghost lore (as well as in mainstream religion).[19]

Patterns of Ghost Beliefs, Experiences, and Media Consumption

Reflecting their cross-cultural popularity, ghosts are one of the most common features of paranormalism in the United States. Slightly over 40% of Americans believe that places can be haunted by spirits (see figure 4.7). If we include those who have not decided one way or the other

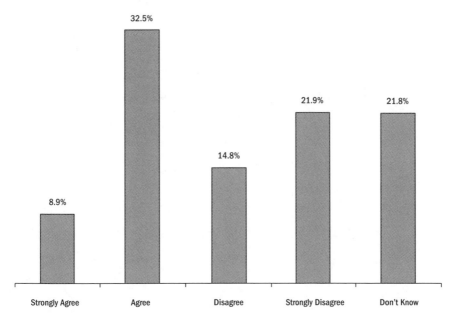

Figure 4.7. Places Can be Haunted by Spirits (Chapman University Survey of American Fears, 2015, n=1541)

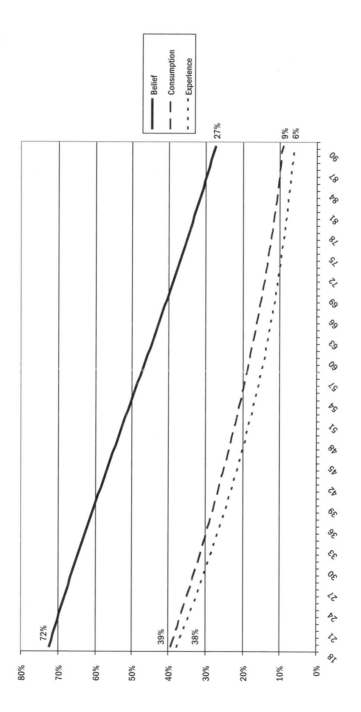

Figure 4.8. Ghost Belief, Media Consumption, and Experience by Age (Baylor Religion Survey 2005)

about the reality of hauntings ("don't know"), the number climbs to nearly two-thirds of Americans (63%).

To assess the sociological patterns of ghost belief, experience, and media consumption, we examined three binary measures: belief in ghosts (absolutely or probably vs. all other responses), whether someone has ever experienced a haunting (yes vs. no), and whether someone has read about ghosts through books or websites (yes vs. no). There are higher levels of interest in ghosts among women, religious seekers, and most especially, the young (see figure 4.8). For instance, 72% of eighteen-year-old Americans believe in ghosts, while 39% of eighteen-year-olds have experienced a haunting and/or consumed ghost-themed media. In sharp contrast, for Americans age ninety, the probability of ghost belief (24%), experience (9%), and media consumption (6%) is much lower.[20] Ghost belief, experiences, and media consumption appear to be on the rise among younger generations of Americans, likely reflecting the ebb of institutional forms of religion among these cohorts, a pattern consistent with other Western countries.[21]

The hunt for ghosts allowed us to experience the allure of both *discovery* and *enlightenment*. Most of the investigators attempted to document the presence of spirits with their array of specialized equipment, hoping to engage in an act of discovery. Every possible "hit" on one of those devices produced high levels of excitement. Alternative explanations, such as the reflection of a camera lens in a window, were readily accepted, but groups held out hope that the *next* event captured on a device would remain unexplained. For mediums like Don Staggs and Gloria, however, the quest was not to gather scientific proof, but to understand the spirit world and to help those spirits when possible. No one can prove that such "impressions" originate with a ghost, but sensitives and mediums provide narrative details and comfort to the haunted that EMF meters cannot provide. Ultimately, spending time with ghost hunters was not about the ghosts. It was about the *people* who believe in and directly experience ghosts.

Ghost (or analogous) beliefs and experiences are prevalent and highly flexible concepts, allowing them to exist, persist, and thrive even in ostensibly secular, rationalized cultural contexts.[22] Their ability to transcend the ordinary in modern life confers upon spirits a potential for deep literary, metaphorical, and experiential power. By existing simultaneously within and beyond time, space, and life itself, the constraints of rationality can be shattered by phantasm, at least temporarily. Rather than banishing such beliefs to the past as "superstition," modern life provides spirits with ample space to haunt the present.

Still, this begs the question: How does belief in one type of supernaturalism such as ghosts relate to supernaturalism that is espoused by mainstream religious groups? Given that, for instance, ghosts and angels are very similar concepts (nonmaterial spirits with humanlike intentions), does belief in one lead to belief in the other? Like so many topics involving the paranormal, the answer defies simplistic assumptions.

5

Round Trip to Hell in a Flying Saucer?

Now the Spirit speaketh expressly, that in the latter times
some shall depart from the faith, giving heed to seducing
spirits, and doctrines of devils
—1 Timothy 4:1 (KJV)

Even though national surveys show a marked increase in the percentage of people in the U.S. who report no religious affiliation, Americans
are still a predominantly religious people.[1] In 2014, more than 70% of
Americans claimed affiliation with some type of Christian tradition.
Forty-five percent identified as Protestant, 24% as Catholic, and 5% as
"other" Christian, which generally represents conservative, nondenominational Christian sects. On the other hand, 21% do not affiliate with a
religious tradition and 3% report affiliating with organized groups outside of Judeo-Christian traditions. Forty-three percent of Americans
reported attending religious services at least once a month, and another
23% maintained *some* contact with a religious group by attending at least
once a year.[2] The majority of Americans also hold relatively traditional
beliefs. Nearly three-fifths have no doubts that God exists (58%), and
over three-fourths (78%) believe that the Bible is a divinely inspired,
"true" document.[3]

Given the high level of faith among Americans, the popularity of the
paranormal in the United States may be tied to the fate of conventional
religion. To the extent that the paranormal is in direct conflict with
conventional religion, its growth may remain limited to the minority of
Americans outside of conventional religion but still open to the supernatural. On the other hand, should conventional religion decline, as has been
occurring in the U.S. for the last quarter-century, this could open the door
to a revival of interest in alternative spiritualities and paranormal topics.

There is an alternative to tying the fate of the paranormal to the
growth, stability, or decline of conventional religion—the possibility that

religious Americans will accept paranormal beliefs as a *complement* to their religious beliefs. Clearly, at least some Christians must be interested in the paranormal judging by the prevalence and popularity of related television shows, books, podcasts, websites, and movies. Perhaps religious individuals simply do not see a conflict between believing in angels and ghosts at the same time, or simultaneously reading the Bible and UFO literature. Is there any harm in a Catholic visiting an astrologer? Or a Baptist hunting for Bigfoot?

Throughout American history there have been sporadic movements that directly tested the boundaries of Christianity by attempting to fuse Christian ideas with paranormal concepts. One of the most audacious of these was George Adamski's endeavor to bring Jesus to the flying saucers.

Jesus on a Flying Saucer

A colorful character by all accounts, George Adamski founded the Royal Order of Tibet in the 1930s to espouse his "cosmic philosophy," and attracted a small following. He had little formal schooling but enjoyed being called "professor" by eager students. By the 1940s, Adamski was living near the Mount Palomar observatory in California, working as a short-order cook. Fortuitously (his critics would say by design), Adamski began to claim UFO sightings just as interest in the subject was reaching new heights in the late 1940s. In October 1946 while peering at a meteor shower through his telescope, Adamski claimed that he spotted an object "similar in shape to a giant dirigible."[4] Adamski began to make frequent trips to the desert near his home, believing that "spaceships" might choose to land in less populated areas.

On November 20, 1952, Adamski and six associates traveled to a barren area near Desert Center, California, spent the morning exploring, and sat down to eat lunch at about noon. At that time a plane passed low over their heads, drawing the group's attention to a "gigantic cigar-shaped silvery ship without wings or appendages of any kind" hovering nearby.[5] According to his later recounting of the events, Adamski experienced a strange "feeling" that he must move to a location nearby. He asked his friends to drop him off there, and he then moved to a position about a mile away. Once safely alone, he claims to have seen a flash in the sky, followed by the appearance of a "beautiful small craft," which descended into a nearby cove. As he took pictures of the vicinity, he noticed a man standing near the entrance of a ravine. Upon approach, Adamski realized that he was face to face with an extraterrestrial:

> Now for the first time I fully realized that I was in the presence of a man from space—A HUMAN BEING FROM ANOTHER WORLD! . . . The beauty of his form surpassed anything I had ever seen. And the pleasantness of his face freed me of all thought of my personal self. . . . He was about five feet, six inches in height and weighed—according to our standard—about 135 pounds. . . . He was round faced with an extremely high forehead . . . and average size mouth with beautiful white teeth that shone when he smiled or spoke. As nearly as I can describe his skin the colouring would be an even, medium-colored suntan. And it did not look to me as though he had ever had to shave, for there was no more hair on his face than on a child's. His hair was sandy in colour and hung in beautiful waves to his shoulders, glistening more beautifully than any woman's I have ever seen.[6]

Adamski asked the being where he came from, but the long-haired spaceman apologetically shook his head to indicate that he did not speak English. Thankfully, he and the alien managed to communicate through a combination of "feelings, signs, and above all . . . telepathy."[7] The being indicated that he was part of a friendly landing party from Venus visiting Earth out of concern for recent nuclear testing. If humans do not change their ways, he warned, they will destroy themselves and surrounding planets. Having delivered this dire warning, the alien indicated that he had to leave and returned to his craft, which ascended out of sight.

Far tamer than the lurid UFO abduction tales of the 1980s and 1990s, Adamski's story was revelatory at the time. A ghost-written account of the event was tacked onto a recently completed compendium of UFO reports written by Desmond Leslie and published under the title *Flying Saucers Have Landed* in 1953.[8] The book was a great success and went through several printings. Adamski became a minor celebrity, appearing on radio shows, lecturing to large groups, and even meeting Queen Julianna of Holland in 1959, who had shown an interest in UFOs.[9] He followed up with two sequels, *Inside the Spaceships* and *Flying Saucers Farewell*, that recounted continued adventures with his "space brothers" including trips to outer space and a visit to a giant mothership.

Whether by accident or design, Adamski's tales represented an attempt to merge the paranormal with conventional religion by incorporating Christian symbolism. Jesus, it seems, was an alien incarnated on Earth to help humans learn to be peaceful. In *Flying Saucers Farewell*, Adamski devotes considerable space to demonstrating biblical support for his claims, including the argument that the space people are the biblical angels:

> The idea of angels having wings growing out of their shoulders and wearing long robes, was instilled in the minds of present-day people by the great artists who pictured them as such. The Bible has always described them as ordinary men from other worlds.[10]

He is even more direct, later in the same book: "Many people want to know if the space people are Christians. I would say they are better Christians than we are."

Adamski's attempt to merge Christianity with flying saucers did not succeed. His personal fortunes faded in the early 1960s. Some of his most ardent fans became disenchanted after his 1962 claim that the space brothers took him to Saturn to attend a conference.[11] Photos of spaceships included in his books were viewed with suspicion and proved easy to fake. Moreover, his eyewitness descriptions of outer space did not match the experiences of astronauts. Critics also noticed the astonishing similarities between Adamski's "nonfiction" works and *Pioneers of Space: A Trip to the Moon, Mars and Venus,* a science fiction novel he had published in 1949. Nevertheless, Adamski proved to be the template for the UFO "contactee" movement.[12]

Following Adamski, other contactee accounts typically included Christian symbols and themes.[13] The late George King (1919–97) received channeled messages from "cosmic masters" such as Mars Sector 6, Mars Sector 8, and Jesus himself (a Venusian, according to King).[14] The audacious King even claimed that Jesus personally endorsed his book *The Twelve Blessings*.[15] King's mother, Mary, was invited by the aliens to take a trip to space on January 19, 1959. Ever the proud mother, she brought a copy of her son's book to a rendezvous point where she was picked up by "a Space Craft Commanded by a Being known as MARS SECTOR 8." The craft traveled deep into space and entered a mothership wherein Mary King met "The Great Master Jesus Himself." Jesus thumbed through the book, blessed it, and kept the copy for himself.

Laura and the Chair of Knowledge

Although the movement certainly had its heyday in the 1950s and 1960s, there remains the occasional contactee representing this curious merger of Christianity and the space age, as we learned by visiting Laura Cyr, a formal postal worker who lives in Washington State.

Late one evening in the spring of 1984, Laura was driving home after visiting a friend in Auburn, Washington. Her favorite route was a calm road that wound past Lake Tapps. Back then the area was rural with scattered farms and ranches and the occasional herd of elk. Nowadays upscale developments and apartment complexes have scattered the animals, and the few remaining farms are surrounded on all sides by suburban mini-mansions. As Laura rounded a bend near a marshy area, she saw what she thought were orange headlights in a field. She immediately felt very tired and pulled her car to the side of the road. As she approached the lights in a daze she realized that they were attached to a strange, landed craft shaped like a piece of Skittles candy.

Figure 5.1. Laura Cyr at the location of her contactee encounter

Next to the strange craft stood two odd-looking creatures beckoning to Laura. Between five and six feet tall in height, they had bronze skin, lightbulb-shaped heads, and large black eyes. She agreed to enter the saucer, which then ascended into the heavens and docked with a "mile-long" craft in Earth's upper atmosphere. The aliens somehow erased or hid her memories every time she left the ship, Laura told us, but upon boarding she immediately realized that she had been there many times. The aliens onboard knew her as "Saleetha," and in preparation for boarding she had shed her earthly body, exchanging brown hair for blonde, her earthly clothes for a silver jumpsuit.

By now it was almost midnight, and the commander of the vessel's night shift anxiously greeted her. Laura recognized the handsome being as an old friend and beamed when talking about him. "He was like a big puppy," she said, "so happy to see me again!" Unlike the creatures that

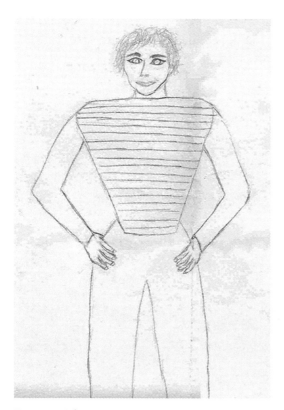

Figure 5.2. The captain

had transported her to space, the commander was humanoid with white skin and blonde hair. She kindly drew him for us.

The commander brought Laura to a balcony overlooking the "well," a multistory opening in the vessel with a gigantic black computer taking up part of the vessel's curved walls. Other humanlike aliens sat in chairs that floated in midair, in front of an array of monitors and controls. Laura/Saleetha was awestruck by the simplicity of the obviously advanced computer system.

After a short elevator ride, Laura's friend led her to the commissary for a meal. She was stunned by the vibrant colors in the room: the rose-colored walls, draperies, and valances, even the tables and chairs. Sitting among a group of friendly humanoids, Laura ate a delicious meal consisting of some sort of vegetable protein formed and shaped to look like a chicken patty, and a drink, which looked and felt like green shampoo but tasted of delicious sugar water.

Once Laura was refreshed and reacquainted with the ship, the commander finally told her the purpose of this visit. The aliens were training Laura for some obscure future purpose, at which point she would be

Figure 5.3. The bridge

needed to help Earth in a crisis. On each of her trips to the mother-ship Laura received a related lesson of her choosing. The commander directed her to a room occupied by a computer and a large chair, similar to what one might find in a dentist's office.

As Laura sat in the chair, the commander adjusted a strange, conelike device attached to a metal arm, until it rested on her temple. Following instructions she selected the subject about which she wanted to learn and the "intensity" at which she wished to learn it. Laura decided to learn about holistic medicine. Fearing that "maximum intensity" learn-ing would be overwhelming, she chose medium intensity, sat back, re-laxed, and allowed information to be relayed into her brain.

The commander was pleased with Laura's efforts. "What you need to know is now in your mind," he told her, "and there will come a time when you need this information to help others." With a sad look on his face the commander told Laura that this concluded their visit. He gave her a necklace, "a gift given to you because you have come to this point," but had to tell her that it could not leave the ship. The two hugged warmly before he led her to the two bronze-skinned escorts. The beings dropped Laura off at her truck, her memories somehow erased. They

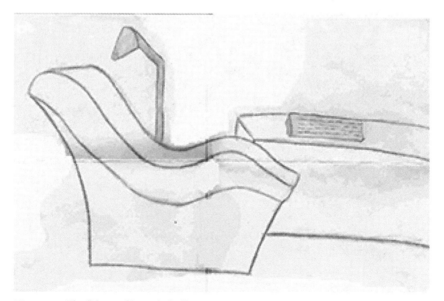

Figure 5.4. The "chair of knowledge"

could not erase, however, a nagging sense in her mind that she had had a "spiritually transforming experience." Eventually Laura sought out a hypnotist to help recover her memories of the events.

A Small Step from Jesus to UFOs?

Like many of the contactees of the 1950s, Laura sees no conflict between her UFO encounters and Christianity. At various times she has attended a Roman Catholic church, and is very attracted to the teachings of the Unity Church. She told us that her flying saucer experiences complement that faith. After all, Laura's experiences are teaching her to be a healer and to help others when they really need it, an inherently Christian message. Besides, she said, Jesus is also an enlightened being and probably a space person as well.

The contactee movement did what many other new religious movements have tried to do—promote their new ideas while drawing heavily upon the beliefs and practices of the existing culture.[16] Religion scholars recognize that new religions have an easier time selling their ideas if they can somehow couch them in concepts with which potential converts are already familiar.[17] In a largely Christian culture, this means that new religious groups would be wise to include elements of Christianity in their belief systems. The Church of Jesus Christ of Latter-day Saints (Mormon) is a key example in this regard. The early Mormons were considered extremely deviant by many Christians,[18] chased across the country for their new revelations about visits by Jesus to the New World, beliefs about plural marriage (since redacted), and doctrine regarding personal ascension to godhood. Yet the mere fact that the LDS church includes the Old and New Testament among its holy books certainly aids in its outreach to Christians, as attested to by the phenomenal growth rate of the church in Christian areas.[19]

Susan Palmer's research with the Raëlians documents the many parallels in their theology and the Judeo-Christian version of creation. Yahweh is the name of the leader of a team of alien scientists who landed on Earth and created the first humans (i.e., Adam and Eve); there is even a Noah's Ark equivalent. Yahweh, convinced of the evil nature of humans by Satan, the head of an Elohim organization opposed to human creation, destroyed Earth with a nuclear holocaust. Lucifer (bearer of light), an opponent of Satan and stranded on Earth, managed to save two of each animal in a spaceship that orbited Earth until the radiation levels returned to normal. Yahweh and Satan are in a perpetual struggle over the state of humans on Earth: Yahweh sees humans as good and redeemable, while Satan sees humans as a failed experiment that must be destroyed.

The Raëlians are awaiting the advent of Elohim in the year 2035. Raël is the current Elohim prophet who is tasked with instructing humans how to prepare for the coming of the Elohim: unite in world peace and build an embassy for them in Israel. Why Israel? The Jews are chosen people in Raëlian theology. They were created by the cross-breeding of the aliens and the daughters of the humans created by the Elohim. The Raëlians spend considerable effort to convert Jews to the cause and to convince them that Raël is the Messiah. It is imperative that Israel provide the Raëlians land to build the embassy. Upon returning to Earth, and provided the prophecies have been fulfilled, the Elohim will share with humans all of their knowledge and technology. If we fail to heed this prophecy, the Elohim will allow us to destroy ourselves in a nuclear holocaust.

The group has also incorporated a number of Judeo-Christian practices, rituals, and symbols into their belief system. Raëlians are expected to give 11% of their incomes, although like Christians, only a small percentage actually tithe the full amount. There is a baptism, or transmission ceremony, in which Raël dips his hands in a bowl of water and then holds the head of the recipient, linking her/him with the Elohim in telepathic communication. They have a "holy ground"—UFOland in Valcourt, Quebec—which will be replaced by the Raëlian embassy in Israel, once it is constructed.[20]

All of this implies that attempts to merge Christianity and the paranormal just might work. After all, there are many similarities between these two spheres. Christian and paranormal beliefs frequently share a spiritual orientation: a belief that the entirety of the world cannot be fully explained by conventional science and materialism.[21] Many of those same beliefs are non-falsifiable and cannot be directly challenged (or supported) by scientific research. Of course certain religious beliefs have a distinct advantage over paranormal beliefs in that they enjoy widespread acceptance in American culture. Given that the United States is predominantly Christian, belief in God, heaven, hell, the resurrection of

Jesus, and the virgin birth are more culturally acceptable, or "normal" supernatural beliefs. Belief in psychic powers, ghosts, and UFOs, however, lack the benefit of association with the dominant religious belief system. Are "normal" supernatural beliefs mutually exclusive to paranormal supernatural beliefs and experiences? To understand why paranormal beliefs and experiences may vary according to the theological conservatism or liberalism of religious traditions and identities, we must take a diversion into the world of economics.

The Economics of Paranormal Exploration

In the simplest terms, classic economic theory attempts to understand the workings of the marketplace by analyzing the movement (production, consumption, and distribution) of scarce "goods" and the motivations of the key actors involved. Economics typically focuses upon scarce items, for there is little to study when a particular entity is available to everyone. If oil were as plentiful as the soil it is found in, then modern history would not have been partially determined by attempts to control its discovery, manufacture, pricing, and distribution.

The most creative economists apply the concepts of goods and scarcity far beyond the marketplace. Love is a scarce commodity, as is happiness, career satisfaction, personal freedom, health, and well-being. People greatly value such nonmaterial rewards and are willing to exchange other material and nonmaterial goods to get them. Seeking love will usually require some money, but it will take an even greater investment of time and emotional energy. We have all experienced the give-and-take of everyday life, even if we do not view it through the lens of markets. Economists focus upon the human desire to avoid risk in such exchanges. Just as good investors try to find the right combination of risk and reward in their business dealings, we all try to do the same in other spheres of life. Put another way, humans do their best to secure the outcomes that they want in the most certain and least costly way possible.

Economist Laurence Iannaccone argues that such principles can also be applied to seemingly personal and ephemeral subjects including faith and personal religiosity.[22] Religion claims to offer some of the greatest rewards imaginable, such as salvation and eternal life, satisfactions not available through other means. People will be highly motivated to seek such rewards and desire as much certainty as possible that they will attain them. Religious acts, argues Iannaccone, "have the character of risky investments," for those engaging in religious activity cannot know for certain if their faith will be rewarded in the manner that they desire.[23] As would any sensible investor, religious consumers will attempt to reduce their risks by holding "diversified portfolios of competing religious assets."[24] In other words, Iannaccone argues that it is human nature to hedge our bets with regard to religion: given the option, people will naturally explore many different religious and spiritual alternatives. A particular religious "consumer" may attend services at one church, while consulting psychics and reading about alternative spiritualities. Should one religious investment strategy "fail," then at least there is another possibility for salvation to fall back upon.[25]

Holding a "portfolio" of competing religious goods may be good for the believer, but it is not particularly healthy for the religious groups involved. People have only a limited amount of time, effort, and resources, so the more they spread those resources around, the less they have to give any one of them. Religious groups that do not actively curtail outside spiritual exploration will become plagued with lackadaisical members who attend rarely and give little of their time and money to further the group goals.

Economists often refer to the concept of a "free rider" to explain a key problem that some groups encounter. A person who manages to sneak onto a bus without paying the toll has gotten a free ride. The bus will reach its destination with or without his money, an amazing bargain to be sure. The problem is, if everyone acts like our free rider, then the bus will no longer have the money to operate and nobody will get a ride. Religious organizations are also forced to deal with the free-rider problem: many people would prefer to reap the benefits of belonging to a religious organization without having to offer anything in return. The stereotypical "Christmas Catholic" is the ultimate free rider, enjoying Mass once a year but avoiding services for the rest. People who want to get married in their church but have little interest in it otherwise are another example of free-riderdom.

One way a religious group can reduce the number of free riders is to make strict demands of its members.[26] If a congregation makes it clear to potential members that weekly attendance is expected, and if they enforce that rule either through peer pressure or by more official means such as dismissal, then free riders will leave to find a less demanding home. In the same vein, requiring members to dress or act in a certain way or placing prohibitions upon behavior makes the cost of minimal participation outweigh the potential benefits for the marginally religious. Groups that have strict rules, regulations, and expectations serve to limit the religious portfolios of their members. In strict religious groups, "[p]otential members are forced to choose: participate fully or not at all."[27]

Iannaccone's creative work suggests that religious groups with conservative theologies and high expectations of members will be strongly motivated to restrict members from involving themselves with other religious or spiritual activities. Following his line of reasoning, we would expect that Evangelical Protestants would develop a strong resistance to the paranormal. Indeed, as our UFO contactee friend Laura learned, Evangelicals do not simply believe the paranormal to be an "economic" threat, but a threat to the soul.

That "Flying Saucer Religion"

Laura may not see a conflict between her flying saucer experiences and Christianity, but her father was not in agreement. Laura's relationship with him was most certainly troubled—at times he had physically abused her and even spent some time in prison. While incarcerated, Laura's father "found God" and became a devout Pentecostal who "believed in the Bible word for word." When Laura told her father of her UFO experiences, he was dismayed. "I don't like this spaceship religion," he told her. UFOs are not spoken of in the Bible and therefore they must be Satanic in nature, he argued.[28] When Laura reiterated that the aliens she encountered seemed friendly and peaceful, her father was unimpressed. "If a spaceship lands and an alien comes out, I know what that alien really is . . . a demon or devil." Laura's father is not alone in his beliefs.

Many Evangelicals and other conservative Christians have a negative view of the paranormal. Christian supernatural beliefs are accepted and expected; supernatural beliefs outside of the Christian purview are discouraged, challenged, and avoided, not embraced.[29]

A visit to a Christian bookstore will reveal a slew of books warning of the dangers of the New Age and paranormal,[30] including the vastly popular *Darkness* series by Frank Peretti, wherein the New Age movement plays a central, villainous role. In these novels the New Age is not seen as a loosely organized collection of paranormal beliefs, but as a threat to organized religion with realistic power. While the novels are considered fiction, the message has been taken seriously by some Christian groups, some even distributing copies of the novels to their congregations.[31]

As the reaction of Laura's father to her UFO tales illustrates, Christian concern about the paranormal is not limited to divination and psychic phenomena. A number of Evangelical authors have warned of the dangers of UFOs. Ron Rhodes's *Alien Obsession* warns that public fascination with UFOs and other "occult" topics is drawing attention away from Christian messages. Among the pieces of evidence Rhodes uses to prove that extraterrestrials are merely demons and devils in disguise are:

- The "aliens" never say anything that *affirms* the Bible as being God's Word.
- The "aliens" never say anything about man's sin problem and need for redemption.
- "Revelations" from these so-called "space brothers" not only consistently contradict the Scriptures but consistently promote a New Age worldview.
- It is typically people who are already involved in the occult who have [UFO] abduction experiences.[32]

The theme of UFOs as a manifestation of Satan has been echoed in other Christian books,[33] fiction films, and documentaries. The Christian Broadcasting Network's *Newswatch* analysis of UFO lore concludes that alien abductions are the outward and visible expressions of Satan, in which people are put into trancelike states so that it is nearly impossible to distinguish truth from reality.[34]

One might think that the possible existence of an undiscovered ape or hominid would be unthreatening to Christians, but even Bigfoot has not been spared from the ire of some Evangelicals. The authors of a paranormal handbook for Christians warn that Bigfoot might be a demon:

It would appear to us that the question of the existence of these "ape men" hinges upon whether or not they are demons inhabiting the bodies of animals. . . . The fact that (as in the case of UFOs) all, or almost all, of the encounters involved non-Christians may suggest either that there aren't that many Christians roaming the wildest reaches of the earth . . . or that there are demonic forces manifesting themselves on planet earth.[35]

To hear for ourselves about the potential conflict between Christianity and the paranormal, we interviewed a forty-year-old youth minister at a suburban, conservative Baptist church in central Texas. "Sam" is a mild-mannered, intelligent person who worked as a science teacher before moving into the ministry. He is also quite opinionated with regard to the paranormal and the "threat" it poses. In Sam's words, "paranormalists are a greater threat to the Kingdom of God than are atheists." When people engage in paranormal activities, or attempt to mix together Christianity and the paranormal, Sam explained, they are "working for the devil . . . whether they realize it or not." God will only protect Christians from harm, he warns, so long as they avoid such activities.

Sam is particularly concerned about the paranormal's prevalence in American entertainment. "Young people have the paranormal coming at them from all angles today. What popular culture is teaching our kids is that it is okay to believe in anything. The paranormal, all these shows on television, make it hard to teach young people a pure biblical doctrine because they want to mix and match beliefs. It scares me about the future of Christianity in America."

UFOs in the Pews

Evangelical authors who fear that the paranormal is "corrupting" conventional religion may have a valid concern, depending upon how you look at it. It is clear that religion does not entirely "protect" against belief in the paranormal. Despite the warnings of religious leaders regarding the dangers of the New Age, occult, and paranormalism, the majority of people across all religious traditions in the United States hold at least one paranormal belief. Among Christians, black Protestants report the greatest percentage of paranormal beliefs, while Evangelical Protestants report the lowest level. Here we categorize the religious affiliations reported by respondents into seven traditions—Evangelical (conservative) Protestant, mainline (moderate or liberal) Protestant, black Protestant,[36] Catholic, Jewish, other organized religions, and those claiming no religion—using a classification scheme developed by sociologists of religion.[37]

Some Catholics might believe in the reality of UFOs but discount the possibilities of astrology. Other Catholics may be convinced that civilizations such as Atlantis demonstrated advanced technology in ancient times but find tales of Bigfoot silly. But over half of Catholics believe in *something* paranormal. The same goes for Americans in black Protestant traditions, Evangelicals, mainline Protestants, Jews, those of other organized religions, and even those claiming no religion.

Does this mean that Christianity and the paranormal have learned to get along? Not exactly. Figure 5.5 shows the relationship between religious traditions and respondents having had at least one of the following paranormal experiences in their adults lives: called or consulted a medium, psychic, or fortune-teller; read horoscope; lived in a house or place they believed to be haunted; consulted a Ouija board to contact a dead person; or witnessed an object in the sky that they could not identify.

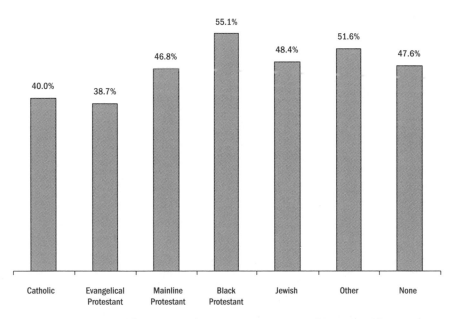

Figure 5.5. Percentage That Have Had at Least One Paranormal Experience by Religious Tradition (Chapman University Survey of American Fears 2014, n=1573). Paranormal experiences include: consulting a psychic or fortune-teller, reading a horoscope, using a Ouija board, seeing a UFO, and living in a haunted house.

While paranormal beliefs are quite prevalent across religious traditions, paranormal experiences are comparatively rare. With the exception of black Protestants and those of "other" religious traditions, a
paranormal experience is reported by less than half of the members of
each religious tradition. Evangelicals alarmed by the paranormal can
take some comfort in the fact that Evangelical Protestants report the
lowest levels of paranormal experience.

Religious Beliefs and the Paranormal

A key distinction and area of great contention between religious traditions, and individual Christians, is their view of the Bible. Some
Christians believe that the Bible is God's literal word, and that everything in the Bible is exactly as God meant it to be. In practice, taking the
Bible literally is quite difficult if not impossible. Two devoted Christians
might disagree as to the literal meaning of more opaque passages. Nevertheless, literalists clearly have a different view of the Bible's meaning
than those who believe it reflects the will of God, but was not dictated
by God. Such people imagine a Bible that must be interpreted in light
of current events. Others believe that the Bible may in some way reflect
God's message, but that it has been significantly tampered with by
human hands and interests. Finally, the most skeptical conceive of the
Bible as a book of fables and stories.

Conceptions of the Bible shape views on controversial moral or social
issues upon which biblical verses are thought to pass judgment. For example, conservative Christians who decry gay marriage often reference
biblical prohibitions on homosexuality (such as Leviticus 18:22, KJV)
which states: "Thou shalt not lie with mankind, as with womankind:
it is abomination." Christian supporters of gay rights argue that such
passages should not be taken literally as they are either reflections of
the historical circumstances in which the Bible was recorded, or do not
mean exactly what they say—perhaps this passage simply means that
men should not engage in casual sexual relationships with other men
outside of committed relationships.

It is also reasonable to expect that views of the Bible impact how
people view the paranormal. Consider the instructions that Moses presented to the Israelites in the Torah:

When thou art come into the land which the LORD thy God giveth thee, thou shalt not learn to do after the abominations of those nations. There shall not be found among you any one that maketh his son or his daughter to pass through the fire, or that useth divination, or an observer of times, or an enchanter, or a witch, or a charmer, or a consulter with familiar spirits, or a wizard, or a necromancer. For all that do these things are an abomination unto the LORD: and because of these abominations the LORD thy God doth drive them out from before thee. Thou shalt be perfect with the LORD thy God. For these nations, which thou shalt possess, hearkened unto observers of times, and unto diviners: but as for thee, the LORD thy God hath not suffered thee so to do. (Deuteronomy 18:9–14, KJV)

The New Testament provides its own anti-paranormal sentiment:

 Now the works of the flesh are manifest, which are these; Adultery, fornication, uncleanness, lasciviousness, idolatry, witchcraft, hatred, variance, emulations, wrath, strife, seditions, heresies, envyings, murders, drunkenness, revellings, and such like: of the which I tell you before, as I have also told you in time past, that they which do such things shall not inherit the kingdom of God. (Galatians 5:19–21, KJV)

For Christians with a literal understanding of such verses, paranormal phenomena are not simply silly or misguided, but a possible route to damnation. The Bible does not "protect" one entirely from the paranor-

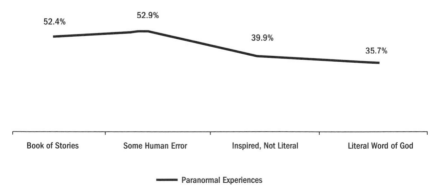

Figure 5.6. Paranormal Experiences by View of the Bible (Chapman University Survey of American Fears 2014, n=1573). Percentages represent those with each view of the Bible who report at least one paranormal belief.

mal, however (figure 5.6). More than 50% of those who believe the Bible is a book with some human error claim at least one paranormal experience. And even though the likelihood of reporting a paranormal experience decreases with more conservative interpretations of the Bible, more than one-third of biblical literalists still report at least one paranormal experience.[38] With regard to paranormal experiences, it is possible that more conservative views of the Bible color the *interpretation* and labeling of arguably paranormal experiences.

Religious Behavior and the Paranormal

A similar pattern holds for religious behavior (see figure 5.7). Slightly more than 57% of those who report attending religious services several times a year report having at least one paranormal experience. As one moves away from this moderate level of religious practice, paranormal experiences decrease markedly. Slightly less than half of those who never attend religious services report having at least one paranormal experience. Looking only at the left half of the chart, one might become convinced that religion and the paranormal walk hand in hand. Once attendance is greater than several times per year, however, the likelihood

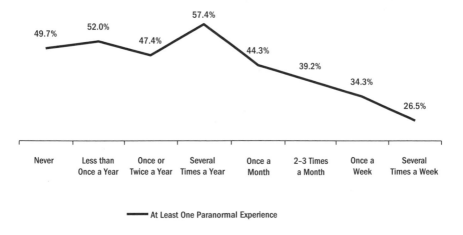

Figure 5.7. Paranormal Experiences by Religious Service Attendance (Chapman University Survey of American Fears 2014, n=1573). Percentages represent those at each level of service attendance who report at least one paranormal belief and/or at least one paranormal experience.

of holding a paranormal belief or having a paranormal experience drops dramatically. People who attend church two to three times a month are much less interested in the paranormal than monthly attenders, and those who fill the pews every week are less interested still.

Religiosity and the Paranormal: It's Complicated

Putting these pieces together, it is clear that the type of religious person least likely to report paranormal beliefs or to have paranormal experiences is a devout Evangelical, biblical literalist who frequently attends church services. This is due in part to the anti-paranormal rhetoric of some Christian pundits, which has its origins in a literal interpretation of certain Bible passages, but also serves to drive away members who are not willing to commit fully to the church and a single belief system. At the same time, atheists are also not the most likely to hold paranormal beliefs or experiences. It appears that the dismissal of the idea of God also leads to the dismissal of paranormal phenomena.

In figure 5.8 we examine how paranormalism varies by religious belief. In this case religious beliefs consists of those topics that are closely

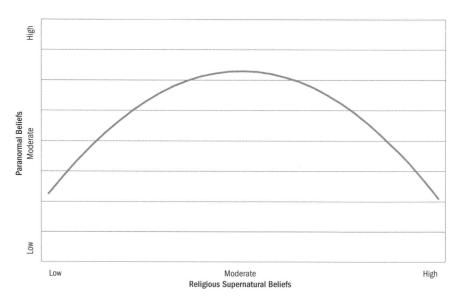

Figure 5.8. Relationship between Paranormal Belief and Religious Belief (Baylor Religion Survey 2005, n=1721; scales based on Baker and Draper 2010)

associated with conventional religion in the United States, such as the belief in angels, demons, heaven, and hell. Someone with a higher score on the religion scale believes strongly in the reality of the angelic and demonic. A person with a higher score on the paranormal scale expresses greater levels of belief in UFOs, monsters, astrology, and other paranormal concepts. It is immediately clear that high levels of religious belief and high levels of paranormal belief do not tend to go together. People at the highest levels of religious belief express lower levels of paranormal belief.

But it is also clear that extremely low levels of religious belief do not produce high levels of paranormalism. For paranormalism to thrive, it appears that a person must have a moderate level of belief in the religious realm. Put another way, paranormalism and conventional religiosity exhibit a curvilinear relationship with one another.[39] As we noted, it's complicated.

Selling Saucers

What does all of this mean for the troubled relationship between Christianity and the paranormal? To whom should an up-and-coming psychic try to sell her services? Should the next budding contactee call the local Baptist church to advertise his lecture about meeting Jesus on a flying saucer?

While exclusivist religious groups may have some success in curtailing paranormal interest, no group is entirely immune. The majority of Americans believe in something paranormal, no matter what religious (or secular) tradition they belong to. It is also clear that a measure of faith opens people up to the paranormal. Rationalists who entirely reject the idea of faith in "conventional" supernatural concepts are unlikely to be attracted to unconventional supernatural topics either. It is people with mid-levels of commitment to conventional religions who have greater paranormal interests. Someone who attends church *sometimes* and believes that there is *something* supernatural about the Bible is the most likely to develop an interest in or already believe in paranormal topics. It appears that religion can have a conditioning effect that, unless actively curtailed, indeed makes the paranormal but a small step away.

6

Paranormal Subcultures

I (Chris) have included a section on the paranormal in sociology courses since 1996. Over this period, I have noticed a dramatic increase in the basic understanding that many students have about paranormal phenomena. Early in my career, discussing topics such as UFO abductions required a detailed overview of the nature of the claims, the reported "aliens" involved (little gray creatures), and the meaning of terms such as "missing time" and "implants." As time passed students began nodding with awareness (and sometimes impatience) as I explained topics that had previously been confined to the fringes of society. I have learned to begin each class on the paranormal by asking the students themselves what is involved in a UFO abduction, the urban legends about Ouija boards, and the nature of Sasquatch, and am amazed by students' ability to draw perfect representations of "Grays" on the board, talk breathlessly about legends of Ouija boards conjuring demonic entities, and describe the habits of the elusive man-beast.

To be clear, student awareness of these topics is not necessarily an indicator of *belief*. Some express considerable skepticism about paranormal claims. Other students are particularistic, perhaps finding Bigfoot credible, but UFO abduction stories outlandish. In rarer cases, students will discuss a paranormal experience they have had, or one reported by a friend or family member. Regardless of their personal orientation toward the paranormal, students appear to increasingly share a basic knowledge of its claims.

Knowledge is but one means by which people interact with a subcultural belief system. In their pioneering research, sociologists Charles Y. Glock and Rodney Stark noticed that any two people may identify themselves as "very religious," yet mean entirely different things by it.[1] There are five primary ways that people manifest their personal religiosity, they argued. For some, (1) being religious is most importantly about *belief*; one must believe without doubt in the tenets of one's faith. Or perhaps (2) being religious means that one has religious *experiences*, such as feeling born again or receiving answers to prayers. For others, (3) one's *knowledge* of the doctrines and documents of the faith are proof of devotion. Still others feel religious because (4) they frequently engage in religious *practices* such as attending religious services and praying. Finally, religiosity can be gauged by (5) proving that one's faith requires accepting *consequences*, such as restrictions on behavior. An individual's involvement with a religious organization could be adequately summarized by knowing one's levels of belief, knowledge, practice, experience, and consequences.

While Glock and Stark focused their attentions upon religion, their ideas have much wider applicability. What they labeled as five dimensions of religiosity could easily be considered five dimensions of involvement in any belief system, hobby, or interest group. For example, consider members of People for the Ethical Treatment of Animals (PETA). Some will have a strong faith in the cause but do little else. There will be other members for whom belief is simply not enough. They will participate in PETA activities and may even be willing to engage in risky behaviors for the group. As with any group, there will be PETA members who have no real sense of group history or a deep understanding of its mission or methods. Perhaps they have joined for social reasons, or they simply have a deep belief in animal rights that does not necessitate an understanding of PETA itself. This raises the possibility that even within the same organization or area of interest, different types of people will be involved in different ways.

The same ideas apply to levels of involvement with the paranormal. Any given person's involvement with the paranormal would be composed of a combination of five elements:

Belief: The extent to which an individual believes in a paranormal topic or topics

Experiences: The extent to which an individual has experienced the paranormal topic in question (has seen a ghost, sighted a UFO, seen a Bigfoot, etc.)

Knowledge: The extent to which an individual is aware of the history and details of a paranormal topic

Practices: The extent to which a person engages in activities related to a
paranormal subject (attends conferences, joins organizations, joins group
activities)

Consequences: The extent to which a person has suffered negative outcomes,
such as ridicule, as a result of their interest in a paranormal subject

With the exception of skeptics,[2] people interested in the paranormal
as a cultural phenomenon, and the occasional curious onlooker, engagement with the paranormal typically involves some level of belief. That
does not mean that belief always comes first. In some cases a person will
develop a paranormal belief as the result of having a paranormal experience. We have met many people during our research who claim they
never believed in UFOs, Bigfoot, psychic phenomena, and the like until
"it" happened to them.

Chapter 3 examined those who hold paranormal beliefs and have
paranormal experiences. For some, involvement with the paranormal
will end with belief or an experience. For example, a person may have
a strong belief in ghosts because of an uncle's encounter with a restless
spirit, but have no interest in pursuing the subject further. Indeed, it
is quite possible to have belief in a paranormal subject with very little
knowledge of its particulars. People who follow their horoscopes reli-
giously may have no idea exactly *how* one is supposed to be influenced
by the stars. And just because a person has seen a UFO does not mean
that he or she has an awareness of UFO history. Judging by the prevalence of paranormal beliefs in American society, only a handful of those
who believe in UFOs, ghosts, and other paranormal subjects ultimately
engage in paranormal practices such as attending UFO conferences or
joining a ghost hunt.

This chapter examines those who move beyond paranormal belief
and experience into a deeper involvement in a paranormal subculture.
We explore the world of people who expand their knowledge of the
paranormal by purchasing paranormal books, visiting paranormal websites, and attending conferences and less formal get-togethers. Finally,
we take a close look at the most dedicated members of a subculture—
those who actively engage in the pursuit of their quarry. To do so, we
enter one particular paranormal subculture, people who research and
hunt for Bigfoot.

Wild Man of the Woods

By many accounts, a mysterious ape-man known variously as Bigfoot or Sasquatch has long inhabited the United States. Native American myths and legends include a rich body of tales of hairy, manlike beasts that roam the forests.[3] Depending on the tribe, such creatures are known as *Wendigo, Tornit, Strendu, Chenoo, Oh-Mah, Sookum,* and a host of other names.[4] "Sasquatch" is merely an anglicized version of *Sokqueatl* (or *Ssosq'tal*), used by Salish-speaking tribes.[5]

As far back as 1818, the *Exeter Watchman* reported the sighting of an "animal resembling the Wild Man of the Woods" near Ellisburgh, New York.[6] In his 1893 memoir, *The Wilderness Hunter,* Theodore Roosevelt recounted a harrowing tale told to him by a hunter/trapper known only as "Bauman."[7] The story goes that Bauman was trapping with a friend in the Bitterroot Mountains of Idaho and Montana. The men noticed that something was raiding their camp whenever they went out to check their traps. Bauman awoke one evening to see a large, dark shape standing outside his lean-to; he fired his weapon at the shape. Over the next few days, the men felt that they were being watched and followed by something that stayed hidden just within the trees. The men ultimately became unnerved and decided to leave the mountains. To expedite their departure, Bauman went to collect traps, and his partner remained to pack up camp. Upon returning to camp, the frightened trapper found the mutilated body of his friend. Bauman fled the scene as quickly as possible.[8]

The creatures continued such aggressive behavior in fantastic accounts from the early twentieth century. For example, Fred Beck claimed that he and three other miners were attacked by "mountain devils" while working their claim near Mount Saint Helens. The men had been hearing strange whoops and hollers from unseen animals for several days when Beck spotted a strange creature staring at him from across a small canyon. He immediately opened fire:

> The creature I judged to have been about seven feet tall with blackish-brown hair. It disappeared from our view for a short time, but then we saw it, running fast and upright, about two hundred yards down the little canyon. I shot three times before it disappeared from view.[9]

That evening the miners' cabin was attacked, perhaps in response to Beck's aggression. At least three large, hairy creatures circled the cabin, pounded on the walls, tossed rocks, and jumped on the roof. At one point a hairy arm reached through a chink in the wall and grabbed one of the men's axes. Beck turned the head of the axe before the creature could pull it outside. During the assault, the men alternated between huddling in fear and firing their guns at the roof and through the walls.

Just before daylight, the attack ended. Beck and his friends fled the scene, but not before he fired parting shots at another creature he saw standing at the edge of the canyon: "I shot three times, and it toppled over the cliff, down into the gorge, some four hundred feet below."[10] The area where the incident purportedly occurred was nicknamed "Ape Canyon" after the story appeared and still bears that name today.[11]

An equally harrowing encounter also stems from 1924, although it was not reported until 1957.[12] Albert Ostman, a Canadian lumberjack, claimed to have been kidnapped by a Sasquatch while camping in British Columbia. The creature simply picked the frightened man up, sleeping bag and all, as he slept one evening. Slung uncomfortably across the beast's shoulder, Ostman endured a long hike until they arrived at a canyon. There he was held captive by four Sasquatch. His kidnapper was a large male Ostman called the "old man." Also present were an older female and a younger male and female, perhaps children of the older couple. A small cache of supplies that Ostman had stashed in the bottom of his sleeping bag provided his avenue of escape. Each morning Ostman boiled coffee and took a pinch of snuff as the apelike family watched with curiosity, resulting in a scene seemingly straight out of a slapstick film. After about a week of watching, the old man grabbed Ostman's can of snuff and swallowed it whole. It did not sit well. The beast tried to soothe his stomach by emptying Ostman's can of cold coffee, grounds and all, into its mouth. As the old man doubled over in pain with his frightened family attending him, Ostman quickly gathered his gear and fled.[13]

Despite such dramatic reports, Bigfoot proved merely an occasional curiosity until August 1958. A construction crew was preparing a roadbed outside of Klamath, California. On August 27, Gerald Crew discovered large humanlike tracks (sixteen inches long and seven inches wide in places) around his bulldozer. Although the tracks were destroyed once roadwork resumed, they reappeared every few days. The foreman, Wilbur Wallace, later reported that something tossed an enormous, seven-hundred-pound spare tire into a gulley near the work site, further disturbing the crew. Finally, a wife of one of the crewmen wrote to the *Humboldt Times* about the worksite's visits from "Big Foot," and a series of stories in local newspapers followed. There is good reason to suspect that the entire incident was a prank played by the contractor,[14] but the societal impact was real. When wire services transmitted the local newspaper story countrywide, Bigfoot finally had a name.[15]

The creature's popularity soared from this point on, and it has become an indelible part of American popular culture.[16] Bigfoot has been the star of movies throughout the past several decades, ranging from cult films such as *The Legend of Boggy Creek* (1972) to family fare such as *Harry and the Hendersons* (1987) and *Little Bigfoot* (1997), and a more recent influx of "found footage" horror films such as *Willow Creek* (2013), *Happy Camp* (2014), and *Exists* (2014). Bigfoot has battled the *Six-Million Dollar Man* and sold snacks in a series of "Messin' with Sasquatch" commercials for Jack Link's Beef Jerky (2006–present). It has even crossed over into video games. The fifth entry in the popular *Grand Theft Auto* series (2013) allows a player to transform into Bigfoot after locating and consuming peyote plants hidden throughout the game world. In the action game *Assassin's Creed 3* (2013), set during and after the American Revolution, the player investigates rumors of a hairy man-beast, only to find a hermit to be the source of the tales. A wide variety of Bigfoot-related apps are available for smart phones, including games in which the user tries to find "evidence for Bigfoot" (*Bigfoot: Hidden Giant*), an app that plays purported Bigfoot vocalizations (*Bigfoot Calls*), and a tool that allows the user to insert a Bigfoot into any photograph they take with their phone (*Bigfoot Camera Prank*).

The popular media often depicts Bigfoot/Sasquatch as a solitary creature roaming the Pacific Northwest. Most believers think of Bigfoot as a separate *species*. Witnesses have claimed sightings of males and females, adults, juveniles, and children. Books, websites, and documentaries outline migration routes, speculate on dietary habits, and even provide population estimates. One source estimates that between fifteen hundred and two thousand adult Sasquatch inhabit the Pacific Northwest alone.[17]

Unlike the protracted interactions present in the early tales of Beck and Ostman, the modern Bigfoot report typically involves a very brief sighting of the hairy beast as it flees from the witness. Many such sightings occur as the furtive creature quickly crosses the road in front of a startled driver, as in the following report from Beltrami County, Minnesota, in 2013:

> My 20 yr daughter was driving. I was in the passenger side..going south towards town on Irvine Ave. it was close to xmas..a yr and a half ago. was around 8pm. a huge..fast upright thing ran in view of our headlights..and in front of the oncoming car headlights. I saw from the waist up and arms pumping. whatever I saw took only 2 to 2 and a half strides to clear shoulder to shoulder. I saw it on the right shoulder.went ahhh..an involuntary reaction by the time I finished, it was gone. I asked my daughter if she saw that..she said she saw something..but thought it was a whirlwind. I told her what I saw. We wanted to go back the next day to see is [sic] we could see anything unusual but it was like 30 below and didn't.[18]

This recent report from Minnesota lacks great detail, but when witnesses claim to have gotten a close look at a Bigfoot they report a hairy, ape-like face with a heavy brow and large nostrils.[19] In some famous cases large, pendulous breasts are reported, but most appear to involve adult males.[20]

That Bigfoot is a creature of the Northwest is also a popular misnomer. Washington, Oregon, and California have high numbers of reports, but Bigfoot sightings have been reported from every state except Hawaii. The Bigfoot Field Researchers Organization (BFRO) provides a popular website that collects sighting reports.[21] As of November 2015, Washington State claims 613 reports, California has 413, and Oregon 242. Yet Florida, Illinois, and Ohio rank only behind Washington and California with 306, 270, and 259 Bigfoot reports, respectively. Even tiny, coastal Rhode Island claims five reports. Residents of states across the union have collected local reports and their own encounters into an abundance of self-published, vanity, and small-press books, such as *The Mogollon Monster: Arizona's Bigfoot*; *Bigfoot Encounters in Ohio*; *The Maryland Bigfoot Digest*; *Swamp Bigfoot: Tales of the Louisiana Honey Island Swamp Monster*;

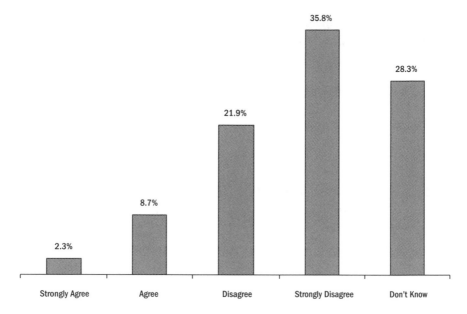

Figure 6.1. Bigfoot Is a Real Creature (Chapman University Survey of American Fears 2015, n=1,494). The 2015 CSAF asked respondents their level of agreement with a series of statements about paranormal topics.

Bigfoot in Mississippi; *Sasquatch: Alabama Bigfoot Sightings*; and *50 Years with Bigfoot: Tennessee Chronicles of Co-Existence.*[22]

Ubiquity does not guarantee acceptance, however. With a few exceptions, scientists have dismissed the possibility of Bigfoot.[23] The American public is equally skeptical about the creature's existence. Only a small percentage either agree or strongly agree that Bigfoot is a real creature (11%), although nearly a third remain uncertain (Don't Know) about the issue (see figure 6.1).

Frustrated Bigfoot advocates point to a mountain of evidence. Thousands of supposed Bigfoot footprints have been cast in plaster by researchers. There are an abundance of photographs and enough purported films to warrant their own book-length listing.[24] Bigfoot hunters have collected samples of claimed Bigfoot hair and feces. Most scientists, however, are simply not convinced of the *quality* of this evidence. The films, photos, and foot castings are obvious hoaxes, they argue. The feces and hair samples must be from known animals; the many sightings are simply misidentifications of bears, if not outright hoaxes themselves.

How different types of Bigfoot believers respond to public skepticism about their quarry is a key distinction between them. Less than half (41%) of those who believe in creatures such as Bigfoot have ever read a book about the subject, consulted a website, or otherwise researched the subject.[25] The interest of *casual believers* is limited to watching the occasional Bigfoot documentary or turning up the TV when a sighting is reported on the local news. The casual believers we have talked to are relatively uninterested in and unaffected by the skepticism of the scientific community. For them Bigfoot is simply one more item added to a paranormal shopping cart that includes UFOs, ghosts, and psychic phenomena. It is something that is believed in but rarely inspected.

Both scholars and the press have too frequently painted all those who believe in a particular paranormal subject with the same brush. We have found most dedicated pursuers of paranormal subjects to be different from what we call casual believers.

Paranormal Research

As we found with paranormal beliefs and experiences, there is a surprising amount of paranormal research going on in the United States (see figure 6.2). Many Americans are taking their interest in the paranormal beyond casual, unconsidered belief. Some subjects are more popular than others, but more than half (53%) of Americans have researched at least one paranormal topic.

Have you ever read a book on, consulted a website about, or researched the following topics?	% Answering Yes
The prophecies of Nostradamus	28
Ghosts, apparitions, haunted houses, or electronic voice phenomena	25
Astrology	24
UFO sightings, abductions, or conspiracies	23
Mysterious animals, such as Bigfoot or the Loch Ness Monster	21
Mediums, fortune-tellers, or psychics	13
The New Age movement in general	12

Figure 6.2. American Paranormal Research (Baylor Religion Survey 2005, n=1721)

We asked Americans if they have ever read a book on the paranormal, consulted websites, or otherwise researched six different paranormal subjects. The most popular of these subjects was the prophecies of Nostradamus. Nearly one-third of Americans were sufficiently intrigued by the French seer's claims of a fiery end to the world to delve into the subject.[26] Four topics closely follow Nostradamus in popularity. Close to one-fourth (25%) of Americans have read about or researched the world of ghosts, apparitions, haunted houses, and/or electronic voice phenomena. Twenty-four percent of us have delved into astrology. Nearly the same number are fascinated by UFO sightings, abductions, or tales of government UFO conspiracies. Bigfoot, the Loch Ness Monster, and similar beasts are not quite as popular, but have, at least at one point, attracted the attention of one-fifth of Americans (21%).

Given that psychics, mediums, and fortune-tellers are one of the most heavily advertised aspects of the paranormal, we were surprised to find it to be one of the least popular subjects for Americans to research; only about 13% of Americans show a deeper interest in the subject. Even fewer (12%) have researched the New Age as a movement, which suggests that the term is of little meaning to most Americans.

It is possible, however, to predict with fair accuracy the specific subjects that will interest a particular type of person. Overall, the paranormal is popular, but certain subjects are more popular among some segments of the population than others. One of the most consistent and powerful predictors of enthusiasm for paranormal subjects is gender.[27] Men and women are, quite simply, attracted to different paranormal topics (see figure 6.3). Even when taking into account differences in marital status, education, income, personal religiosity, and age, men are still more likely than women to develop an interest in "cryptozoology" (the study of Bigfoot, the Loch Ness Monster, and other mysterious creatures), UFO sightings, abductions and conspiracies, and the prophecies of Nostradamus. Women are more interested in astrology, psychics, fortune-tellers and mediums, and the New Age in general. If there is a trend here, it appears that men are somewhat more interested in "concrete" paranormal subjects. In theory at least, it *would* be possible to capture, kill, or find concrete physical evidence for the existence of Bigfoot, lake monsters, or extraterrestrials—and men seem to enjoy

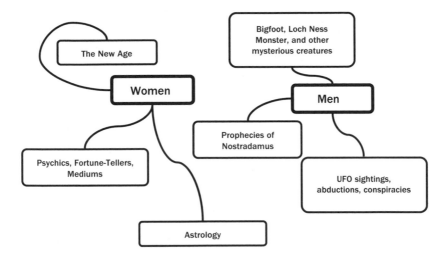

Figure 6.3. Gender and Paranormal Research (Baylor Religion Survey 2005, n=1721)

the hunt.[28] Women have greater interest in more ephemeral topics related to personal destiny and self-improvement. Put another way, we find that men are more likely to take a *discovery* approach to the paranormal. Women are more likely to pursue the paranormal for purposes of *enlightenment*.

Given the wide diversity of topics that fall under the rubric of the paranormal, it is not surprising that enthusiasts vary quite widely. For example, unmarried people are, on average, significantly more interested in the New Age and UFO sightings, abductions, and conspiracies than are married people. Yet marital status is not predictive of whether one will become invested in the subject of psychics and fortune-tellers, Nostradamus, or Bigfoot and other monsters. Married people are just as likely as unmarried people to chase Sasquatch.

Using a statistical technique, we can simultaneously consider the relationship between different demographic characteristics and enthusiasm for, and research about Bigfoot, UFOs, or other subjects. This allows us to paint a profile of the "average" person that will delve into each paranormal subculture (see figure 6.4). Different types of people are more likely to move beyond simple belief and into deeper involvement with each paranormal subject.

	Psychics	UFOs	Ghosts	Monsters	Astrology	Nostradamus	New Age
Gender	Female	Male	---	Male	Female	Male	Female
Age	---	Younger	Younger	Younger	Younger	---	---
Race	Other Race	Other Race	Other Race	Other Race	Nonwhite	Nonwhite	Nonwhite
Marital Status	---	---	Not Married	---	Not Married	---	Not Married, Not Widowed
Income	Lower	Lower	Lower	Lower	Lower	---	Lower
Education	Higher	Higher	---	---	---	---	Higher
Political Affiliation	---	---	---	---	---	Democrat	---
Religious Tradition	Other Religion	Other Religion	Evangelical, Mainline, Catholic, Other Religion	Mainline	Catholic, Other Religion	Catholic, Other Religion	Non-Mainline, Non-Catholic, Other Religion
Church Attendance	Lower	Lower	Lower	Lower	Lower	Lower	---
Biblical Literalism	Lower	Lower	Lower	Lower	Lower	Lower	Lower

Figure 6.4. Profiles of Paranormal Researchers in the United States (Baylor Religion Survey 2005, n=1721)

For each topic of interest, we examine the extent to which researching a topic is related to gender, age, race/ethnicity, marital status, income, education, political preference and several measures of religiosity, including religious tradition, frequency of religious service attendance and biblical literalism.

Taken together these factors paint a detailed picture of what people who delve into paranormal topics are like, statistically speaking. For example, the person most likely to have researched "monsters" such as Bigfoot or the Loch Ness Monster is a younger male with a lower level of income who is not white or African-American, and who is a member of a mainline Protestant church, although he does not attend very often and holds a liberal view of the Bible. The person most likely to have researched astrology is a younger, unmarried, non-white female. Similar to a monster researcher, she will tend to attend church infrequently and have a liberal view of the Bible, although in this case, Catholics and those of non-Judeo-Christian religions tend to be most attracted to astrology.

Several demographic factors proved especially important in predicting paranormal research. Gender has an impact on most topics, although ghosts are of equal interest to men and women. Income is also a common predictor of paranormal research, although it tells us nothing about those interested in the prophecies of Nostradamus. Race is a consistent predictor across all paranormal topics, with the general finding that whites are less interested in each, controlling for other factors.

However, as we found in chapter 5, religion plays an extremely important role in predicting interest in the paranormal because paranormalism often operates as an alternative belief system to conventional religion. Consequently, those who are heavily invested in conventional religion may be less attracted to the paranormal. Indeed, our three measures of religiosity—religious tradition, religious service attendance, and biblical literalism—are the most consistent predictors of paranormal research, with both religious tradition and biblical literalism being significant predictors of research in all topics and service attendance predictive of all but New Age research. Put simply, with the exception of ghosts, where Evangelical Protestants express some interest, paranormal research is not the province of conservative religion. Those who frequently attend traditional religious services are simply less likely to examine alternative belief systems. It seems frequent churchgoers are unlikely to be researching the paranormal when they get home on Sunday. A person is even less likely to put down a Bible that he or she believes is the literal word of God to pick up a book about psychic powers.

While demographics and religiosity play a role in paranormal research, perhaps a stronger role is played by preexisting *belief* in that subject. Put simply, someone is more likely to research Bigfoot if he believes that Bigfoot exists. Certainly there are skeptics who research paranormal subjects, but they are far outnumbered by believers (see figure 6.5). Of those people who do not believe in Bigfoot, the Loch Ness Monster, or other monsters, less than one-fifth (18%) could be bothered to investigate further, but true believers are highly motivated to do so. Someone who believes in Bigfoot and other creatures is more than twice as likely to acquire knowledge about the subject as someone who does not believe.

Having a paranormal experience is an even more powerful entry point to researching paranormal subjects. Of those Americans who claim to have seen a UFO, nearly half (48%) have researched the subject (see figure 6.6). Only a handful of those who have not seen a UFO have any interest in researching the subject. Of course, chicken-and-egg argu-

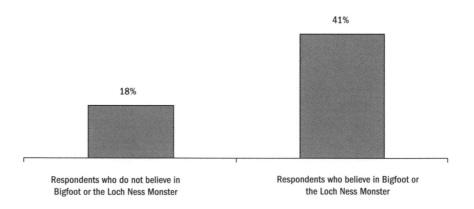

Percentage of respondents who have read a book on, consulted a website about, or researched Bigfoot, the Loch Ness Monster, or other mysterious creatures

41%

18%

Respondents who do not believe in Bigfoot or the Loch Ness Monster

Respondents who believe in Bigfoot or the Loch Ness Monster

Figure 6.5. Paranormal Belief Correlates with Paranormal Research (Baylor Religion Survey 2005, n=1721)

ments necessarily arise with such data. It is possible that people come to believe in Bigfoot or other paranormal topics because they have studied them. It is also quite likely that some people have paranormal experiences only *after* they have researched a subject at length, what could be formulated as the "social construction of reality factor." After all, there are many books available that tell one where to go to find ghosts or to have the best chance to see Bigfoot, or that provide instruction on how to develop psychic powers. Nevertheless, in our time spent with people who have had paranormal experiences, it is clear that those experiences often marked major turning points in their lives.

One of the most common ways to delve deeply into a paranormal subject, Bigfoot or otherwise, is to attend a related conference or fair. Psychic and New Age fairs are easily found in most major cities. UFO enthusiasts benefit from many regular conferences from which to choose. Those who are fascinated with claims of crashed flying saucers can attend annual festivals in Roswell, New Mexico. Starworks USA provides an annual conference where attendees can hear presentations from a variety of famous UFO witnesses and UFO "experiencers," in addition to learning about the process of meditation. The International UFO Congress conference offers its own film festival in addition to well-

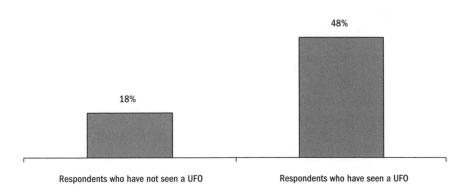

Figure 6.6. Paranormal Experience Correlates with Paranormal Research (Baylor Religion Survey 2005, n=1721)

known UFO speakers. The UFO Con: The Experiencer Event provides an annual lineup of speakers, all of who claim "other worldly contact and have extraordinary wisdom and knowledge to share."[29]

Bigfoot is also exceptionally well served by conferences. Several states with well-developed Bigfoot lore are host to their own events, such as the annual Ohio Bigfoot Conference, the Honobia Oklahoma Bigfoot Conference, the Original Texas Bigfoot Conference, and the Florida Skunk Ape Conference.

With the exception of curious locals, the occasional skeptical on-looker, and the press, people who attend such Bigfoot conferences are passionate. They are not content with mere belief nor satisfied with the research they can do on their own. They want to meet Bigfoot celebrities face to face, purchase the latest Bigfoot products, trade stories from the field, and hear tips from veteran hunters. Some of them have taken it upon themselves to answer skeptics. They hope to learn tips and tricks that will help them find proof of Bigfoot that scientists cannot ignore. To visit such a Bigfoot conference is to meet some of the beast's most dedicated enthusiasts.

Bigfoot Knowledge

At 6 p.m. on a breezy Thursday on the coast of Washington State, hundreds of Bigfoot enthusiasts waited in line for entry to the third annual Sasquatch Summit. Billing itself as the state's premiere Bigfoot conference, the gathering took place over three days in November 2015 at the Quinault Beach Casino, just a few miles outside the sleepy, oceanfront town of Ocean Shores. As the first author (Chris) and a colleague, Ed,[30] patiently waited our turn to register, we listened to the hum of conversation around us. An older man and his son, each wearing Bigfoot-themed T-shirts, quietly discussed a recent Bigfoot sighting near Ocean Shores. Two younger men talked about their hope of meeting Thom Cantrall, one of the day's speakers. Others simply complained about the length of the line.

Once we had registered and received our official Sasquatch Summit T-shirts and lanyards, we entered into a world of Bigfoot vendors. SasquatchPrints.com manned a booth selling a wide assortment of topical T-shirts. One displayed an image of Bigfoot crouched near a stream with the label "Bigfoot Gone Fishin'," another had a set of Bigfoot footprints trailing into the distance. Nearby, BigAssSquatch sold a series of stylized prints, T-shirts, and Christmas ornaments with Bigfoot themes. Other vendors provided Bigfoot jewelry and lunchboxes, plaster replicas of purported Bigfoot footprints and handprints, and even Sasquatch-themed caramel corn, SasQrunch.

Stepping into the Great Hall, we found a room of nearly six hundred seats. Nearly two-thirds of those seats were already occupied. Many other attendees were walking the perimeter of the room, where each of the day's speakers was provided with his or her own table. The aforementioned Thom Cantrall, who has reported numerous close encounters with Bigfoot, sold copies of *Sasquatch: Search for a New Man* and *Sasquatch: The Living Legend*.[31] Lori Simmons signed copies of her book *Tracking Bigfoot: The Journey Continues*, which promotes her belief that Bigfoot lives in underground tunnels and caves.[32] Biologist John Bindernagel divided his time throughout the day between studiously taking notes in the audience and manning his table of copies of *The Discovery of Sasquatch: Reconciling Culture, History, and Science in the Discovery Process*.[33] Members of two Bigfoot research organizations, the American Primate Conservancy and Olympic Project, sat at neighboring tables, patiently answering questions from attendees and collecting the occasional sighting report. This host of Bigfoot "celebrities" engendered great excitement from the Bigfoot faithful, but would likely not be recognized by anyone outside of the conference.[34]

Remove the element of Bigfoot, and there is nothing particularly unique about this. Most Americans belong to one or more subcultures, sometimes without even realizing it. A subculture is simply any group that possesses characteristics that distinguish it from the wider culture. Mutual hobbies and interests or any other shared characteristic such as age, race, social class, or geographical location can become the basis of a distinctive group with shared values and behaviors. Youth can be described as a subculture, having shared interests, lingo, styles of dress, and habits that differ from the rest of the population. The youth subculture itself can be further subdivided based on favorite music styles, particular hobbies, region of the country, relative age (adolescents vs. tweens vs. teens), and in any number of other ways. A shared passion or characteristics can spawn a subculture that baffles outsiders. There are

Figure 6.7. Meeting a Bigfoot celebrity: Bob Gimlin at the 2015 Sasquatch Summit in Ocean Shores, Washington. Left to right: Christopher Bader, Bob Gimlin, L. Edward Day.

biker subcultures and Goth subcultures. There is a NASCAR subculture and a Twilight subculture; subcultures for hunters and for comic book collectors. NASCAR has its own celebrities that are completely unknown to those who do not like watching people drive fast in circles. Stan Lee, a godlike figure to many comic book enthusiasts, would engender little excitement at the Indy 500. Members inside any subculture demonstrate their devotion to their subject by being familiar with its key personalities and history.

This particular subculture was most abuzz at the attendance of a thin, spry, eighty-four-year-old cowboy from Yakima, Washington, by the name of Bob Gimlin. Bob is such a celebrity in the world of Bigfoot that he had been brought to the event without even the requirement of giving a presentation: his mere presence was enough to electrify the crowd. Bob wandered the vendor area, taking pictures with thrilled attendees, including me (see figure 6.7). We were handed cameras on a number of occasions to snap a photo of an excited fan with his or her arm around the perpetually grinning Gimlin. As one attendee posted on the Sasquatch Summit website after the conference: "Meeting Bob Gimlin was my dream and I got to meet him, so don't say dreams don't come true!"

Indeed, Gimlin unwittingly served as a method of distinguishing the few casual believers in attendance from the serious Bigfoot enthusiasts. On several occasions we overheard whispered conversations as those who knew Gimlin's importance to the Bigfoot subculture informed, and occasionally admonished, their compatriots.

Gimlin's claim to fame is in being the "Gimlin" part of the famous Patterson-Gimlin film, which shows a purported Sasquatch.[35] In October 1967 Bob and his friend, the former rodeo rider Roger Patterson, visited Bluff Creek, California, in hopes of capturing a Bigfoot on film for a planned documentary. Patterson had previously written a book on Bigfoot and believed that the Bluff Creek area was a good spot to search for the creature.

As luck would have it, the duo was rounding a fallen tree in a creek bed on their horses in the early afternoon of October 20 when they spotted a large, dark creature about six or seven feet tall that rose up from a crouched position and walked across a gravel sandbar.[36] The strange, stocky figure was covered in black hair with the exception of small parts of its face. It had arms that hung below its knees and pendulous breasts. For fifty-three seconds of shaky 16mm footage, the figure shambled across the sandbar toward the tree line. At frame 352 it turned its head to look at Patterson, one arm swung in front of its body, the other to its back. This frame of film has been reproduced countless times and its subject, often nicknamed "Patty," became the face of the Bigfoot movement.[37] Patty, in fact, appeared throughout the vendor tables in various forms, her visage emblazoning shirts, bumper stickers, prints, and other merchandise.

In addition to the P-G film, we heard of other famous pieces of Bigfoot evidence at the Summit. For example, Ron Morehead's talk centered around the "Sierra Sounds," a series of strange sounds recorded by Morehead, colleague Alan Berry, and others during visits in 1972–75 to the Sierra Nevada Mountains in central California. Morehead claims that a group of Bigfoot creatures regularly approached the group's cabin. By hanging a microphone from a nearby tree branch, Morehead and Berry captured over ninety minutes of Bigfoot "vocalizations" that have since become a regular subject of debate in Sasquatch circles.[38] The Sierra Sounds formed the centerpiece of a presentation on day two by

Scott Nelson, a retired Navy cryptologic linguist (an expert in identifying foreign languages).

Nelson has become convinced that the Sierra Sounds recordings represent the language of a heretofore unknown primate. In an animated presentation, he played clips of the recordings, walking back and forth across the stage. For example, he played a long audio track of what he believes to be an adult male, adult female, and baby Sasquatch arguing back and forth. "Listen for something that doesn't sound human," Nelson exhorted the crowd. When one of the "creatures" made a chuffing noise, Nelson loudly mimicked it several times, snorting into his microphone. "Humans don't make noises like that," he told the audience. "And hoaxers wouldn't think to do it." Most amazingly, Nelson believes that he has begun to decode Bigfoot language based on the Sierra Sounds and distributed the Sasquatch Phonetic Alphabet (SPA), also known by its more formal designation, the Unclassified Hominid Phonetic Alphabet (UHPA).[39] Skeptics have been quick to pounce on Nelson's work as an exercise in pseudoscience.[40] Should Nelson's analysis have cracked Bigfoot language, it is a scientific feat worthy of great note. At the very least, he has produced the beginnings of a mythical language, a feat akin to the development of Klingon within the Star Trek subculture.

Indeed, interacting with a subculture oftentimes necessitates the learning of a new language, for a defining characteristic of a subculture is the development of a specialized vocabulary, known as *argot*. Shared interest in a subject naturally leads people to make distinctions that are of no interest to outsiders. For those involved in the world of role-playing video games, it is useful and necessary to distinguish MMORPGs from single-player games and to know the difference between turn-based and real-time combat.[41] Those with no patience for battling goblins and dragons on their computers find this to be so much boring trivia—they are all just video games. Explore any hobby or interest group and you will find similar categorization systems, which serve the useful function of distinguishing insiders from outsiders. One becomes a valued member of a subculture by learning its lingo, often under the tutelage of more senior members. Put another way, *knowledge*, identified by the use of specialized language and communication, is a key marker of membership in a subculture.

As researchers in the paranormal arena, we have had to become fluent in the argots of a number of different subcultures. We learned the difference between UFO contactees and abductees and what an abductee meant when she said aliens had placed an "implant" (tracking device) in her brain or that she had birthed a "hybrid" (a half-human/half-alien child). To navigate the world of ghost hunters we learned the workings of EMF detectors, the differences between residual and intelligent hauntings and human and inhuman entities, and how to spot "orbs" in our photography and listen for EVPs in our tape recordings.[42]

In addition to learning about key pieces of purported Bigfoot evidence, we had to learn many other pieces of the Bigfoot argot to successfully navigate its conferences. For example, Bigfooters speak of the "shoot/don't shoot" controversy, with some Bigfoot hunters advocating the killing of a Bigfoot specimen, since it seems that only a body will attract the attention of mainstream science. To those on the "don't shoot" side of the fence, it could be potentially deadly to an obviously endangered species to take even one specimen. If Bigfoot is a close relative to humans, it may even be considered murder.

At the Sasquatch Summit we heard of "vocalizations," used to refer to the Sierra Sounds and other purported Bigfoot screams and howls heard in the woods. Several speakers and attendees talked about "habituation," the process of acclimating Bigfoot to a particular property or location in the hopes of repeated visits. Habituation may be facilitated by "gifting," or leaving small objects out for Bigfoot, with some "gifters" reporting that the creature leaves its own gifts in return (such as rocks or animal bones or even a pair of sneakers).[43] We learned about long lines of alleged Bigfoot tracks, or "trackways," such as the recent "London Trackway," consisting of seventy-two plaster casts recovered near Cottage Grove, Oregon, in 2012. An impressive display of plaster casts at the back of the Great Hall allowed attendees to view the London Trackway in person.

The 2015 Sasquatch Summit provided us with a window into the world of Bigfoot enthusiasts. The knowledge and passion on display highlighted the meaning of these events to believers. For sociologists, attending such an event immediately raises questions about its composition. What types of people are here? What do they believe? Are they mostly people coming to find out if Bigfoot is real or not? Or are they already committed believers when they walk in the door? Unfortunately, data on attendees at paranormal conventions is exceedingly rare and we can only paint impressionistic portraits of the 2015 Summit. But in

2009 we were afforded the unique opportunity to document the world of a Bigfoot conference thanks to the generosity of the North American Wood Ape Conservancy (NAWAC).[44]

Profiles in Bigfoot Hunting

In some form or another, the NAWAC has been in existence since 1999. At first the group called itself the Texas Bigfoot Research Center (TBRC) and entirely focused its efforts upon the Lone Star State. Readers who have not visited Texas (or only its western portions) may be under the impression that the state provides no cover for a large, hairy beast. In fact, much of Texas consists of rolling hills and trees, and east Texas is covered with miles upon miles of dense, swampy forests. Indeed east Texas is home to a long tradition of tales of hairy wood creatures, sometimes called "Wooly Boogers."

By 2007 the TBRC had reorganized itself as a nonprofit organization and officially changed its name to the Texas Bigfoot Research *Conservancy*. At this time the leadership structure of the group changed and its original founder, Craig Woolheater, left the organization. Even more recently, members became frustrated with the negative baggage associated with the term "Bigfoot" and decided one more name change was in order:

> [I]n the minds of many, "Bigfoot" remains a solitary, presumably magical creature along the lines of the Tooth Fairy or Jack Frost. Eventually, the term "Bigfoot" was appropriated by the media as a proxy for the humorously improbable interests of simpletons and not the concern of serious, practical people. . . . To that end, after long consideration by and following a unanimous vote of this organization's Board of Directors, we are pleased to announce that from this point forward, the Texas Bigfoot Research Conservancy (TBRC) shall be known as the North American Wood Ape Conservancy (NAWAC).[45]

As of this writing, the NAWAC focuses its efforts upon research projects to document the existence of "wood apes" and no longer holds annual conferences. Thankfully, we met the group prior to this time and were generously provided the opportunity to survey the members of its 2009 meeting in Tyler, Texas.

Of five major cases and purported pieces of
Bigfoot evidence, with how many is respondent familiar?

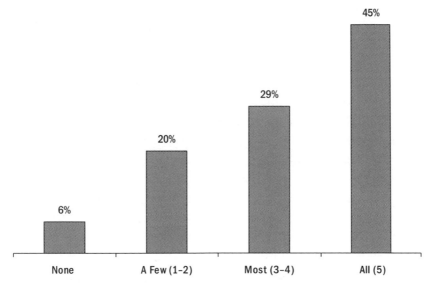

Figure 6.8. Bigfoot Knowledge among Attendees of a Major Bigfoot Conference

We arrived at an auditorium in downtown Tyler on the morning of the first day of the conference. Nearly four hundred conference attendees poured in the doors and registered at the front desk to listen to a day full of Bigfoot-related speakers. The group handed out a questionnaire prepared by the authors to all who enrolled for the event and encouraged attendees to complete the surveys throughout the day, providing us with an unprecedented window into the makeup of the Bigfoot faithful.

As we walked around the lobby collecting surveys and answering questions, we quickly noticed how serious those in attendance were about the subject. These were not people new to the study of Bigfoot, nor were they only curious locals just hoping to have a laugh at the Bigfooters' expense. This was a distinctive, hardcore Bigfoot subculture. We saw much joking around, lighthearted banter, and hugs between old friends. But most of the people who showed up had been deep into the subject for years, about half (49%) for over twenty years. When asked if they knew of several famous pieces of Bigfoot evidence, including the Albert Ostman kidnapping case, the Patterson-Gimlin film, a recorded scream of a purported Bigfoot known as the Ohio Howl,[46] the plaster cast of a supposedly reclining Bigfoot known as the Skookum Cast,[47] and the Memorial Day footage (1996) that shows a Bigfoot running across a meadow,[48] nearly half in attendance were familiar with all of them (see figure 6.7). Another two-thirds were familiar with most of the presented evidence.[49] These attendees were already Bigfoot experts when they entered the conference.

From these Bigfoot experts we heard many additional terms to add to our developing Bigfoot lexicon. Nearly one-fourth (24%) of those in attendance claimed to have heard the screams, howls, or chatter of a Bigfoot. Using a technique known as "call blasting" some Bigfoot hunters attempt to entice the creature to speak by playing purported Bigfoot screams, sounds of animals in distress, recordings of a baby crying, or any other noise believed to be a possible attractant to a curious Sasquatch at high volume in the woods.

Twenty-six percent of the Bigfoot hunters at the conference had experienced "wood knocking," the sound of wood knocking on wood. This so-called wood knocking is believed to be a form of non-vocal Sasquatch communication wherein a Bigfoot bangs sticks on the trunks of trees to communicate with other nearby Bigfeet. On occasion Bigfoot hunters will pick up a branch and try wood knocking themselves in the hopes of hearing an answer from the deep woods.

Of course, the ultimate experience of a Bigfoot researcher is to see the beast itself, known as a "visual" among Bigfoot hunters. Only twenty-three people at the conference had been lucky enough to actually see a Bigfoot, although another ten people think they may have seen one but are not absolutely certain. The holy grail would be to capture that visual on camera, the modern equivalent of the Patterson-Gimlin film. Presenters discussed a number of methods by which they might accomplish this goal, often in quite technical terms. Speaker Jerry Hestand discussed the NAWAC's "Operation Forest Vigil" in which dozens of motion-activated cameras have been attached to trees in areas of Texas and Oklahoma known for Bigfoot sightings. Bill Draginis, an engineer, discussed the "Eye-Gotcha" photographic system that could be placed in such areas.

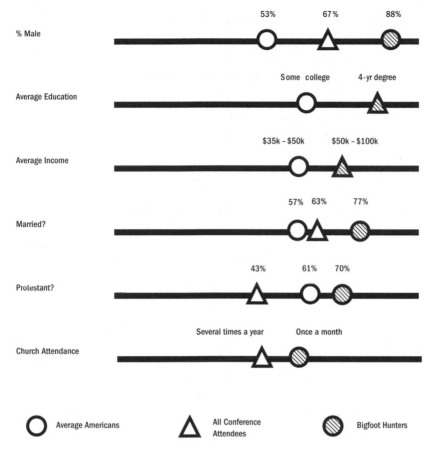

Figure 6.9. Profile of Bigfoot Researchers and Hunters: Attendees at the Texas Bigfoot Research Conservancy's Annual Conference, Compared to National Averages

Being well acquainted with the NAWAC before we attended the conference, we already knew that its members did not fit the stereotype of paranormal believers. Nevertheless, we were still surprised by the staid nature of the conference and the conventionality of most of those in attendance. We found the conference attendees to be of two broad types. Some of those in attendance were true Bigfoot hunters—members of the NAWAC, Bigfoot Field Researchers Organization, or some other Sasquatch research organization. In fact, nearly one-fifth of those in attendance had taken the step of joining such an organization. The remaining attendees were simply Bigfoot enthusiasts with an interest in the subject that has not yet developed to the level of organizational membership.

Comparing these two groups of people to the general population provides some interesting findings (see figure 6.9).

Unless one defines a person as "strange" simply *because* they express an interest in Bigfoot (and we realize that some would use that definition), the Bigfoot enthusiasts at the all-day Sasquatch event were remarkably normal, everyday people. The average Bigfooter was married and above average in education and income (with a four-year degree from a college or university and earning $50,000 a year or more). If conference attendees were slightly unconventional, it was in terms of religion. While the majority of Americans (61%) are Protestant in some form or another, less than half of the Bigfoot enthusiasts claimed affiliation with a Protestant denomination. They also attend religious services several times a year, which is less frequent than the national average of once a month.

If we separate out those in attendance that are members of Bigfoot hunting organizations, however, we find a very conventional group of people. One might even call them hyper-conventional. There was not a statistically significant difference between all conference attendees and Bigfoot hunters in terms of average education and income, but Bigfoot hunters were more likely to claim a Protestant affiliation and were in line with the average American in frequency of church attendance. There was the occasional obvious eccentric, such as an angry truck driver from Dallas who pinned us in a corner to discuss theories of Atlantis, but these types were the exception, not the rule. For the most part we were among very normal people talking about a very strange subject.

Of course, the NAWAC as an organization and its conference fostered a very particular image of Bigfoot, one that might attract a certain sort of attendee. This is an issue to which we will return in chapter 7.

Practice: Hunting Bigfoot

If people who seek paranormal *knowledge* by reading books, scanning websites, or attending conferences can be characterized as more involved in a paranormal subculture than those who simply hold a belief or have had singular experiences, then *practice* may truly separate the dabblers from the serious enthusiasts. There are a number of ways that someone with an interest in a paranormal subject can put that interest into practice. Someone with an interest in ghosts can join a ghost-hunting club. Budding astrologers and psychics can attempt to use their powers. Monster enthusiasts, on the other hand, must enter the field to search for their quarry.

When the three authors joined some NAWAC members on a hunt for Bigfoot, we witnessed something much different than the lighthearted, casual experimentation of Anaheim's Holistic Health & Spiritual Fair. These men were single-minded, focused, and serious in their quest to bring Bigfoot into the light of day. "Bigfoot ain't no unicorn," one member told us, "and we will prove it."

December, 2006: Big Creek Scenic Area, Sam Houston National Forest, Texas

"David" is a forty-something ex-air force intelligence officer and now manager of a bank in a central Texas. In 2004 he caught a brief glimpse of a five- to six-foot, manlike creature, covered in reddish brown hair, jumping across a trail in the woods of Liberty County, Texas. "Mitch," also in his forties, played basketball in college and now works with computers near Temple, Texas. He has been interested in Bigfoot since he was a child. After seeing David give a lecture about Bigfoot, Mitch began visiting the woods on ad hoc Bigfoot hunts. While driving through the countryside with his brother, he spotted a Bigfoot run across the road in front of his truck. A friendly, quiet man, Mitch's "beginner's luck" led him to formalize his quest for Bigfoot with the TBRC. "Keith," a surgeon, is also in his forties. Over six feet tall with salt-and-pepper brown hair, Keith had not seen a Bigfoot but believed he has been close. On a recent excursion he heard "something" knocking on trees and pounding rocks together in the forest. Although serious in his interest in Bigfoot, Keith also joked continually about the benefits of the hunt. "I get to spend my weekends chewin' tobacco and eatin' what I want." Indeed, we were astonished at the volume of meat Keith was able to cook and consume from a portable oven in the back of his pickup.[50]

The three men graciously allowed us to accompany them on a field investigation to the Big Creek Scenic Area in the Sam Houston National Forest, outside of Cold Spring. Per David's instructions, we wore camo

Figure 6.10. A "call blaster"

clothing (newly purchased from Wal-Mart) and brought enough food to make it through the evening. Early in the afternoon, we met at David's home and helped him pile five large plastic tubs of equipment into the back of his truck. After about three hours of driving, we pulled into a hunter's camp: a clearing in the woods with a dumpster and several pads on which we could pitch our tents.

As we set up camp, David informed us of the evening's plan. Our goal was to attempt to attract any Sasquatch that might be in the area via call blasting. David pulled a cooler from the back of his truck and opened it for us. Inside was his call blaster—a small device with dials and knobs attached to a loudspeaker. Throughout the night the call blaster played the purported Bigfoot screams, the sounds of animals in distress, and the whoops of gibbons.

Shortly after 10 p.m. we hopped in their car and followed David and the other investigators to a series of trails a short distance from our camp where Keith had experienced wood knocking. We parked at the trailhead and gathered around David's truck to receive instructions. By this point the temperature had dropped below thirty degrees, leaving the authors feeling ill prepared.[51] We shivered uncomfortably and hopped from foot to foot to keep warm.

David was dressed from head to toe in camouflage clothing. He stored cameras, flashlights, water, and other supplies in the multiple pockets on the outfit; an imposing .357 Magnum strapped to his hip. The gun was there only to protect us against "indigenous wildlife," he informed us. In 2006, David fell on the "don't shoot" side of the shoot/don't shoot Bigfoot debate. He could see "no good reason" for shooting at a Sasquatch, even though a real body would provide indisputable evidence of the creature's existence. He would use his gun only if a Sasquatch attacked or if we were threatened by other dangerous animals, such as wild boars. In more recent years, David's opinion on the matter has shifted. He now believes it is essential to gather a "type specimen" to prove the existence of "wood apes."

As David showed us his gun, Keith fiddled with his "new toy," a bizarre headlamp with two glowing lights attached to its top. By pressing a button, he could switch between white and red lights that sputtered and died when he moved too quickly. The red light was supposed to keep it from being visible to creatures without the capability to pick up the different coloration of the light. We avoided talking directly to Keith lest we had to look directly into the painfully bright lights.

The group's newest call blaster featured a remote control. It is possible that Bigfoot is deterred from investigating sounds produced by a call blaster because it hears or smells the humans operating the device, David told us. Therefore, we placed the unit and its speakers in the crook of a tree deep in the woods and retreated. The team then spread out. Each of the authors was paired with one of the investigators and followed his partner to a location in the woods. Keith would activate the blaster via remote. Ideally, a curious Bigfoot would walk right past us on its way to investigate the sounds coming from the call blaster.

It is an eerie experience to crouch by the side of a path, deep in unfamiliar woods on a bitterly cold evening, waiting for a terrifying howl to erupt from the call blaster. Between each blast, Keith would wait for responses from the local wildlife and then try again. For those of us who had no idea when the next blast would come, these waits were nerve-wracking. The sudden sound of chattering gibbons echoing off the trees caused one researcher to fall to the ground from his crouching position. Unfortunately, the experiment did not seem to produce an immediate response from resident Sasquatch. An irritated cow responded to one call blast, and we greatly annoyed the local dog population. We shudder to think of how we must have terrorized any unsuspecting campers in the area.

After an hour of call blasting, David yelled for the team to gather. We quietly marched single file back into the woods to retrieve the blaster and speakers. Several events occurred during the walk that intrigued the NAWAC investigators, as outlined in the group's written report of this excursion:

> [A]t approximately 11:30 p.m., the investigators . . . heard several sounds like extremely loud knocks on trees. Also noteworthy: investigators . . . were overwhelmed with a very obnoxious odor smelling very much like an animal that had been immersed in garbage. The knocks seemed to be in response to [our] broadcasting playbacks of gibbon and gorilla vocalizations.[52]

The authors indeed heard what sounded like something knocking on a tree and briefly noticed a foul odor, akin to that of an animal carcass. We could not locate the origin of the smell, as it came and went. Perhaps the source of the smell was moving or the wind was shifting the smell of a fixed object. Unfortunately, we are not sufficiently familiar with the Texas woods, or its wildlife, to know potential sources for such phenomena. Nevertheless, David, Mitch, and Keith were excited by the possibility of having attracted a Sasquatch to the area. "We'll come back in the morning and look for more evidence," David told us.

A Trackway

A fitful night's sleep and a hot breakfast at a local diner later, our group returned to the call blasting location. We split into two teams. Keith and Mitch asked Joseph to follow them in one direction; Carson and Christopher followed David in another.

Figure 6.11. David finds a track

David slowly walked along a creek, hopping from side to side, scanning the ground carefully, most of which was hard-packed and covered with leaves. Our best chance of finding the tracks of any Bigfoot drawn to the area by our call blasting was in the soft, wet sand around the creek, he reasoned. After searching for about twenty minutes, David said, "I think we've got something here fellas!" He knelt next to the creek and brushed leaves away from an impression in the sand.

David's cautious optimism transformed into excitement as he examined the "potential hominid track." He pointed at the indentation in the ground and at what appeared to be toe prints. It certainly looked like the track of a person, but we are not experts on animal tracks and so cannot speculate on what animals could make these tracks. "It's not a raccoon," he said. "It's not a fox or a horse or a hog either. There are only two things it could be—a human or a Sasquatch." As he scanned the area, David found what he likened to a heel print to the left of the full print. Across the small creek were what he thought might be knuckle prints. He speculated that a Bigfoot might have knelt beside the creek, resting on one hand and scooping a drink of water with the other. The NAWAC made plaster casts of the tracks, which now reside in their evidence collection. These tracks were featured in the episode "Swamp Stalker" of a now defunct History Channel series known as *MonsterQuest*.[53]

Paranormal Complications and Consequences

In our research we have found that the paranormal is difficult to predict. As social scientists we hope to answer questions when possible, not simply raise new ones. But we are compelled to note that attempts to predict who will engage the paranormal often ignore the multitude of different ways that a person might interface with a paranormal subculture or belief. Some people will simply hold an unexamined, uncritical belief in one or more paranormal subjects and their interest will go no further. Some of those who are inclined to believe in UFOs, ghosts, or psychic powers think about those subjects rarely unless asked. Other people have had what they perceive to be a paranormal experience. Sometimes a psychic experience, Bigfoot sighting, or other mysterious encounter will have a dramatic impact upon a person's life, upending paradigms and upsetting established ideas about the cosmic order. For others a ghost sighting merely provides a fun story to tell one's children around the campfire, no more, no less. Still others will be compelled by a belief or experience to study the topic further through reading books, visiting Internet sites, and watching documentaries. A small subset of these casual researchers will be funneled into even deeper levels of a paranormal subculture and will start attending psychic fairs or UFO conferences. A select few will become psychics, ghost hunters, and UFO watchers themselves.

The point being, not only do different types of people become attracted to different paranormal beliefs and have different types of paranormal experiences, different types of people will be more attracted to different levels of involvement in a paranormal subculture. For example, those who have spent time researching the subject of Bigfoot online, as well as through books and documentaries, tend to be younger males who infrequently attend church and who live on the West Coast. Yet a different type of person is attracted to the highest, most serious levels of the Bigfoot subculture and joins the hunt for Bigfoot. We cannot speak to other paranormal subcultures, but within the Bigfoot hunting subculture, at least some of the people at its most involved levels are quite conventional in other aspects of their lives, contrary to public expectations.

In the time we spent with Bigfoot hunters, we found them to be well aware of the way they are perceived by outsiders. David, Mitch, and Keith all have much to lose by "being branded as nutcases," David told us. Mitch's uncle and brother continually make fun of his fascination with Bigfoot. David is careful who he tells at work, concerned that people will not trust a Bigfoot hunter to manage their banking. Keith would not dream of telling his fellow surgeons about his quest for the beast. The men's devotion to their quest allows them to press on in the face of public scorn, not that they would not change how others perceive them if they could. Their willingness to accept the consequences of their quest for Bigfoot evidence separates them from casual Bigfoot believers and from those who visit Bigfoot websites or watch *Finding Bigfoot* once in awhile. Their focus on proving Bigfoot's existence appears largely motivated by vindication, and they dream of the day that the scientific community is forced by the weight of evidence to announce to the world that Bigfoot is indeed real. They think of themselves as normal people who just happen to have seen or believe in Bigfoot. They appear to be correct in this regard.

The willingness to be unconventional is a key distinction that separates people who are involved in the paranormal. Some are willing to face the social consequences of exploring the full range of the paranormal. Others try their best to maintain conventional lives in the face of limited paranormal interests. As we explore in the next chapter, those who are unconcerned about the consequences of paranormal belief are truly different from the rest of us. For once, the paranormal will become less complicated.

7

Paranormal People

There are several popular and academic ideas regarding people who believe in the paranormal. Sociologists and social commentators such as Karl Marx have argued that religious and paranormal beliefs are the province of the downtrodden, searching for supernatural solutions to earthly troubles. Other religion scholars have theorized that paranormal beliefs represent comparatively new and fringe elements of the religious marketplace. New ideas tend to be adopted first by elites, and therefore, some argue, the paranormal is the province of those with higher educations and incomes.

Outside the halls of the academy a broader stereotype is often applied to paranormal believers—people who believe in or have experienced the paranormal are "different." People who do not believe in the paranormal are perceived to be normal; those who believe in paranormal topics are considered weird, unconventional, strange, or deviant.

There is a big problem with this simplistic assessment—believing in something paranormal is not deviant, at least statistically. When asked if they believe in the reality of six different paranormal subjects including alien visitations, UFOs, Bigfoot, mediumship, telekinesis, and hauntings, more than half (52%) believe in at least one (see figure 7.1). In a strictly numerical sense, people who do not believe in anything paranormal are now the "odd people out" in American society, with less than half (48%) dismissive of all seven subjects. What this means is that distinguishing between people who do and do not believe or experience the paranormal may be less interesting than finding out *how much* of the paranormal they find credible.

Very few Americans (2%) believe in all six of these paranormal subjects. Only about 11% believe in four or more. What this means is a slight majority of Americans are not entirely dismissive of the paranormal but display a form of particularistic skepticism. Some believe strongly in aliens and Bigfoot, but find the claims of psychics incred-

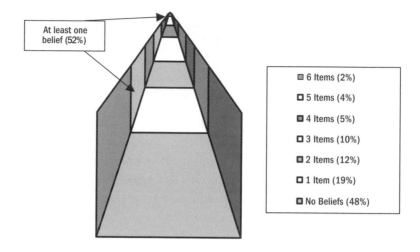

At least one belief (52%)

6 Items (2%)

5 Items (4%)

4 Items (5%)

3 Items (10%)

2 Items (12%)

1 Item (19%)

No Beliefs (48%)

Figure 7.1. The Paranormal Pyramid: Percentage of Americans Holding Simultaneous Paranormal Beliefs (Baylor Religion Survey 2014, n=1474)

ible. Some believe wholeheartedly in haunted houses and the ability to communicate with the dead, yet have little patience for claims of psychic powers.

To put it simply, people who believe in the paranormal can be placed along a continuum ranging from paranormal particularists, who believe strongly in one aspect of the paranormal or have had a single type of paranormal experience, to paranormal generalists, who hold multiple different types of paranormal beliefs and may claim multiple different types of paranormal experiences.

Throughout this book we have dispelled many stereotypes about the paranormal, but in this chapter we find that some popular notions about the paranormal do indeed fit. In our fieldwork and in our data we have noticed that there are strong demographic differences between paranormal particularists and paranormal generalists. Sometimes paranormal generalists are quite unconventional and do indeed inhabit the fringes of society—you just have to know where and how to look.

To understand the important differences between these paranormal generalists and particularists we will first revisit two people we met earlier in the book.

Laura, Paranormal Generalist: "I Refuse to Limit Myself"

In chapter 5 we introduced Laura, who claims to have been taken aboard a UFO in 1984. Aboard this ship she met a group of friendly, humanlike extraterrestrials and their commanding officer. Laura was connected to an advanced computer system to receive lessons about holistic health and medicine that she would someday use to help the planet. Following her lessons and an amazing meal, Laura was returned to Earth unharmed. Laura's story is not particularly unusual within the UFO subculture. It fits in rather nicely alongside those of George Adamski, Billy Meier, and other UFO contactees who have received wisdom from their humanlike space brothers.

But Laura is not like other people we have met who have had a singular UFO experience. She does not obsess over UFO tales and does not seem to dwell on this particular experience unless asked about it. The reason? She lives a life filled with paranormal beliefs and experiences, and her visit to space was but one of many.

On a rainy weekend, I (Chris) visited Laura at her home in Federal Way, Washington, to chat about her varied beliefs about the paranormal. Laura lives in a mobile home in what she cheerfully described over the phone as a "trailer park that has seen better days." Having retired from a job with the post office several years previous, Laura now lives on a fixed income but is "busier than ever" with her reading and hobbies.

One of her strongest interests is Native American spirituality, which I noticed immediately upon entering her well-kept home. As a puppy jumped at my legs and an older cat stared petulantly from behind a chair, I looked around the room. Nearly every surface had a popular representation of Native Americans on it. To my left was a small bookshelf. Covering the wall above it was a series of small collector plates, each emblazoned with reverent paintings of Native Americans. In one, a chief in full headdress sits on the back of his horse, his arms out to his sides. In another, a medicine man communes with a wolf in the forest. On top of the bookshelf was a resin statue of three wolf heads, howling at the sky. Across the room and on top of another bookshelf was a two-foot-tall teepee made of cloth. A large ceramic maiden doll with feathers in her hair was standing inside the teepee. A dream catcher hung from the ceiling in a corner. Paintings of saintly Native Americans filled the open wall space. They sat near streams, danced in fields, and gazed at totemic animals in the sky.

I asked Laura about this obvious interest in Native Americans. She is one-eighth Native American, she said, and finds these groups to be the "most in touch with nature and most in touch with their inner spirituality." She further believes Native American tribes to be the descendants of star ancestors as "they have legends about coming from the sky." To explore further, Laura recently joined a "Medicine Wheel" formed by a local shaman. The creation of medicine wheels or sacred hoops was a common practice among Native American tribes, who used them as calendars and for various healing rituals and rites of passage. Most often the wheels were physically laid upon the landscape using stones. Lines of rocks radiated outward in a circular pattern from a center point of stones.

Recently, the symbol of the sacred circle has been adopted in paranormal circles, and it is this blending of the old and the new that Laura practices. She describes her Medicine Wheel as "basically Northwest Indian astrology" and symbolic in nature. Sometimes when the group meets, they do not bother to lay out a wheel on the ground. Each member is given an animal representation based on their birth dates. Laura is a bear, a natural leader. In the group's irregular meetings, they stand in a circle and meditate, often focusing upon their animal representations.

Laura also told me with pride of her membership in a "Grandmothers Meeting." Although Laura has several grandchildren, this group is not only for grandmothers in the literal sense. Rather the grandmother is a "symbol that represents an aspect of the divine that has come to heal the Earth." Grandmothers represent the "yin," Laura said. She continued:

> Yin energy finds the divine in the world as it is. People flooded with yin energy look at the forest and marvel in its beauty. Yang energy looks at a forest and sees the profit that can be made from its woods or from building on it. Yang represents movement and change. Yin is peace. When the two are in balance, the world works as it should. When they are out of balance there are problems. The world has too much yang now. That is why we have wars.

The grandmothers believe that by coming together and meditating they can raise the level of yin in the world, thereby bringing renewed peace, prosperity, and balance to the planet. When not meditating with her Medicine Wheel or at a Grandmothers Meeting, Laura pursues a dizzying array of other paranormal interests. She once signed up for astrology courses at a New Age school, but soon realized that she would have to invest considerable time, energy, and money to become a truly proficient astrologer and withdrew her enrollment. She still occasionally reads a book on astrology, but now has more interest in numerology, which "just makes sense to [her]."

She has attempted automatic writing at times, wherein the "writer" holds a pen or pencil over a pad of paper and enters a trancelike state during which the writer's hand scribbles out messages and drawings. Some think these messages are from the writer's subconscious; others believe that aliens, ghosts, angels, or other entities enter the writer's body and use this opportunity to communicate. Laura has a strong interest in Bigfoot and believes the creatures come in more humanlike and more beastlike varieties. Both versions of Bigfoot escape detection via the ability to become invisible, even though several of her friends claim to have seen one.

Laura has not spotted Bigfoot herself, but she has many other paranormal experiences. It seems that as a young girl Laura was duck hunting with her father near a swamp in southern California. She was crouched next to her father behind some tall grass waiting for ducks to fly overhead when she heard a male voice in her head yelling at her. "Laura! Move your head! Now!" it said. She ducked down and at that very moment heard a gunshot. It seems that duck hunters on the other side of the swamp had fired at a duck crossing in front of Laura's position. If Laura had not ducked, she claims, she would have been shot directly in the face. She believes that the voice she heard was that of a guardian angel sent to protect her. Her father was not so warned, however, and was hit in the face. He lived the remainder of his life with bullet fragments embedded in his forehead.

Laura also believes that she has lived a number of past lives. She was sent to Earth eighty thousand years ago by a consortium of extraterrestrial "higher beings" called the Goodly Company. Members of the Goodly Company share an agenda of helping to promote peace throughout the universe. Laura was involved in the creation of the human species. She has memories of observing Neanderthal man with a team of other higher beings. They would look for the selfless Neanderthals—the ones who helped others and not only themselves. These noblest specimens were used for breeding in creating the human race.

As part of her life journey, Laura occasionally lived among the early humans. In a recent correspondence, she told of her experience with wooly mammoths:

> I was [once] a young unmarried woman of a small band of cave dwellers. Our people were starving. Our medicine man went into the between worlds and talked to the leader of the Mammoths. He pleaded for a sacrifice from one of them so our people would not die. The old Mammoth agreed ONLY if one of our children was sacrificed as well. Their children were as precious to them as ours were to us. The shaman agreed.
>
> On a certain day my parents came and were so excited. I was massaged with grease and my hair was straightened and flowers were put on me and in my hair. I was excited too. I thought that a mate had been found for me and I was to be married. I was brought out to a jumble of rocks that overlooked a narrow strip of plain between two cliffs. All the people were there and the shaman was telling us how this was a good day. The Mammoth were coming and we would eat. The day was beautiful and sunny and the rocks were warm. It seemed like fall because the grasses in the valley were golden. The Mammoths started walking through the valley but too far away for our hunters to reach them. The shaman had me sit on the rock and lay back. He told my parents to hold my arms. They looked bewildered but did it. Quickly the shaman took a knife and stabbed me in the heart. Everyone was horrified because this sort of thing had NEVER been done before. My parents were devastated because they had not been told. I was startled and then I was out of my body watching.
>
> A young female Mammoth with a beautiful shining golden coat turned away from the herd and walked close to the wall where our people were. She looked me straight in the eye and I was dumbfounded by the intelligence and beauty I saw there. Our hunters pushed down boulders and killed her. She knowingly sacrificed herself because I was sacrificed. And the people lived.[1]

Once the human race was firmly established, Laura says, extraterrestrials sent Jesus to Earth to teach us further. Laura was also around to help with his mission. During Jesus's time she lived as an old widow named Rachel. She became extremely close friends with Jesus after traveling with him and the apostles. Jesus was crucified, says Laura, because he was so good at changing people's mind. "He brought out the best in everyone and the powerful people couldn't stand it." Laura/Rachel could not bear to witness the crucifixion of Jesus but afterward became a vocal advocate of his message. Eventually, she also became an irritant and was stoned to death for "talking to [sic] much about Jesus."[2]

Learning so much about her own past lives has opened Laura up to new revelations. She believes that we are all connected to a big "Oversoul," and that each individual person is merely an extension of it. Those who tap into the Oversoul can tap into the lives and experiences of others, something that Laura has learned to do. She experiences not only her own past lives but can relive and reexperience the past lives of people she has never even met.

Were a UFO author to interview Laura, she would probably ask her only about adventures aboard a spaceship and label her a "contactee." A professional astrologist or numerologist would find a budding initiate in Laura. Someone producing a documentary on guardian angels might have interest in her story. She would be the perfect call-in guest for a talk show about past lives. But Laura is not any one of these things. She is all of them, simultaneously. She lives in a paranormal world where each day can bring a new paranormal experience or interest in a new paranormal topic. She knows that she is not like most people and takes pride in her unconventionality.

In chapter 6 we introduced David, a Bigfoot hunter from Texas. He has devoted himself to finding conclusive evidence for Bigfoot's existence since he sighted the creature in 2004. Nearly all of David's free time is spent in the woods searching for Bigfoot or helping with the operations of the North American Wood Ape Conservancy. Someone who had not met David and Laura might lump them together—they both claim to have had an experience that we have labeled paranormal in this book. But in almost every other way, they could not be more different. To understand this difference, we must first visit a controversy within the Bigfoot community regarding the nature of their quarry.

The Woo Woo Factor

A key challenge that has faced Bigfoot believers over the years has been the subject's frequent association with other aspects of the paranormal.[3] To those outside Bigfoot circles, the subject is akin to ghosts and astrology. Sasquatch is something for the tabloids or a silly story with which to end the local evening news. The anthropologist Jeff Meldrum, one of the few academics to openly express an interest in Bigfoot, ruminated on this issue in his book *Sasquatch: Legend Meets Science*:

> Unfortunately, the legitimate search for elusive animals had become embroiled in the mix of the mystical and the pseudoscientific. Accounts of lake monsters and wildmen continue to be the stuff of sensational supermarket tabloids. Walk into a bookstore in search of reading material on Bigfoot and you will most often be directed to the occult section, somewhere between Bermuda triangle and crop circles.[4]

Attendees at the 2015 Sasquatch Summit (see chapter 6) agreed on many things, such as the importance of the Patterson-Gimlin film to the study of Bigfoot and the meaning of key terms. But we certainly experienced one point of disagreement at the event (albeit a friendly one). Exactly what is Sasquatch anyway? Some presenters described a creature that resembles an undiscovered primate, nonmalevolent and certainly not a monster, but a wild animal nonetheless. Others talked about Bigfeet as more humanlike than animal, perhaps a tribe of undiscovered, wild humans. But the most pronounced distinction between Bigfoot camps lies with Bigfoot's possibly mystical nature.

During his presentation, Tom Baker, a senior manager for Amazon Logistics in Seattle and member of the Olympic Project (a Bigfoot research organization based in Washington State), presented data gathered from reports submitted to the group. As a statistical data analyst, Baker has expertise in developing data and metadata and searching for meaningful patterns within those data. His presentation, titled "Statistical Analysis of Sasquatch/Human Interactions (The Journey Continues)," displayed mapped Bigfoot sightings in Washington. He carefully explained the concept of standard deviations to the audience and described how he could use them to search sighting data for locations, reported behaviors,

You	Creature
Olympic Peninsula	7 feet, 3 inches tall
August	422 pounds
9:00pm - 11:00pm	Dark brown hair
Driving down a woodland road	Walking down or near a road
Elevation between 1,000 and 2,000 feet	It may scream
	It may be rocking back and forth

Figure 7.2. The Typical Washington State Bigfoot Sighting (Presentation by Tom Baker of the Olympic Project at 2015 Sasquatch Summit in Ocean Shores, WA)

times of day, and other characteristics of Bigfoot encounters for outliers. Putting all of these pieces together, Baker outlined the most common features of a Bigfoot sighting in the state.

Baker's presentation operated upon a key underlying assumption. To intuit the migratory patterns and behaviors of a creature based on such data assumes that said creature is predictable and earthly—some form of primitive human, relic hominoid, or undiscovered primate. Others at the conference did not see Bigfoot the same way.

For example, Samantha "Sam" Ritchie operates a blog called "Planet Sasquatch" (http://planetsasquatch.blogspot.com). Samantha did not speak at the conference, but ran a table advertising her blog. She claims to be a "sensitive" who can communicate with Sasquatch. Far from being an animal, Samantha told me, Bigfoot is a "spiritual, benevolent entity" that has the ability to cloak itself, appearing fully or partially invisible at will. In her opinion, people should spend more time attempting to commune with the Bigfoot people than hunting them, and the fact that many at the conference refuse to admit that Bigfoot is a spiritual being is more a reflection on them than the creature.

"People are operating at different levels," she continued. "At level 1 are people who just don't believe in Bigfoot at all. At level 2 are people who believe that they are just monkeys. At level 3 are people who think they are some form of Neanderthal. Level 4 are those who at least think it's some type of human."

"I'm up here," she said raising her hand above her head, "at level 7." "This is for people who understand that Bigfoot is more than a creature and is a paranormal entity." Despite differing with some others at the conference about the nature of Bigfoot, Samantha said that everyone gets along for the most part. "When I am talking to someone at a lower level—I try not to freak them out too much."

One of the final speakers at the conference did not share Samantha's concerns about "freaking people out." On Saturday afternoon, Thom Powell, a science teacher at Robert Gray Middle School outside of Portland, Oregon, took the stage for his talk, titled "What Is Bigfoot?" An entertaining, charismatic speaker, Powell immediately warned the audience about his perspective on Bigfoot: "I'm a little more on the paranormal side." "I'll warn you now," he continued, "so that you can get out of the room."

Powell used to think that Bigfoot was likely an undiscovered creature and joined the Bigfoot Field Researchers Organization to help document its existence. Some cases he investigated for the BFRO changed his mind about the nature of the beast. For example, a couple reported that Bigfoot was stealing items from a freezer they kept in a shed. Powell placed a camera near the freezer and the thefts stopped, but the couple then reported that the Bigfoot activity had relocated to the woods nearby. When Powell moved the cameras to those woods, the freezer was raided again. Clearly Bigfoot was smarter than a typical animal, he thought. On another occasion, Powell spent a long evening sitting on a chair near some woods far from his home. He would knock on his chair three times, await a possible response and then do so again. The night went by without incident. Powell made the long drive back home. As soon as he stepped from his car, he heard three loud knocks coming from the woods. Either a Bigfoot had chased him home to play this prank, or the creatures had the psychic ability to transfer information to one another; a sort of "coconut telegraph," he called it.

Such experiences led Powell to focus on "understanding, rather than scientific evidence." He began noting similarities between Bigfoot and other paranormal phenomena such as lake monsters, ghosts, and UFO sightings and abductions, all of which involved mysterious camera and electronic failures (making it difficult to capture conclusive evidence), strong senses of fear or dread, and claims of telepathic contact. He has become further convinced Bigfoot and UFOs are connected. It is possible, Powell said, that "Sasquatches are footsoldiers for the ETs." After all, both UFOs and Bigfeet emanate from underground hideouts and there have been many reports of Bigfoot-type creatures seen emerging from UFOs or jumping out of "portals." All of these insights have led Powell to posit that Bigfeet, which he prefers to call "Forest People," have certain characteristics, which he outlined on a slide:

- Language
- Advanced communication: Definite yes
- Telepathy: apparently
- Superior intellect
- Contempt for cameras in particular
- Contempt for Scientific documentation in general

Powell recognizes that his perspective is uncomfortable for those who prefer to view Bigfoot as an undiscovered primate. He displayed a slide that showed two cartoon characters screaming at one another. Titled "The Two Camps of Bigfoot/Sasquatch Researchers," one of the characters was labeled "Paranormal (Woo-woo)," the other "Flesh-and-Blood (Scientific)." "The science camp says to me," said Powell, "'Thom you are ruining it for us and making us look bad to science.'" His reply to those who do not like his connection of Bigfoot and the paranormal:

Bigfoot is considered paranormal by the general public. Only in the Bigfoot community do we distinguish between Bigfoot and the paranormal.

In a conversation with another speaker at the Sasquatch Summit, I broached the subject of Powell's presentation.[5] The speaker, who had earlier presented on the biological characteristics of Bigfoot, laughed at the mention, dismissing Powell and others with similar views as part of the "woo woo factor" that the Bigfoot field has to endure.

Indeed, Powell is but one of several figures within the Bigfoot subculture that have emerged to vex such Bigfoot naturalists. Since 1983 former logger Stan Johnson has claimed telepathic communication with the "Bigfoot Peoples," peaceful forest beings who worship the Christian God. "The first time I met Sasquatch he got up and prayed . . . to God, and to Jesus Christ," Johnson claimed.[6] Through a Bigfoot named "Allone" (of the Rrowe family of Bigfeet), Johnson has learned that the Bigfeet are visitors from the fifth dimension who travel in UFOs. Originally from the planet Centuris, the Bigfoot Peoples were rescued by the inhabitants of nearby Arice when their planet was about to be destroyed. The Bigfeet lived happily with the humanlike people of Arice until an evil ruler came to power, forcing many to find another home. Sometime before the last Ice Age, some of the Bigfeet made their way to Earth, where they were forced to contend with rampaging dinosaurs and aggressive cavemen. Compounding their problems was a troop of evil Bigfeet sent to Earth by the evil conqueror. After many bloody skirmishes, the good Bigfeet fled to various corners of the globe. Allone warned Johnson that the bad Bigfeet remain especially numerous in Russia, China, the mountains of Oregon, and parts of Washington and Canada.[7]

One of the greatest thorns in the sides of more staid Bigfooters was the late Jon-Erik Beckjord (1939–2008), whom Thom Powell cited as an inspiration. Beckjord regularly appeared on radio talk shows and TV programs such as *The Today Show* and *Late Night with David Letterman* to espouse his unique theories about Bigfoot. We were able to speak to Beckjord by phone shortly before his death to learn more about his unique perspective.

"We should have captured Bigfoot by now if it was flesh and blood," he told us. He went on to explain that a hunter should have shot one of them. Would it not be possible to follow the footprints of such a large beast until we found one? Why hasn't a Bigfoot been struck and killed by a car? Those who favor a simple, naturalistic origin for Bigfoot have provided their own responses to such criticisms.[8] Beckjord believed he had a more reasonable answer. Bigfeet "cannot be caught or shot" because they are shape-shifters that can "manipulate the light spectrum they're in so that people can't see them." They can also use telepathic powers to sense the presence of humans. Further, Bigfoot creatures share a "space-time origin and connection with UFOs, and come from an alternate universe by a wormhole."[9]

David, Paranormal Particularist: "That UFO Nonsense"

In our time with members of the North American Wood Ape Conservancy, we observed how little patience David and most other members have for connecting Bigfoot to the paranormal.

With a diverse, dedicated, professional, and talented roster of over one hundred members, including biologists and other professionals, the NAWAC proposes that the source of the Bigfoot phenomenon is a biological entity, probably an unlisted large primate. The organization is actively engaged in activities designed to test that hypothesis. The group seeks to enhance the credibility of Bigfoot/Sasquatch research and facilitate a greater degree of acceptance from the scientific community.

NAWAC members dream of Bigfoot moving out of the tabloids and into the academy, but Bigfoot paranormalists threaten these ambitions. With their outlandish theories and colorful personalities, Powell, Beckjord, and others further convince already wary academics and government agencies that Bigfoot is a fringe topic, from which serious people should stay away. "We have lots of scientists that quietly support us," David told us, "but they don't say it publicly because they are worried about their reputations."[10] To date most have not taken the time to truly examine their evidence, David told us, but merely dismiss it out of hand.

NAWAC members make a point of talking about their level of skepticism to counteract the perception that Bigfoot is a silly subject. "Just because I hunt Bigfoot doesn't mean I believe everything I hear. I'm a skeptic," one told us. At NAWAC meetings we have heard speakers who spent as much time debunking potential cases as they did presenting exciting new pieces of evidence.[11] More importantly, David told us, the group is very careful to avoid being caught up in "that UFO nonsense." Those with a more paranormalist view of Bigfoot are unlikely to agree with the clear biological stance outlined in the group's materials, and if they were to join they would find little hearing for their theories. This is not to suggest that the NAWAC is rude or close-minded; they just have a clear perspective on the nature of their enterprise.

Popular and academic discussions often treat the paranormal as an either/or proposition. Either you are "normal" and do not believe in topics such as Bigfoot, UFOs, and psychic phenomena, or you are deviant and believe in the paranormal. The reality is—yes—much more complicated. Among paranormal believers we find a strong distinction between people like Laura, who see their involvement with the paranormal as a lifelong exploration of the unknown in many forms, and people like David, who are seeking credibility and focus upon only one subject. David tries very hard to make sure that his topic of interest is not associated with other paranormal topics. Laura sees the paranormal as an interconnected web of beliefs and experiences; she is a paranormal person. David has almost reluctantly found himself involved in the study of Bigfoot and will not cross the line into other topics.

The differences between David and Laura may seem idiosyncratic and unique to their biographies, but in fact, we can predict with some accuracy what type of person will become involved in one or many aspects of the paranormal.

The Paranormal as Deviance

To explain and predict why someone might become a paranormal particularist like David and other members of the NAWAC versus a paranormal generalist like Laura, we turn to research by scholars of deviant and criminal behavior. We want to be clear about several points though. The reader might ask why we would apply theories of deviant and criminal behavior to people who believe or participate in the paranormal. Does this mean that we think that people who visit astrologers are potential criminals or that UFO believers are weird and dangerous?

Typically, it is the bizarre examples of a phenomenon that become the most heavily publicized. Consider homicide in the United States. Judging by news coverage, popular police dramas, and reality series, one might be left with the impression that most murders are committed by strangers and that serial killings are on the rise. The opposite is true. Most homicide victims are killed by someone they know, usually in the heat of passion, as in cases of domestic violence.[12] Law enforcement is well aware of this fact. Most detectives start their murder investigations by interviewing spouses and other in-home family members before moving to extended family members, close friends, and finally acquaintances and co-workers. Only when such leads fail to produce a viable suspect do police seriously consider the possibility that a complete stranger was involved in the crime. There is also no evidence that serial killings are on the increase. Serial killings rise and fall with the overall homicide rate. Serial murders constitute a very small percentage of all murders; we see more serial killings during times of increased violent crime and fewer in less violent times.[13] The reason we have such a skewed sense of what murder is like is that shocking and atypical murders are considered bigger news than "routine" domestic violence incidents.[14]

The same problem applies to coverage of the paranormal. The most eccentric personalities receive the most airplay. Those very rare instances (such as the mass suicide of the Heaven's Gate UFO cult) wherein paranormal believers have been a danger to themselves or others receive so much media attention that they often come to typify the paranormal in the minds of the public. We have run into our share of eccentric personalities while researching this book. But we have also met just as many who are indistinguishable from the average person on the street. People who believe in the paranormal are not to be feared and we do not want readers to think that our application of ideas from criminology and deviance studies means that we have bought into stereotypes about paranormal believers.

To call something "deviant" is not the same as calling it bad, evil, or crazy. Deviance simply refers to beliefs or behaviors that diverge from the norms of society. A more appropriate synonym for deviant would be "unconventional." Unconventional beliefs and behaviors can be bad for society. Criminal acts are a form of deviance, as is holding white supremacist beliefs. At other times, unconventional behaviors and beliefs are beneficial. Rosa Parks engaged in an act of deviance that helped to spawn the civil rights movement. Inventors, entrepreneurs, and scientists often have to think in unconventional ways and break with norms to make advances in their fields. Something is defined as paranormal because it has not yet been recognized by conventional science, organized religion, and conventional society more generally. Therefore, the paranormal is, by definition, deviant, and theories of deviance can sometimes help us understand involvement with the paranormal.

We also must be very clear about another point. Many theories that attempt to explain deviance focus upon criminality, particularly gang violence and juvenile delinquency. This is not surprising, as the reduction of crime is of much greater interest to public officials and granting agencies than is the understanding of noncriminal deviant or unconventional behaviors and beliefs. Our reference to this research does not mean that we believe the paranormal to be akin to criminal behavior.

Stakes in Conformity

Criminologists and deviance researchers have proposed a wide variety of different theories to explain what causes unconventional beliefs and behaviors. Much of this work has assumed that people naturally desire to conform and that it takes a negative event or circumstance to push someone into deviant behavior. In other words, much criminological theory rests on the implicit assumption that people are inherently "good" until something makes them "bad."

The criminologist Travis Hirschi pushed for a different approach to understanding deviance in his landmark book *Causes of Delinquency*.[15] Although he focused his theory upon the explanation of juvenile delinquency and crime, its core ideas have wider applicability and can also be applied to unconventional beliefs and behaviors. Hirschi argued that conformity is not natural for humans.[16] Crime and deviance can provide an easy, quick, and often thrilling means to desired ends. One way to buy a car is to work long hours at a job, slowly saving up the necessary funds to finally purchase a sensible vehicle. It is much quicker to simply steal the expensive sports car that one actually wants. If one is angered or humiliated by someone else, the sensible thing to do is walk away and cool down, when the most gratifying thing to do would be to instantly retaliate. Hirschi's point was simple: most people know the conventional routes they are expected to use to reach desired goals, but unconventional or deviant routes to those same goals are often quicker and more appealing on a base level. So why do people conform at all?

The answer is simple, but insightful. Most people do not act on their base instincts or take the quickest route to desired goals because to do so would be too risky. Consider two men, one of whom has a high-paying job with opportunities for advancement, a higher education, a wife he loves, and children that he dotes on. The other man has had less luck in life. He was never able to go to college and has briefly held a series of low-paying jobs. Recently divorced, he is entirely estranged from his ex-wife and children. Following Hirschi's line of reasoning, the first man should be much less likely to engage in a deviant act, such as visiting a prostitute. Were he to be caught soliciting by police, his name might reach the papers. His wife and children would be humiliated and angry and might never forgive him. His boss and co-workers might find out about the arrest, costing him future promotions or even his job. The other man is not concerned about losing his high-paying job or future opportunities for advancement in his chosen career. With no current desire to reconcile with his wife and kids, he is not concerned about them finding out that he consorted with a prostitute. The temptations of deviance should be less attractive to the first man because he has more at risk, more to lose if he gets caught.

Hirschi and related theorists do not argue that people who do not have a job or who are lonely are inherently criminal. Nor do they argue that people who have much to lose will never deviate, as evidenced by high-profile scandals involving politicians and public figures. They simply claim that people who are more tied to conventional society will be more concerned with conventionality. People who have significant investments in conventional lines of action will be loathe to risk those investments. Someone who has spent years acquiring the advanced education for a high-paying engineering career is less likely to engage in risky behaviors than another person earning low, hourly wages at what he perceives to be a dead-end job. On average, people who have a high "stake in conformity" have more to lose by engaging in deviant or unconventional behavior and should be less likely to be engaged in deviance than people with lesser stakes in conformity.[17] Those with low stakes in conformity are comparatively free to indulge in deviance.

Hirschi argued that a stake in conformity is composed of four elements: attachments, involvements, commitments, and beliefs. Attachment refers to the extent to which an individual has strong relationships with people that he desires to maintain. An individual who has strong attachments will, theoretically, not want to risk the disapproval of these significant others by engaging in deviant behavior. Involvement refers to the extent to which individuals engage in conventional activities. Hirschi argues that an individual who is involved in social clubs, charities, or other such activities will be too busy doing those things to find time to engage in deviant behavior. Commitments of money, energy, or time made in order to obtain a certain lifestyle compose another part of the stake in conformity. Someone who has worked hard and achieved material success will, theoretically, avoid unconventional behavior since it might threaten the investments she has made in a certain lifestyle. The final element of the social bond, belief, assumes that an individual will be less likely to accept unconventional beliefs if she already has conventional beliefs.

People with high levels of attachment, involvement, commitment, and belief will be more likely to be conformists, while people with extremely low levels of each will be more likely to be deviant, unconventional, or nonconformist. People can range anywhere between these two extremes. For example, Hirschi would expect a youth with an average number of strong attachments to be more deviant than a youth with a high number of attachments, but less deviant than a youth with no valued relationships.

Hirschi's ideas help us to predict how involved someone will become in the paranormal, both in the specific examples of David and Laura, and in the trends we find in our national surveys. There is strong evidence that a person's stake in conformity helps to predict her level of involvement in the paranormal. People who are wedded to conventional society are less attracted to paranormal beliefs. They will tend to have no paranormal beliefs or to be paranormal particularists like David. People with lower stakes in conformity lean toward the more unconventional in general and are more likely to be paranormal generalists, like Laura. To demonstrate this trend, we examine each element of a stake in conformity in turn.[18]

Attachment

The attachment element of a stake in conformity refers to the extent to which an individual has strong relationships that she desires to maintain. It is risky to engage in deviant or unconventional behaviors if doing so will result in ridicule or shame from family members, friends, and co-workers. Depending upon the behavior in question, one may end up losing those relationships if the deviance is discovered. Someone who lacks such relationships is comparatively free to deviate—they do not have to factor the opinions of others into their decisions.

Although we did not ask respondents to our national surveys how many friends they currently have, we can examine one measure of attachment—marital status. Marriage is a marker of conventionality in American society. A number of studies have found that people who are married tend to be more conventional in a variety of ways.[19] They take fewer risks, have fewer social problems such as addiction to drugs and alcohol, and are likely to have higher levels of physical and mental health.

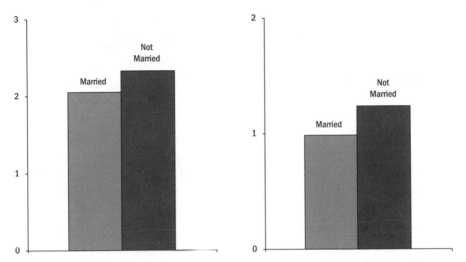

Figure 7.3. Attachment: Number of Paranormal Beliefs and Experiences by Marital Status (Chapman University Survey of American Fears 2014, n=1573). Married respondents hold 2 paranormal beliefs on average compared to 2.4 for respondents who are not married. Difference in means is significant at p<.001. Married respondents on average have had slightly less than one paranormal experience (.98), compared to respondents who are not married, who report more than one (1.2).

To see if marital status relates to the paranormal, we compare the number of paranormal beliefs and number of paranormal experiences claimed by married and unmarried people. In 2014 we asked Americans about six different paranormal beliefs. We asked if the respondent believes in ancient, advanced civilizations such as Atlantis, psychic powers, Bigfoot and other monsters, UFOs, hauntings, and astrology. We then counted the number of items in which the respondent believes. Some people have a score of zero, meaning they do not express belief in any of these items. A person who scores a "1" believes in only one item. Such a person is a paranormal particularist, who believes in, for example, Bigfoot, but is dismissive of other phenomena. A person that scores a "6" is a true paranormal generalist—he or she believes in all of these phenomena. In a similar vein, we can assign a paranormal experience score to each respondent by asking if the respondent has consulted a horoscope; visited a medium, fortune-teller, or psychic; lived in a placed believed to be haunted; used a Ouija board to contact a spirit; witnessed a UFO; and/or had a dream that later came true.

The number of paranormal beliefs a person holds and the number of paranormal experiences claimed is indeed related to marital status (see figure 7.3). People who are married hold fewer paranormal beliefs on average than those who are unmarried.

Belief

Travis Hirschi's argument that conventional beliefs will tie a person to conformity is straightforward. People who are conventional or traditional in the way that they think or in what they believe will be less attracted to ideas or beliefs that are outside of convention. In our surveys we found strong evidence that conventional belief is a deterrent to the paranormal. People who have more conventional beliefs in other spheres are simply less likely to hold paranormal beliefs or to have paranormal experiences.

Political preference is one indicator of the types of beliefs a person holds. About a fourth (26%) of Americans self identify as liberals. Over a third (36%) identify as conservatives. The remainder self-identify as moderates. It would be incorrect to claim that identifying as either liberal or conservative is unconventional or deviant in the United States, but clearly conservatives have, by definition, more traditional attitudes on most social issues.[20] Thus, we might expect the claiming of a conservative identity to tie a person more tightly to conventionality and deter experimentation with the paranormal. Indeed, we find such a trend (see figure 7.4).

Conservatives are significantly less interested in the paranormal than liberals and moderates. Extremely conservative people believe in fewer than two of the paranormal subjects we asked about (Atlantis, UFOs, monsters, psychic powers, hauntings, and astrology) on average. Moderates and liberals believe in more than two of these subjects, on average. A similar relationship holds for paranormal experiences. Claimed paranormal experiences fall directly as the level of conservatism rises. Put another way, extreme conservatives are least likely to claim paranormal experiences, extreme liberals the most likely.

Chapter 5 explored the complicated relationship between conventional religion and the paranormal. In particular, we discussed how conventional religion often acts as a competing paradigm to the para-

Paranormal Beliefs

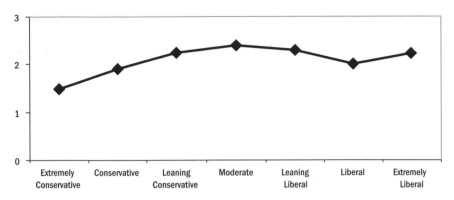

Paranormal Experiences

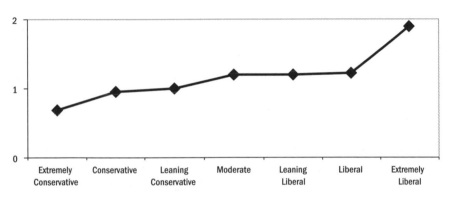

Figure 7.4. Belief: Number of Paranormal Beliefs and Experiences by Political Preference (Chapman University Survey of American Fears 2014, n=1573). All differences are statistically significant.

normal. Some religious groups will allow their members the freedom to investigate alternative beliefs while stricter groups will discourage or forbid such behavior.

Religion can also be thought of in a different way—as a sign of conventionality, at least in the United States. Certain religious beliefs are held by most Americans. For example, the majority (78%) report affiliation with a Christian denomination of some type (Catholic, Evangelical Protestant, mainline Protestant, black Protestant). Differing from majority religious beliefs is, in certain cases, a sign that a person is willing to embrace unconventional worldviews.

A succinct means by which to gauge the conventionality of an individual's religious views is his conception of God. Sociologists have found that conceptions of God impact a variety of other beliefs and attitudes.[21] Nearly two-thirds of Americans believe in God without doubts and another 12% believe in God, even if they sometimes have doubts (see figure 7.5). About 6% have no opinion or simply do not know what God is. Of greatest interest for the current purposes are the remaining two views of God. A small percentage (7%) of Americans are atheists who do not believe in anything beyond the physical world, including God. Since such people exhibit skepticism toward the supernatural in general, they should be unlikely to hold paranormal beliefs, despite the unconventionality of non-theism.

Another 12% of Americans refer to God as a "cosmic force" or higher power. These people eschew terms such as "God" that imply a singular figure or a man in the sky. This is too abstract for many Americans, who ascribe feelings, emotions, and judgment to God. In other words, imaging God as a "force" is a relatively unconventional belief in American society. Holding this belief about God may indicate that an individual is open to unconventional supernatural beliefs as a whole. Indeed, this appears to be the case (see figure 7.6).

People who do not believe in God or who do not know about God reported the fewest paranormal beliefs. People who believe in God with or without doubts were not significantly different from one another in terms of paranormal beliefs. But those who hold an unconventional view of the supernatural, seeing God as a cosmic force or higher power, are most likely to believe in a greater breadth of paranormal subjects.

Involvement

Although a rather large body of research generally supports Hirschi's ideas, the concept of involvement is problematic.[22] Hirschi argued that people should be less deviant to the extent that their time is filled with conventional activities such as youth groups, clubs, and volunteering. Similar to the popular idea that "idle hands are the devil's playthings," he argued that youth who have unsupervised free time are more likely to

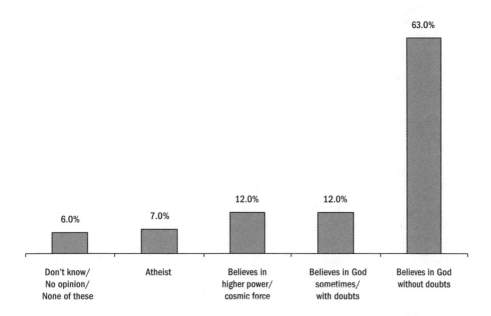

Figure 7.5. Conceptions of God in the United States (Baylor Religion Survey 2014, n=1474)

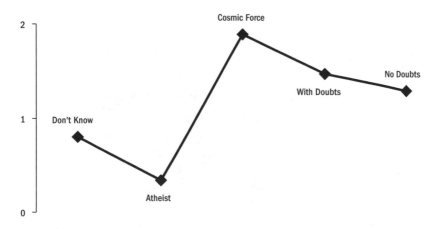

Figure 7.6. Belief: Number of Paranormal Beliefs by Conceptions of God (Baylor Religion Survey 2014, n=1474)

get into trouble because they are bored or simply have more time to do so. There is, in fact, little evidence from studies of juvenile delinquency or crime that involvement in conventional activities has an independent effect upon levels of deviance.

Similarly, there is no evidence that involvement in conventional activities deters belief in the paranormal (see figure 7.7). We asked respondents to a national survey to indicate if they had engaged in any of the following activities in the past twelve months: donated blood, attended a club or organizational meeting, met with a community leader, attended a meeting where there was a discussion of local or school affairs, and/or volunteered. Using these data, we can categorize people as either being involved in their community (doing one or more of these things) or not involved (doing none of them). People who engaged in such activities report about the same number of paranormal beliefs and experiences as those who are entirely uninvolved in the community. The minor differences between the involved and uninvolved are not statistically different. Put another way, one cannot assume anything about another person's propensity toward the paranormal if all that is known is how much he or she volunteers. The local Cub Scout leader may have seen a UFO.

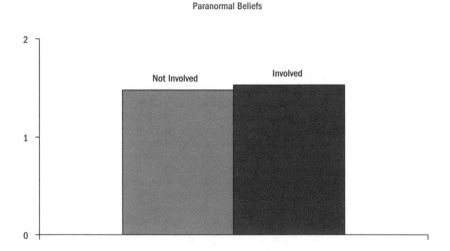

Figure 7.7. Involvement: Number of Paranormal Beliefs by Involvement in Community Groups (Chapman University Survey of American Fears 2014, n=1464). The differences in paranormal beliefs between these categories were not statistically significant.

Commitment

Commitments of money, energy, or time made by a person in order to obtain a certain lifestyle make up the final stake in conformity. People who have worked hard and achieved material success will, theoretically, avoid deviant behavior since it might threaten the investments they have made in a certain lifestyle. Following this line of reasoning, those who are in high-paying careers with potential for advancement and those who have worked hard to obtain a higher education should be more wedded to the conventional system.

We find strong evidence that the investment of time, money, and energy required to obtain a college degree appears to curtail paranormal belief and experience (see figure 7.8). People who do not have a college degree report greater numbers of paranormal beliefs and experiences. Those who have obtained a bachelor's or more advanced degree exhibit significantly lower levels of paranormal belief and experience.

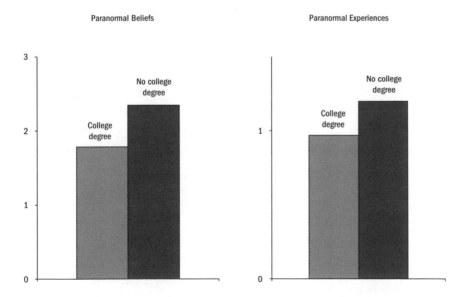

Figure 7.8. Commitment: Number of Paranormal Beliefs and Experiences by Education (Chapman University Survey of American Fears 2014, n=1573). Analysis compares respondents who received a bachelor's degree (or higher) with those who did not. All differences are statistically significant.

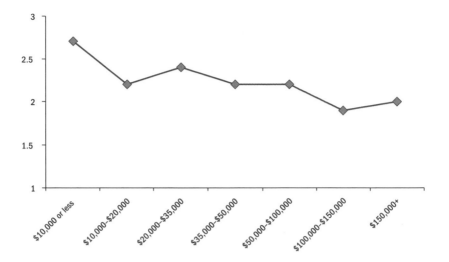

Figure 7.9. Commitment: Number of Paranormal Beliefs by Income (Chapman University Survey of American Fears 2014, n=1573). The same pattern exists when examining the number of paranormal experiences reported by respondents. As income increases, number of paranormal experiences decreases.

A similar relationship holds for income. People who have achieved a higher level of income have theoretically invested themselves in the furtherance of a high-paying career or job and have more to lose by engaging in deviant or unconventional behavior. Paranormal beliefs do, in fact, steadily decline as income increases. People who have lower levels of income have a strong tendency to believe in a wider variety of paranormal subjects than those at higher levels of income. Those at the lowest levels of income ($10,000 or less a year) believed in nearly three (2.7) paranormal subjects on average, while those making $150,000 a year or more believe in two on average (see figure 7.9). Importantly, while income level matters, people at all levels of social standing still average at least some paranormal beliefs.

Conventionality and the Paranormal

With the exception of involvement in community activities, there are relationships between aspects of individuals' stakes in conformity and how much of the paranormal they find credible. Attachments to others

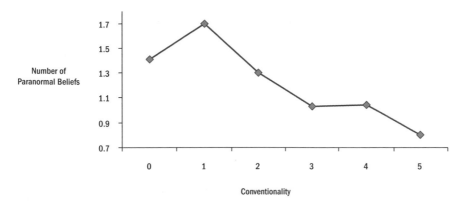

Figure 7.10. Conventionality and the Paranormal (Baylor Religion Survey 2014, n=1474). Conventionality scale ranges from 0 to 5, indicating whether or not a respondent is married, conservative politically, has a high income ($50k and above), a college education, and believes in God without doubt. A person who scores five on the scale is married, conservative, college-educated, believes without doubt in a traditional conception of God, and has a high income. Differences in number of paranormal beliefs are significant across different levels of conventionality.

appears to limit engagement with the paranormal, as do traditional beliefs and investments one has made in a conventional life such as a higher education. The relationship between conventionality and the paranormal becomes even clearer when all of these factors are considered together.

We assigned respondents to our survey with an overall stake-in-conformity score ranging from zero to five based on their marital status, political leanings, beliefs about God, income, and education. Respondents with a five have a very conventional/traditional life; they are married, Republican, believe in God without doubt, have a higher income and a college education. Someone with a zero is unmarried, non-Republican, did not acquire a college degree, does not believe in God without doubts, and earns a lower family income. People with a mixture of these characteristics—e.g., unmarried but Republican, high income but lower education and so on—would score somewhere near the middle of the index.

The relationship between stakes in conformity and paranormal beliefs is clear. As stakes in conformity increase, paranormal beliefs and experience steadily and markedly decrease (see figure 7.10). A person with the highest stakes in conformity accepts, on average, less than one paranormal belief. This is nearly half the level of belief exhibited by those with the lowest stakes in conformity.

In our time with David and Laura it became clear that they had distinctly different ways of living their lives and distinctly different views about the paranormal. David knows that some people think he is strange and told us of occasions when people have ridiculed his interest in Bigfoot. David has reason to be concerned with being branded as strange. With the exception of Bigfoot, he leads a conventional life. A veteran of the Air Force, he shares a tidy house with his wife on the outskirts of a small Texas town. During the week he manages a bank and makes a good living. On the weekends he faithfully attends a small, conservative Baptist church. He is a born-again Christian holding very traditional views of God as a father and the Bible as the word of God. Traditional religious views are coupled with conservative political views. He is a member of the National Rifle Association and consistently votes Republican.

In many ways Laura is David's mirror opposite. While David lives in the Bible belt, Laura proudly resides in what she described as the "unchurched West where the outdoors is your chapel." David is happily married, and Laura is "proudly by myself." Laura fills her time with activities and hobbies in retirement; David hands out loans at the bank.

Laura labels herself a Christian, as does David, but clearly she has something different in mind than he does. When asked to more specifically describe her personal religious or spiritual beliefs, Laura struggled. "I am a Christian . . . but I would also say that I am more spiritual than religious." She imagines a world connected to a multitude of beneficial entities and higher powers, rather than a single, personified God, and she sees Jesus as a special being sent to Earth by high powers, not as the one and only son of God.

As someone who is strongly bound to conventional society, David is tentative and cautious in his paranormal belief. He believes in one subject only—Bigfoot—and is rankled by its definition as "paranormal." David wants to redefine Bigfoot as a purely zoological mystery as opposed to a supernatural one. He has no patience for UFOs, ghosts, astrology, or other paranormal matters. To believe in such things is a threat to his self-image as a normal guy who just happens to hunt Bigfoot.

Laura is liberal and unconventional—and proudly so. Compared to David she is relatively free to explore "deviant" beliefs. She does not risk her career, her relationship, or contradict her personal faith by exploring alternative ideas. Her friends accept her varied interests, if they are to remain her friends. Where David is focused and driven to prove his quest is normal, Laura has long ago left concerns about normality behind. "People put so many blinders on themselves," she told us, "and I refuse to limit myself. I'm open to everything. It's all part of the fabric of life." Public discourse about the paranormal tends to devolve into separating people who believe in the paranormal from people who do not. This distinction is not particularly useful. In previous chapters we found that it is difficult to predict who will be attracted to individual paranormal beliefs. After all, half of Americans believe in something paranormal.

What truly distinguishes most Americans from one another is not whether they believe in a paranormal topic, but rather how many subjects they find credible. People who are very conventional otherwise are likely to believe in a single paranormal topic. These people are often indistinguishable from the average American in terms of their beliefs in other spheres and the way that they live their lives. Paranormal generalists who simultaneously believe in UFOs, ghosts, Bigfoot, astrology, psychic powers, and Atlantis are likely to be quite unconventional. They are not dangerous or mentally ill, they simply live in a different cultural universe than the rest of us.

8

Darkness and Light

As we have reiterated, some might say bemoaned, throughout this book, the paranormal is a messy subject in many ways. The subjects themselves are elusive. Bigfoot is hard if not impossible to catch. Ghosts fade into nothingness, UFOs fly away before cameras are at the ready, and psychic powers rarely perform upon demand.

If that was not a big enough problem, agreed-upon definitions of our objects of study are equally elusive. When is something paranormal? One person's paranormal is another person's normal. Should Bigfoot be labeled paranormal? Some of the Bigfoot hunters we have talked to are baffled that we lump together ESP, flying saucers, and ghosts with what they consider to be an undiscovered animal.

Complicating matters further is the thorny issue of distinguishing religion and the paranormal. At first glance religious and paranormal phenomena appear to be one and the same. The belief that the Bible is God's word and belief in the physical resurrection of Jesus are just as resistant to scientific proof as astrology, auras, and flying saucers. Yet religious beliefs have the benefit of widespread acceptance, cultural continuity, and a strong organizational backing.

Previous research (including our own) has found that Americans tend to distinguish between these two realms of the supernatural. In American society conventional religious beliefs are a sign of conformity, paranormal beliefs a potential sign of deviance. Should you happen to mention to your new neighbors across the street that you are a Presbyterian, banker, and Seahawks fan,[1] none of these pieces of information elicit much concern from most people. Should you tell the neighbor that you are a banker, Seahawks fan, and a practicing astrologer, they may consider you a bit kooky.

Unfortunately, the subject of this chapter will complicate matters even further. There are a number of beliefs and experiences that straddle the border between religion and the paranormal. Consider once again the diverse collection of topics and subjects that appear in the paranormal section of bookstores. Scattered among the UFO books, astrology training manuals, and collections of ghost tales you are likely to find books that discuss sightings of the Virgin Mary, stories of demons, possessions, and exorcism, as well as collected tales of claimed miraculous healings and rescues by guardian angels. Perhaps we should not be terribly surprised by this, given our findings in chapter 5. Very religious and irreligious people are less likely to report having had a paranormal experience than those who have moderate levels of religiosity (figure 5.5).

Books on the same topics will also be found in most Christian bookstores and in the Christian section of general bookstores. An exorcism tale can carry different meanings depending upon the type of book in which it appears. A book targeted at Christian audiences is likely to frame exorcisms as proof of the reality of Satan and a warning to Christians to get right with God and avoid the "occult." A book meant for general audiences will treat exorcisms as a fascinating and frightening mystery but will avoid explicit religious overtones or suggestions that a conversion to Christianity is a means of avoiding possession. A Christian author may write of the power of Ouija boards, but rather than focus upon it as a potential means to contact a dead relative, the object is feared as an instrument through which demons may attack the unwary.[2]

Exorcisms, Virgin Mary sightings, guardian angel tales, and the like serve as a potential bridging area between religion and the paranormal. Perhaps an interest in such topics will lead conservative Christians to develop an interest in paranormal subjects, such as UFOs and ESP, or maybe an interest in guardian angels could draw an otherwise nonreligious person into a faith.

This chapter explores some of the contested ground between religion and the paranormal by examining who believes in manifestations of evil such as Satan, demons, possession, and Satanic conspiracies, as well as manifestations of "light" such as guardian angels, speaking in tongues, miraculous healings, and other powerful religious experiences.

Darkness: From Presidential Discourse to the End of the World

As part of the long run-up of public events preceding the 2008 presidential election in the United States, the two main contenders, Senators Barack Obama and John McCain, traveled to Saddleback Church, one of the largest megachurches in the country, to take questions from pastor and best-selling author Rick Warren. Rather than being a debate in the traditional sense, the evening consisted of separate interviews for both men. The candidates were not able to hear one another's responses.

Among the various topics covered, Warren asked each candidate about his understanding of the nature of evil in the world. Specifically, Warren asked "Does evil exist? And if it does, do we ignore it? Do we negotiate with it? Do we contain it? Do we defeat it?" The responses given by each candidate provided a glimpse into their moral framework of good and evil, and how these perceptions connected to policy issues. Senator Obama responded:

> Evil does exist. I mean, I think we see evil all the time. We see evil in Darfur. We see evil, sadly, on the streets of our cities. We see evil in parents who viciously abuse their children. I think it has to be confronted. It has to be confronted squarely, and one of the things that I strongly believe is that, now, we are not going to, as individuals, be able to erase evil from the world. . . . Now, the one thing that I think is very important is for us to have some humility in how we approach the issue of confronting evil, because a lot of evil's been perpetrated based on the claim that we were trying to confront evil.[3]

In effect Obama claimed that evil did exist and was multifaceted, as it could take the form of genocide, poverty, crime, or child abuse. Although he believed that measures should be taken to confront these issues, he also qualified that evil could not be eradicated, and that people should be careful about what is done in the name of confronting evil, as often the responses to such issues could also be morally reprehensible.

Senator McCain then took the stage for his interview and was eventually given the same question concerning evil, to which he responded:

> Defeat it. A couple of points. One, if I'm president of the United States, my friends, if I have to follow him to the gates of hell, I will get bin Laden and bring him to justice. I will do that. And I know how to do that. I will get that done. No one, no one should be allowed to take thousands of American—innocent American lives. Of course, evil must be defeated. My friends, we are facing the transcended [sic] challenge of

the twenty-first century—radical Islamic extremism. . . . And we have—and we face this threat throughout the world. It's not just in Iraq. It's not just in Afghanistan. Our intelligence people tell us Al Qaeda continues to try to establish cells here in the United States of America. My friends, we must face this challenge. We can face this challenge. And we must totally defeat it.

In arguing that evil must be defeated, McCain connected evil primarily to the issue of threats posed by radical Islamic sects and global terrorism. Related to this perception of evil and the broad issue of terrorism is an array of specific policy issues concerning war, border patrol, immigration, and attitudes toward methods of social control generally. The belief that evil must be defeated translated into approaching the issues that were linked to it with a veracity and tenacity necessary to achieve its defeat. Warren's question was an insightful way to draw out the differences between the two candidate's philosophies. Obama offered a more abstract and gray (rather than black-and-white) conception of evil than did McCain (or did then president Bush).

Ultimately Obama garnered 52.7% of the popular vote and won the presidency, but his narrow victory in the polls is reflective of key differences between Americans, one of which is different underlying conceptions of evil. Americans are deeply divided on the nature of evil. Researchers have found that a person's views about the nature of evil and the role of evil in the world impact other behaviors and beliefs. For instance, beliefs about Satan were a strong predictor of participation in social movements, rallies, petitions, pickets, and membership associated with the Moral Majority movement in the 1980s and 1990s. Strong views of religious evil are also associated with intolerance of homosexuality.[4] When it comes to Satan's power, Americans are split down the middle, with a little more than half expressing an absolute belief in the reality of a dark counterpart to God. A little less than half of Americans believe that Satan has access to an army of demons with which to further his goals (see figure 8.1).

Like it or not, Satan is a part of American life, and his impact is felt in the pews and in popular culture. Belief in Satan is higher than in any of the paranormal topics we have discussed so far in this book. In the United States, more people believe in a real Satan than in Bigfoot,

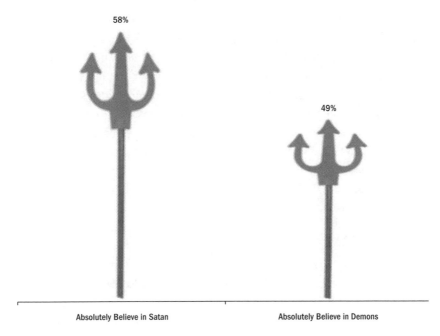

58%

49%

Absolutely Believe in Satan

Absolutely Believe in Demons

Figure 8.1. Belief in Satan and Demons in the United States (Baylor Religion Survey 2014, n=1474)

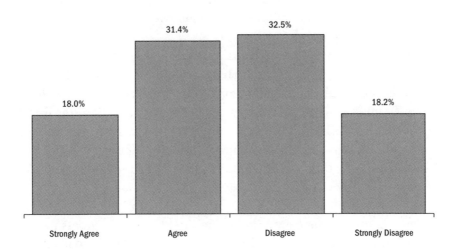

31.4%

32.5%

18.0%

18.2%

Strongly Agree

Agree

Disagree

Strongly Disagree

Figure 8.2. Satan's Power: Satan Causes Most Evil in the World (Chapman University Survey of American Fears 2014, n=1573)

psychics, and modern alien visitations combined.[5] Only the belief in haunted places (at about 41%) approaches the level of belief in Satan.

It is one thing to believe in the devil, another to grant him great power. The famous and terrifying film *The Exorcist* and television shows such as Discovery Channel's *The Exorcist Files* depict Satan as having the power to control unwary humans via demonic possession. Some Americans view Satan's power as less personal, but more insidious, viewing happenings in the world through a supernatural lens, with its evils being due to the machinations of Satan. Indeed, nearly half (49.4%) of Americans believe that Satan causes most evil in the world (see figure 8.2).

Who Believes in Supernatural Evil?

People differ in the extent that they see life as a struggle with supernatural evil. Different individuals have greater or lesser certainty about the existence of hell. Some people believe in the reality of the devil, but are less certain about the existence of his army of demons. Still others believe that the world will experience an Armageddon-type event, wherein the devil will marshal his forces of evil against the world. Taken together, we can assign respondents to our surveys an "evil score" based on how many of these four items they express belief in (see figure 8.3). People who have scores of zero believe in none of these phenomena. People who score a "perfect" evil score of four view the world as a battleground between good and evil.

More than a third of Americans (40%) do not ascribe much power to the forces of supernatural evil, having evil scores of zero. Such people reject the idea of a hell and do not foresee an Armageddon event ending life as we know it. They are skeptical about the existence of the devil and dismissive that he has a host of demons to command. By contrast about one-fifth of Americans attribute greater power to supernatural evil and clearly view the world in a different way than someone who is skeptical even about the devil's existence.

Not surprisingly, belief in supernatural evil is strongly related to religious tradition. Evangelical Protestants and black Protestants have a much stronger belief in the reality of supernatural evil than do mainline Protestants, Catholics, Jews, those of other religions, and those who report no religion (see figure 8.4).

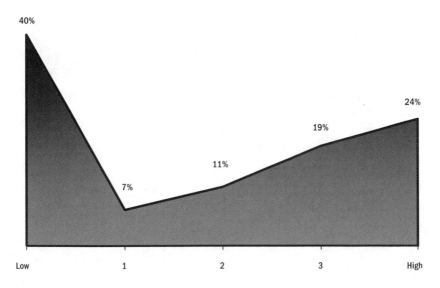

Figure 8.3. Strength of Belief in Religious Evil in the United States. Mean=2 (Baylor Religion Survey 2014, n=1474).

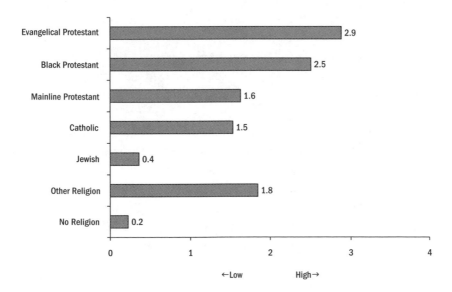

Figure 8.4. Evil Scores by Religious Tradition (Baylor Religion Survey 2014, n=1474)

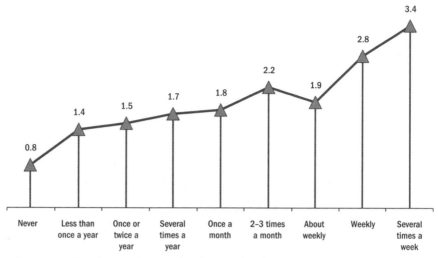

Figure 8.5. Church Attendance and Evil Scores (Baylor Religion Survey 2014, n=1474)

The person most likely to believe in devils, demons, hell, and Armageddon will also be a person that takes the Bible literally. The average biblical literalist has an evil score (3.0) more than seven times that of a person who thinks of the Bible as a work of literature (.41).[6] The more frequently a person attends religious services, the greater their belief in supernatural evil. Scores steadily and significantly increase with increasing church attendance (see figure 8.5).

When it comes to social and personal characteristics, it can be a bit more difficult to predict who will see the world as a spiritual battleground. Men are no more likely to hold such views than are women. Age is of no consequence—young and old alike are just as likely or unlikely to fear an impending Armageddon and believe in demons, devils, and hell. Once we use statistical techniques to remove the effects of religiosity, race does not directly impact evil scores (more on this later).

What does matter when it comes to predicting beliefs about evil is a person's social status as measured by education and family income. The more education acquired, the less likely people are to believe in supernatural evil (see figure 8.6). Evil scores also decline dramatically with increased income (see figure 8.7).

The person most likely to view Earth as a spiritual battleground between good and evil is a conservatively/traditionally religious person

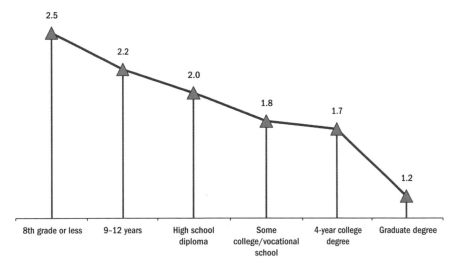

Figure 8.6. Education and Evil Scores (Baylor Religion Survey 2014, n=1474)

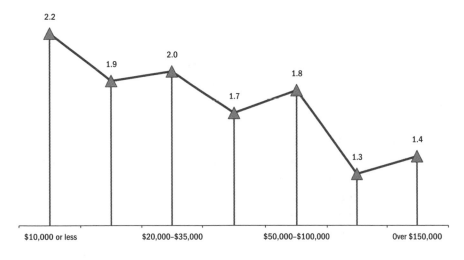

Figure 8.7. Family Income and Evil Scores (Baylor Religion Survey 2014, n=1474)

who is not faring well in the socioeconomic status system by conventional standards. These patterns point to an interesting correspondence between conditions in the material world and one's perceptions about the nature of evil. Those occupying traditionally power-deprived social statuses are also more likely to turn to religion as a coping mechanism to deal with the difficulties encountered in the world.[7] Christianity offers a ready-made explanation for one's suffering to those who desire such an answer—suffering, evil, and misery are the work of evil forces. In a certain way, this is a comforting answer. Suffering is not meaningless or endless. The world is evil and controlled by Satan; it is not supposed to be fair or just. But Satan will be defeated at the battle of Armageddon, and those suffering now will be greatly rewarded later. Attribution litera-ture in psychology suggests that when difficult situations occur, people are more likely to attribute the events to supernatural evil.[8]

Satanic Panics and Scares

Beliefs about Satan's power in the world are powerful and have played an important role in American history.[9] What constitutes the perceived earthly work of Satan evolves over time and varies from group to group, but when people come to believe that Satan is impacting the world directly (or via his minions), the consequences can be quite powerful.

Perhaps the best known example of a scare related to Satan comes from the Salem witch trials, where from February 1692 to May 1693 more than 150 colonial settlers were arrested and charged with being witches. Sociologist Gary Jensen details the "perfect storm" of politi-cal and sociological factors that coalesced to create the witch hunts and ritual executions in Salem. Of particular importance were the lack of strong centralized government for the colony (which was amplified by the 1684 revocation of the Massachusetts Bay Colony's royal charter), an extended period of disease and death, extensive social and familial conflicts within the community, and not least of all a demonological interpretation of disease and misfortune.[10]

The panic in Salem began when the young daughter of Reverend Samuel Parris, nine-year-old Betty Parris, and Parris's niece, eleven-year-old Abigail Williams, began acting strangely. They exhibited be-havior somewhat akin to epileptic fits. The girls threw objects, screamed and cried, ran about the room, and crawled behind and under furniture. At times, they claimed to be pricked by invisible needles and pinched by unseen hands. When word traveled of the Parris girls' condition, other young women became similarly afflicted.

The Puritans of Salem found themselves in a new land, where even their previous religious identity, which centered around criticizing other religious groups, was placed into jeopardy. Without outside groups to castigate and define themselves against, the Puritans turned inward. When faced with a terrifying unknown, people often find, or create, a villain to explain their circumstances and serve as a focus for their anger and worry. This is especially true concerning an unknown involving people who are distinct in some way from the community in question. In other words, people who are viewed as fundamentally different or "other" compared to the majority of people comprising a community can become defined as the "them" that helps create and sustain the "us." A strong out-group offers a community a scapegoat for their trials and tribulations. Having a concrete villain upon which to place one's fears and direct righteous anger serves to comfort and bind together a community.[11] As the sociological truism goes, strong out-groups create strong in-groups.

In Salem, rumors spread that witches were behind the disturbing and unexplained behavioral outbreak. Unfortunately, it is generally not satisfactory for a community to simply believe there is an enemy in their midst: the enemy must be identified and overcome through ritualized punishment. Minority groups, or those who are already considered "strange" for some reason, are typically the first to be identified as the source of a new social problem.[12] In Salem, three women who were already community outcasts for various reasons were the first to be identified as witches.[13]

Accusations multiplied as the community's fear spiraled out of control. A critical turning point occurred when former minister of Salem Village George Burroughs, who was openly skeptical of the witch accusations, was put to death despite his passing of the "tests" given to see if he was a witch—such as reciting the Lord's Prayer correctly—under the pretense supplied by rival minister Cotton Mather that "the Devil has often been transformed into an Angel of Light."[14] From this type of "sealed logic" there is little hope of counterargument. The accusations and ritual executions continued unabated.

The longer the panic continued, the greater the risk each person faced of being identified as a witch. Much of the problem had to do with reliance on so-called spectral evidence. If a purported victim had a dream or vision in which the spirit of an accused witch appeared, the contents of the vision could be entered into court as evidence against the defendant. Since such dubious evidence was considered sufficient, it is not surprising that twenty-nine men and women were ultimately convicted of being witches. Nineteen of the convicted were hanged; one unfortunate soul was crushed to death under rocks. Ultimately the fear ran its course as accusations of witchery subsided and then stopped— particularly once the high-ranking and powerful members of the community began to face accusations themselves.[15]

The Devil Comes to Olympia

The Salem witch trials have become emblematic of how panic can grip a community, a lesson in how unreasoned fear of evil can lead to terrible consequences. Yet today we often view the story of Salem with smug comfort and distance, mocking the backward views of the Puritans and their fear of witches.[16] We assume that, in our enlightened age, such things would not and could not happen again. And yet we have seen many similar incidents throughout U.S. history when people become convinced that Satan is active in the world.

Consider the Ingram case, where the young daughters of a prominent citizen of Olympia, Washington, became convinced that they had been assaulted by a mysterious cadre of Satanists. Despite a complete lack of physical evidence, the girls' hazy recollections of Satanic ceremonies led to the arrest of their father, Paul Ingram, and two family friends. After a dramatic trial that included tales of mysterious underground Satanic cults, human sacrifice, forced abortions with swords, blood drinking, and demonic possession, Ingram was convicted—in 1988.

Prior to these events, the Ingram family led normal lives by all appearances. Raised devoutly Roman Catholic, Paul Ingram met his future wife, Sandy, while attending Spokane Community College. Eventually they moved to Olympia to raise their four children: Paul Jr., Chad, Erika, and Julie. Ingram became a pillar of the community and faithfully attended a local Pentecostal church called the Church of the Living Waters. A former president of the Thurston County Deputy Sheriff's Association and former chairman of the Thurston County Republican Central Committee, Paul was chief civil deputy of the Thurston County sheriff's office at the time of the accusations against him.

In the summer of 1988, Living Waters held a retreat for young, female members at Black Lake Bible Camp in Olympia. Erika, twenty-one at the time, and Julie, eighteen, attended. Karla Franko, a charismatic Christian from California who claimed to have "biblical gifts of healing and spiritual discernment," had been invited to speak. Over the course of the retreat, Franko claimed to have received several messages from the Holy Spirit indicating that some of those in attendance had suffered physical or sexual abuse. Franko's pronouncements created an emotionally charged atmosphere at the camp, with several girls sobbing and becoming hysterical.[17] On the last day of the retreat, as attendants were boarding the bus to return home, Erika broke down and proclaimed that she had been sexually abused by her father. Eventually Julie corroborated Erika's claim of sexual abuse, adding that the abuse had been at the hands of several men.

Julie claimed that from the age of four she had been gang-raped by Paul and his friends who occasionally gathered at the Ingram home for poker games. The church reported the accusations against Paul to the sheriff's department and he was brought in for questioning. Curiously, although Paul claimed that he could not remember a single incident where he molested his children, he admitted to the abuse. He reasoned that the crimes must have happened even though he could not recall them—because he had taught his children to be truthful.

As the prosecution interviewed various parties, the story grew increasingly tangled. Ingram admitted to the abusive poker parties reported by Julie and named several employees of the sheriff's department as participants in these games. Based on these "confessions," two of Ingram's closest friends, Jim Rabie and Ray Risch, were taken into custody. As interviews with family members continued, Erika expanded her allegations. She claimed that her mother had also participated in the abuse. The two Ingram sons, Chad and Paul Jr., added their own allegations. Eventually Paul and the Ingram children started talking of Satanic activity taking place along with the abuse.

In a December 1988 interview with sheriff's department detectives, Ingram remembered—though he could not give specific dates or times—standing near a fire with a person that he thought might be "the devil" next to him. He could hear wailing and moaning all around him as he stood on a platform that looked down on the fire. Ingram claimed he wore an apron with an upside-down cross on it and sacrificed a cat by slicing its stomach open and pulling out its heart.[18] Rabie and Risch, he said, were present at the meeting. Ingram claimed that Risch's girlfriend at the time, Dana, was the "high priestess" of the ceremony, and as a reward for performing the sacrifice, he was allowed to have sex with Dana and another woman. Paul's wife, Sandra, soon added her own stories of Satanism, including a bizarre instance in which Rabie allegedly held her by one hand with an open book in the other, as blood purportedly flowed from the book, across his chest, and onto her.[19]

During the investigation of the Ingram case, detectives became convinced that the mysterious Satanists alluded to by the Ingrams must be practicing some form of mind control. This would explain why the Ingram family's stories often conflicted with one another and why Paul seemed to have great difficulty remembering the incidents of abuse, even though he admitted to being an abuser. It would also explain why Paul occasionally provided clearly false confessions. For example, at one point Ingram reported that he might be the Green River killer—a serial murderer accused of killing dozens of young women near the Seattle-Tacoma International Airport. Though characteristically hazy about dates or specific locations, he claimed that he and Rabie picked up a prostitute near the Sea-Tac airport and murdered her. The Green River Task Force investigated Ingram very briefly but quickly dropped him as a suspect.[20]

Working from their assumption of cultic mind control, the Thurston County prosecutor's office hired Dr. Richard Ofshe, a sociologist and expert on cult activity from the University of California at Berkeley. They hoped that Ofshe would testify for the prosecution about the ability of cults to affect a person's mind. However, Ofshe quickly became troubled by the investigation. His first concern was the credibility of Erika and Julie Ingram as witnesses. He was concerned with Erika's history of making and then dropping abuse charges, as well as with the content of her stories.[21] In particular, Erika's stories contained broad summaries of abhorrent events, but she failed to provide any other information about the group's ceremonies, Ofshe reported:

> Ms. Ingram has been consistently unable to provide me with any details about the content of the rituals or descriptions of even the most mundane events that occurred at the approximately 400 group meetings she claims to have been obliged to attend. Although Ms. Ingram is able to report watching numerous babies being killed, seeing the dead body of

at least one adult woman, having undergone two backyard abortions and having to eat the flesh of her own fetus, she is unable to provide me with an account of the format of the group's meetings or any of the group's non-homicidal rituals. She reports that the group's meetings took about 3 hours. All that she can describe about their conduct is that "they chant."[22]

Further, Ofshe noticed that Paul only seemed to offer tales of Satanism after excessive prompting from detectives; therefore, he decided to give Paul a test. In an interview with Ingram, Ofshe told Paul that one of his daughters and one of his sons claimed that Paul forced them to have sex together while he watched. In fact, no such charge had been made by the children. Ingram could not recall the event at first, but Ofshe pushed him, telling him that he "had to remember," just as detectives had done in previous interviews. When the two men met a day later, Ingram produced a confession:

> Mr. Ingram produced a written confession to acts of sexual abuse of his children in response to the influence of methods I employed. The tactics I used . . . resembled the interview procedures used in Mr. Ingram's interrogations.
>
> I subsequently confronted Mr. Ingram with the fact that he had produced a false confession. . . . Mr. Ingram became quite distraught but steadfastly maintained that the recollections he had in response to my suggestions were as real as his other recollections. Mr. Ingram succeeded in convincing me that this statement was true.[23]

Ofshe noted a similar process of persuasion at work in the recollections of Sandra Ingram. He was especially concerned with the influence of John Bratun, Paul and Sandra's minister at the Church of the Living Waters. Bratun counseled every member of the Ingram family, was allowed to visit Paul in jail, and had even performed a jailhouse exorcism on a distraught Paul. Ofshe was concerned that Bratun's influence had contaminated the case. Bratun admitted to acting as Sandra's spiritual advisor and telling her she was "80 percent evil." Perhaps even more troubling for the case, he provided Sandra with full details of Paul's confessions. Ofshe believed that Sandra provided stories of Satanism as a result of the intense spiritual and emotional pressure Bratun placed upon her. After spending a total of nine days interviewing prosecution witnesses, Thurston County detectives, friends of Erika and Julie Ingram, and John Bratun, Ofshe switched to the defense.

The interviews conducted with Paul's younger son, Chad, were also troubling. Consider the December 8, 1988, interview performed by two investigators, Dr. Richard Peterson and detective Brian Schoening. Peterson and Schoening started the interview by questioning Chad extensively about his childhood and prodded him to remember any strange sexual encounters or abuse. Chad answered all of their questions in the negative, although he did reveal that he had become quite troubled during his teens, even attempting suicide once after a heated argument with his father. The incident piqued the interest of Dr. Peterson, who thought the suicide attempt was somehow related to suppressed memories of abuse. Peterson told Chad that he had been abused but simply couldn't remember it.[24] As Chad continued to deny having memories of sexual or physical abuse, Peterson asked him if he could recall any strange or frightening dreams from his childhood. Chad recalled nightmares of a fat "witch" flying through his window and sitting on his stomach. Peterson and Schoening told Chad that this "dream" was a memory of a real event.[25]

In a turn strikingly similar to what occurred in Salem, Peterson and Schoening attempted to have Chad identify the witch in his dreams. At first, Chad could provide no information. He said the room was dark in his dream, so he could not see the witch's face. A frustrated Dr. Peterson asked Chad to "turn the lights on" in his dream, so that he could see the witch's face more clearly. Chad still could not identify the witch. The only details he could offer were that the witch was a female, had black hair, an oval-shaped face, and brown eyes. At that point Dr. Peterson pushed Chad further, with an interesting offer:

PETERSON: I'll tell you something, you'd have a, you have the right to
    sue these f***** and get as much as you want from 'em.
CHAD: That'd be nice.
PETERSON: You'd *** rights [sic] it'd be nice. Pay for a college education.
CHAD: Yeah.
PETERSON: Pay for a nice car. Get you started in life.
CHAD: Well, I already got a nice car.
PETERSON: Yeah, do you have a BMW?[26]

Soon after this exchange, the cassette tape recording the conversation was turned off. When recording resumed, Chad named Jim Rabie as the witch—the same witch he had previously been certain was a female.

Even with the spectral evidence provided by Chad, the Thurston County sheriff's office was eventually forced to drop its case against Rabie and Risch. Thankfully, unlike in Salem, the courts in Washington could not be convinced to rely solely on the content of dreams to convict, and the prosecution found itself wholly without physical evidence. Erika and Julie Ingram claimed to have attended Satanic ceremonies at least three times a month for seventeen years, seeing hundreds of infants and animals sacrificed at these meetings, but investigators never found a single body, even after digging up the Ingram yard with backhoes. No skeletons, bodies, or any of the elaborate trappings of Satanic rituals were found. The investigators also failed to find a third-party witness to the large Satanic gatherings that purportedly took place over a twenty-year period. Further, physical examinations of Erika and Julie did not support their allegations of rape, mutilation, and forced abortions. In January 1989, Dr. Judith Ann Jacobsen of Providence Hospital in Seattle examined Erika and Julie, concluding that the girls did not appear to have suffered the abuse they reported.[27]

Despite the lack of evidence against him, Paul Ingram pled guilty to six counts of third-degree rape on May 1, 1988. As part of an agreement with the sheriff's office, Ingram accepted a plea bargain in exchange for an assurance that he would not be charged with any additional crimes that might arise from the investigation. Ultimately Ingram started serving his time in a Delaware prison in 1990 where he remained until he was released on parole in 2003. Sandra divorced Paul while he was in prison and, Paul claims, remained convinced of the claims of Satanism until her death in 2006.

Life as an Accused Satanist

On a Monday afternoon, Christopher met Paul Ingram and his second wife for lunch.[28] Ingram was quite friendly, affable, and willing to talk about his case. Over enormous plates of pasta at a Portland, Oregon, chain restaurant overlooking the Willamette River, we chatted about what life is like for the victim of a Satanic panic.

It took awhile for Paul to settle after his release, and he told of some of his problems. At first he moved to his deceased parents' house in Spokane, where he was required to register as a sex offender. Paul's parole officer treated him well, but he often felt unwelcome in the community. The local news stations aired details about his case and announced that the "notorious" Paul Ingram was headed to town. A neighbor who had heard of his case complained to the police that Paul was stalking her, driving by her home in the evenings in a black car. Paul explained to his parole officer that he had no driver's license and no car. The only vehicle that was at least theoretically available to him was his sister's tan van. Ultimately the matter was dropped, but Paul continued to feel the suspicion of his neighbors.

Paul found that his reputation even followed him into the pews. Shortly after visiting a small, nondenominational congregation in Spokane, he decided to join but thought it best to inform the pastor of the accusations against him first. To the pastor's credit he welcomed Paul into the congregation. Shortly after, a member of the church familiar with Paul's case recognized him and complained to the pastor about allowing a registered sex offender to join the congregation. The pastor told a grateful Paul that he should remain with the church despite such objections, but Paul felt that his presence was dividing the church and chose to leave.

Not all was bad in Spokane. Paul soon met Catherine, a nurse recently arrived from Boston. After years on the East Coast, Catherine had decided she needed a change, but she quickly grew bored and lonely in Spokane. People made fun of her thick accent, and she had trouble making friends. Eventually, she joined a dating website and ran across Paul's profile. They emailed back and forth and finally set up a date.

The first date went well. Before their second date Paul asked Catherine if they could meet for lunch. As they sat down at a cafe the next day, Catherine could sense that Paul was very nervous and thought to herself "is he married?" "If only that had been the case!" she joked. Paul blurted out all of the details of his case and then excused himself to go the restroom. "I didn't expect her to be there when I got back. This was her chance to leave." Catherine stuck around. That evening she researched Paul's case online and became convinced that he was innocent of the horrifying charges against him. They had their third date.

In 2004 the couple married. They moved away from Washington State where Paul "never really felt comfortable" and settled in a small town near the Oregon coast. Paul is happy to have found a companion, but he often reflects upon the children from his first marriage. Recently, he has had contact with three of his children. Through extended family members he knows that he now has at least seven grandchildren, but has never seen any of them. Paul looks at the past with "no bitterness, just regret." He wishes that things were different and that he could see his kids, but is determined to make the best of his new life with Catherine.

They are active in a Christian church and have made many friends, although most know little of his troubled past. How do you tell someone, "Oh, by the way I am a registered sex offender, but I'm not guilty of the charges made against me?"

Paul has never lost his deep, personal faith despite all he has been through. It is this faith that gets him through "the rough patches," he said.[29]

Paul's strong belief in the reality of personified evil sealed his fate. Ingram trusted John Bratun, pastor of the Living Waters church, so when Bratun told him that Satan was clouding his memories of his horrifying Satanic activities, Paul believed his pastor. The only way to release Satan's grip upon him, Bratun counseled, was to confess to the crimes against him, whether he could remember them or not. In the end, Paul admitted to being an evil Satanist to avoid becoming an evil pawn of Satan. The irony is not lost upon him.

Unfortunately, hysterical accusations of abuse by covens and Satanic cults have a long and storied history well beyond the Salem witch trials and Paul Ingram case.[30] Outlandish as Ingram's case may seem, it occurred during the height of a societal panic about the existence of powerful, underground Satanic groups and child abuse. The 1980s saw an incredibly fast rise in awareness about such groups and public fear that correlated with this menacing presence; however, as is often the case with such incidents of collective behavior, the response far outweighed any actual threat to society. The rumors of such groups were enough to produce specialists in law enforcement and psychotherapy designed to help patients "recover" memories of abuse, but no physical evidence of such groups was ever produced.

The most notorious incident in regard to the moral panic was the Mc-Martin Preschool trial, in which daycare workers in California were accused of being members of an underground Satanic group possessing supernatural powers, which they used to engage in child abuse. Charges were brought against two workers, followed by a three-year investigation and a three-year trial, including the razing of the school in the search for evidence—none of which was found. Ultimately the trial produced no convictions, but not before costing in excess of $15,000,000 in public funds.

Such tales always appear ridiculous—after the fact. Yet their continual reoccurrence is evidence of the potential power of belief in evil, supernatural forces. In spite of the importance of views of evil to many religions, we should not think even the most conservative and traditional are focused solely upon the evil and demonic. One of the most powerful rewards religion can offer is direct access to the divine via physiologically and psychologically enrapturing religious experiences. Here again we enter the muddy waters separating "religion" from the "paranormal."

Light: From Speaking to God to Angelic Interventions

Nestled in the foothills of the Blue Ridge Mountains in southern Appalachia, an unassuming Pentecostal church sits on the outskirts of a small city. The building is modern, but hardly fancy by any standard.

On a Sunday morning, Joseph and his wife attended services. We were greeted warmly by a well-dressed, middle-aged woman. The hallway from the foyer led directly into the sanctuary, a long room with a low ceiling, standing in direct contrast to the sweeping architecture and high ceilings of more traditional church buildings. Rows of padded folding chairs lined each side of the room. The aisles in the middle and down the side were wide enough to allow free movement, which proved necessary. Toward the front a large podium sat on a slightly elevated portion of the room. To its left a small booth with a drum kit, to the right a flat-screen television embedded in the wall. Directly behind it was a large red banner displaying flames and a flock of doves.

We took a seat toward the back as the pastor and several congregants gathered. Members shook our hands and offered warm greetings, doing their best to make us feel at home in a place where everyone else knew one another. Loud praise and worship music piped over the sound system. The pastor and several members paced back and forth up front, praying aloud and moving their bodies to the frequent swells of the music. Others knelt in prayer or chatted with their families.

As the start of services neared, we heard commotion behind us at the entry to the sanctuary. An older man was clutching a young man in a tight embrace as others gathered around. The impromptu group began to loudly "speak in tongues." Two women ran laps around the right side of the seats as the man collapsed to the floor and the members gathered around him. The pastor took the microphone and exclaimed, "If you're wonderin' what's a-goin' on back there, the prodigal son has come home!" The pastor explained that the man was a member who had not been to church in over a year. His mother and brothers were members of the congregation, and they and the church had been praying for the man to return. As he knelt, doubled over, hands were placed upon him by a large group of members as they prayed aloud in tongues. As the level of jubilation in the group swelled, the pastor jumped up on the first row of chairs and shouted, "I'm here to tell you that God answers prayer! Amen-uh?! And if you turn your troubles over to the Lord he will answer that call-uh!"

The act of speaking in tongues or glossolalia is most frequently practiced in Pentecostal and charismatic churches. It consists of speaking phrases and sounds in an unknown language, usually during a period of religious ecstasy.[31] Believers claim that when speaking in tongues they are using a special, holy language gifted to them by God. To skeptics, however, these utterances are incomprehensible gibberish produced as part of a religious trance induced by a highly emotional setting. For the most part this "language" is unintelligible to listeners, except for a select few who claim to have the gift of "interpreting."

On even rarer occasions a person will speak a recognizable language that she claims not to know, a phenomenon called xenoglossolalia. We did not witness xenoglossolalia, but did watch someone earn the gift of speaking in tongues for the first time. During the service, James, a boy in his late teens with a slightly receding hairline, dressed in jeans, work boots, and an untucked polo shirt, sat in front of us. He was closely flanked by Thomas, a slender, athletic boy with light blond hair who wore dress pants, a business shirt, and a tie. Near the end of the service, the pastor motioned for James to come to the stage. As James went forward, Thomas followed. The minister prayed over James, telling him that "the Holy Spirit" was all around him. James raised his hands—eyes closed—as those around him loudly spoke in tongues and prayed. The church band played on. For the next ten minutes the huddle prayed as the pastor told James that he was on the verge of baptism in the Holy Spirit, if he would only release his self-consciousness and "yield to it!"

About twenty minutes after the pastor had called James forward, a young man burst from the group and ran down the aisle. He was immediately followed by Thomas, who was drenched in sweat, tears streaming down his face. There was joyous pandemonium among the congregation as two men held a weak-kneed James up as he triumphantly spoke in tongues. After a couple of minutes, James ceased speaking in tongues and fell into a tight embrace with the pastor, who was visibly overjoyed by the events.

For They Heard Them Speak with Tongues (Acts 10:46)

Pentecostals share with Evangelicals, "fundamentalists," and other conservative Christians a tendency to view the Bible as the literal word of God, hold restrictive attitudes on moral issues, and focus upon born-again experiences.[32] But while Evangelicals and fundamentalists are strongly focused upon the bedrock of doctrine, Pentecostals emphasize the continual revelation of God's will through the dynamics of religious experience.[33] Pentecostals seek what they believe to be a baptism from the Holy Spirit, which can impart a number of spiritual "gifts" to the recipient. The ability to speak in tongues is but one of these gifts. Others include prophecy, the ability to sense the presence of demons or angels, and supernatural knowledge or wisdom.[34] In addition, one of the "gifts" is the ability to call upon God to heal the physical, emotional, and spiritual pains of the faithful, which we were able to witness that Sunday.

The congregation could barely contain its excitement when the preacher asked members to come forward to "testify." He asked a middle-aged woman to step forward and explained to the congregation that she had been enduring physical and spiritual troubles in her life. The pastor laid his hands on her as the praise-band leader put anointing oil on his hand and touched the woman's head. Soon more than twenty people gathered around her and prayed for her to be healed as she fell back into the arms of those gathered around her.

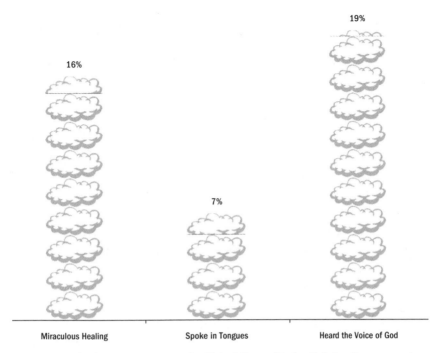

19%

16%

7%

Miraculous Healing   Spoke in Tongues   Heard the Voice of God

Figure 8.8. Religious Experiences in the United States (Baylor Religion Survey 2007)

After almost two hours of singing, dancing, testifying, and religious experiences, the pastor had yet to deliver a sermon. He stood before the group and said, "What more can I say? I could preach, but you all already did. The Lord has healed and we have rejoiced as a lost sheep returned to the fold. Young men have been baptized in Jesus Christ and the Holy Spirit. God is good! I hope we see y'all Tuesday night for Bible study. And don't you leave here without hugging everybody!" With that the extemporaneous, spirit-filled service came to a close.

Recent estimates suggest that there are more than fifteen million self-described Pentecostals in the United States.[35] On any given Sunday, Pentecostals are communing with spirits and angels and speaking in unknown tongues. Yet these are marginal experiences even within the cultural context of Christianity, as only a minority of Americans claim to have experienced a miraculous physical healing, spoken in tongues during a religious service, or directly heard the voice of God speaking to them (see figure 8.10).[36]

When we consider these three experiences together, about 30% of Americans claim having had at least one, if not more of them. And those Americans are distinct in many ways. First and foremost, those who claim such experiences are very religious. The more one attends religious services the more likely she is to report such experiences by a wide margin.[37] This should come as no surprise. Religious experiences are a product of the environment in which they occur. These settings stress specific experiences, are high in emotional intensity, and draw upon specific religious doctrines and narratives to frame the experiences. More than half (58%) of those who believe the Bible is God's literal word report such experiences compared to only a fifth (21%) of those who view the Bible in less literal terms. Evangelicals and black Protestants are much more likely to report speaking in tongues, miraculous healings, and hearing the voice of God than are members of other religious traditions.

There are also some social factors that are associated with intense religious experiences. We do not find age or education to predict such experiences, but do find that women are more likely to claim such ex-

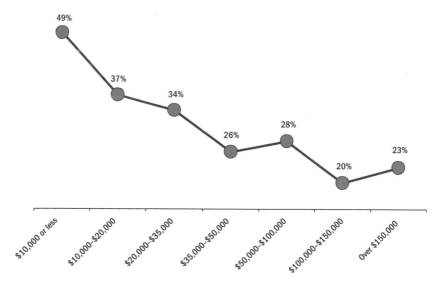

Figure 8.9. Having an Intense Religious Experience by Yearly Family Income (Baylor Religion Survey 2007). Indicates what percentage of respondents at given income level have spoken in tongues and/or received a miraculous healing and/or heard the voice of God speaking to them. Forty-nine percent of those making less than $10,000 a year reported at least one such experience.

periences than men (34% versus 23%), and that unmarried people are slightly more likely (33%) to have such experiences than married people (27%). We found that income was a strong predictor of beliefs about evil, and it is an equally powerful predictor of intense religious experiences (see figure 8.9). Almost half of those who make $10,000 a year or less report speaking in tongues, experiencing a miraculous healing, and/or hearing the voice of God. From there the likelihood of reporting such experiences decreases dramatically. Only about a third of those making $20,000 to $35,000 a year report one or more of these experiences. Individuals at the highest level of income (more than $150,000 a year), are half as likely to speak in tongues, have a healing, or hear the voice of God as those at the lowest levels of income.

Why are intense religious experiences of greater appeal to those at the lowest levels of income? Our visit to another small Pentecostal church provided insight into this matter.

A Gift of Faith from the Lord

About an hour north of Austin, Texas, sits a classic small rural church covered in flaking white paint. The Pentecostal House is the kind of simultaneously quaint and nondescript house of worship that is easy to pass by with barely a glance.[38] On a Wednesday evening, we pulled off the highway access road and into its grass-covered parking lot to attend a service.

We were met by the pastor, Buddy, and his assistant, Tom. Buddy, forty-five years old with sandy brown hair, penetrating eyes, and a crooked smile, has been with the church for twenty years. His wife greeted us warmly and introduced us to their son and young daughter. Tom, a tall man in his sixties with gray hair, served terms as pastor at a variety of conservative churches around Texas before finally settling onto a farm near the Pentecostal House. Numbering only fifteen consistent members, the congregants were very excited by our visit, in spite of the fact that we had told them we were there primarily for observation purposes—we were not looking to join. Nevertheless, they hoped that a passionate Wednesday night worship session might change our minds and net three unexpected new members. To a person, they were welcoming and friendly.

Ricky, a tall, imposing, fifty-year-old maintenance worker, firmly shook our hands. He did not look the part of a small country church member. He was dressed in faded jeans and a well-worn black T-shirt. His arms were banded with tattoos, and his boots were those of a working man, smattered with the traces of hard labor. "This is a church where you meet the Lord," he told us. "We don't judge people by how they look," he said, chuckling as he showed off his tattoos. "Just come three times and you're a member."

Ricky sat near the back with his wife and another, older couple next to them. In front of us three older women shared a pew with an older Hispanic man. The women were stay-at-home moms and secretaries for small businesses. The men worked construction, in factories, or in other forms of manual labor. To them, as one member told us, "worshipping the Lord is fun after a hard day's work." The minister too was empathetic to the plight of a working-class lifestyle, starting his message to the congregation by saying, "I'm not gonna ask ya to stand." His voice rising in volume, he continued, "I know y'all worked hard today. So stay in your seats, but rise up in your hearts to praise Him!"

It was clear from talking to members that they strongly believe in the power of direct contact with the supernatural, and this contact is extremely important to them. A stack of pamphlets in a rack near the doorway testified to "The Truth about the Holy Spirit Baptism." With sufficient faith and obedience, the tract promises, anyone can develop a special relationship with the Lord whereupon they may speak with tongues, lay their hands on one another in healing, and prophesy the future.

Pastor Buddy convinced a soft-spoken man named Gary to tell us of his healing. It seems that Gary had suffered a massive stroke two years ago that left him unable to walk, speak, or squeeze with his hands. Doctors couldn't help him. In an effort to have the supernatural intervene in Gary's life, the group had prayed over him during an impassioned service, laying their hands upon him as they called for God's mercy. Gary felt "a charge," and is convinced that God interceded on his behalf. From that point on he steadily improved. He now walks, although he still favors one side of his body. He seems embarrassed by the slight droop on one side of his mouth, but he speaks without difficulty. And he vigorously and happily shook each of our hands several times throughout the night, demonstrating that his ability to grip has fully recovered. "A gift of faith from the Lord," he told us.

During the service, the pastor repeatedly called upon members to seek a new connection to the divine. Tom would shout at the top of his voice, "If you are hungry for God's glory then you can see God's glory! We want a bigger touch! A new touch! A fresh touch of His love!" All this was a reminder that the faithful must not content themselves with the past, but continually seek to renew their connection to the divine with new experiences.

The call to experience God's love was couched in a warning though. Pastor Tom spoke of a coming judgment: the once-mighty dollar is losing its clout, evil is rampant. The world is like a tree that has been eaten from the inside by insects, he exhorted. It may look strong from the outside, but a coming storm will knock it down, revealing its inner corruption. Sinners will be placed in a "fiery furnace." Neither is it enough to be born again. People must still work hard to convert others and do God's work or they will not be among the favored in heaven. "Anyone in America can be rich if they just work at it," Buddy said. "If you aren't rich already you just haven't tried hard enough. But what's important is to spend your time getting rich in the right way. I'd rather have my treasures stored up in heaven. I'm too happy worshipping the Lord to worry 'bout getting rich here!" The rewards offered by God to Buddy, Gary, and the other working-class congregants were otherworldly, both in contemporary experiences and eternal bliss.

Scholars of religion have suggested that the economically disadvantaged are the most open to intense religious experiences.[39] Religious groups in which most of the members are lower on the socioeconomic ladder tend to have a strong focus upon the rewards offered in the next life. Promises of chariots in heaven and the riches of salvation offer some recompense for the sufferings of this life.

Within these churches, speaking in tongues, receiving healings, and other religious experiences confer status. As we noticed in our observations of Pentecostal churches, those who spoke in tongues received enormous attention and respect from other members. Those at the lower end of the economic ladder have much to gain from such experiences, with less conventional social status to lose from claiming an encounter with the otherworldly. A surgeon who believes she has had religious visions and experienced miraculous healings may well have difficulty convincing her social network that her experiences are the product of divine intervention and not an issue of mental malfunction. A long history of studies indicates that people of lower social status are more likely to be drawn to sects where intense emotive experiences are integrated into the religious culture of the group.[40] In general, such experiences are not typically found in more "traditional" or liturgical congregations.

Angels: Gateway to the Paranormal?

One of the surprises we encountered while investigating American paranormal beliefs and experiences was the prevalence of the belief that one has been saved by a guardian angel. Angels pervade popular culture in books, television shows, and movies. Believers exchange informal testimonials in newsletters and interpersonal conversations about the potential power of angels to influence the world. As of 2011 approximately 60% of Americans reported that they had personally been saved from harm by a guardian angel.[41]

The presence of guardian angels offers a supernatural explanation for events that seem inexplicable. How and why did I survive that accident? Why did I miss the plane on the day it crashed? How did I survive my tour of military duty? We asked respondents to the BRS who reported a guardian angel experience to briefly describe it. These narratives revealed the incredibly diverse ways Americans attribute dramatic (and sometimes mundane) events in their lives to angelic powers.

Reported guardian angel experiences often involve the coincidental avoidance of harm, with stories of the survival of severe accidents or near misses especially commonplace. A self-described "traditional" Catholic reported the following story:

> While camping, I was intent on nursing my baby. A sixty foot snag breaks off and falls on the tent. The snag top breaks off, going over top of the tent and lands one foot from where we were. Tent was destroyed, but we were unharmed. I feel we were protected by guardian angels.

Even the irreligious sometimes attributed such fortuitous "near misses" to the supernatural, as did the following self-reported atheist:

Not sure it was a guardian angel, but some higher force or being caused me to miss Pan-Am flight 759 (in 1982), which crashed on takeoff. Everyone died.

Less common, but still frequently reported, were instances where the respondent claimed angels directly protected him or her from interpersonal violence. For instance, an angel shielded an Iraq veteran from a bomb:

In Iraq a bomb went off. Everyone died, but me, not a scratch. Everyone else was cut in half or in pieces.

In another instance, an angel protected a woman and her children from an attacker:

A crazed man was trying to attack me and my children. He was forcefully lunging and swinging at us. It was like we were protected in a bubble.

In some narratives, people actually see angels, or report supernatural forces changing the material world to protect people from harm. A professional Reiki practitioner and "Tarot psychic" described an angelic encounter this way: "A shaft of light descended thru my body, from my head to my feet when a friend was reciting the Hail Mary Prayer—and I was raised Jewish!" In other stories, loved ones, friends, and even strangers are described as angels. A Jewish man reported:

I jumped head first into a pool filled with snow when I was 5, and I realized I was going to die. The hotel was closed & deserted. Suddenly, the hand of a stranger pulled me out by my foot. I never saw him again.

In sum, stories about angelic intervention are as varied as those who tell them, but all such narratives contain a common element: the belief that the supernatural broke through to influence the material world for the benefit of the believer. Anthropologists have found that belief in intentional agents of the divine is one of the most common supernatural beliefs among humans in general.[42]

While speaking in tongues, miraculous healings, and hearing the voice of God are mostly confined to the realm of conservative Christianity, the guardian angel experience has much wider appeal, being

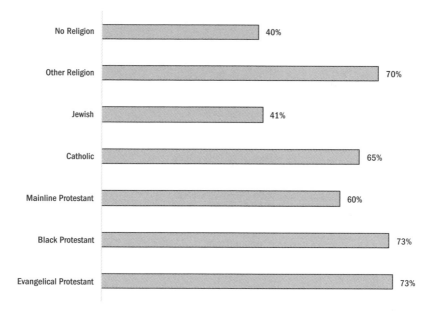

Figure 8.10. Guardian Angel Experience by Religious Tradition (Baylor Religion Survey 2011, n=1553)

common across Christian groups in the United States (see figure 8.10). Nearly three-fourths of Evangelical Protestants and black Protestants (both 73%) claim such an experience. Similarly 65% of Catholics report being protected from harm by a guardian angel, as do 60% of mainline Protestants. Seventy percent of those in non-Judeo-Christian traditions also claim guardian angel encounters. And even 41% of those who claim no religion believe that they have been rescued by mysterious forces, even though they may hedge on whether it was a guardian angel per se, as we saw with the atheist who avoided the plane crash.

While books about angels are quite popular on the Christian shelves, angels also find their way into the psychic realm. At the Holistic Health & Spiritual Fair in Anaheim (see chapter 2), angels (particularly the archangel Michael) shared the stage with other fonts of spiritual wisdom, such as extraterrestrials, ascended masters, dead relatives, and elementals. Indeed, belief in angels can appeal to both "conventional" and "unconventional" supernatural worldviews, perhaps even serving as a gateway between religion and the paranormal.[43]

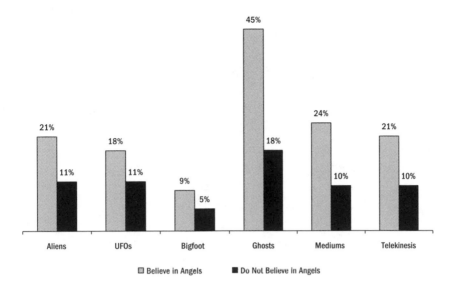

Figure 8.11. Belief in Angels and Paranormal Beliefs (Baylor Religion Survey 2014, n=1474)

Unlike other religious beliefs, people who "probably" or "absolutely" believe in the reality of angels are more likely to believe in paranormal subjects such as ghosts, extraterrestrials, and psychic phenomena than those who do not (see figure 8.11). Here we compare people who believe in the reality of angels with those who do not. Across six forms of paranormal belief (aliens have visited Earth, some UFOs are spaceships from other planets, Bigfoot is a real creature, some places are haunted by spirits, some people can use the power of their minds to communicate with the dead, and some people can use the power of their minds to move objects), people are consistently more likely to believe in the paranormal if they also believe in angels. For example, 21% of those who believe in angels *also* believe in aliens. By comparison, only 11% of those who *do not* believe in angels believe in aliens. The most pronounced difference is seen with belief in ghosts. Nearly half of those who believe in angels (45%) also believe in ghosts. But only 18% of those who do not believe in angels believe in ghosts. Put simply, believing in angels means that you are *more likely* to believe in paranormal topics. Angels are a bridge between religion and the paranormal.

Darkness *and* Light

With the exception of guardian angels, most religious experiences appeal to a fairly narrow segment of the population—conservative Christians, particularly those lower on the socioeconomic ladder. This same population tends to believe in the reality of Satan, demons, possession, and the power of evil forces. Over four-fifths (84%) of those who claim to have spoken in tongues believe that "Satan causes most evil in the world," while only two-fifths of those who have never spoken in tongues believe in an active Satan.[44] Why do these beliefs and experiences cluster together and what purpose do they serve?

A person who believes that God sometimes imparts special languages to a chosen few or is willing to heal the faithful also believes in a world of active supernatural forces. Being a spiritual warrior on the side of righteousness is a very important role, especially in the lives of people for whom important roles may be lacking. It makes sense that people who imagine a very active God will also imagine God's counterpart in order to account for misfortune. Taken together, beliefs about Satan and religious experiences are complementary for those suffering in this world. The presence of a real and powerful evil force helps provide an explanation for worldly suffering. The countervailing presence of good felt via visceral religious experiences proves to those receiving the experience that there is a God that will reward his followers for maintaining faith in the face of evil.

The Christian world is filled with experiences, beliefs, and events that are certainly beyond the "normal." By their very definition religious experiences are the perception of direct contact between an individual and that which is otherworldly. What distinguishes "religious" from "paranormal" experiences is to what source individuals attribute their otherworldly experience.[45] One might therefore expect that someone who is actively experiencing the supernatural in their church services and believes in the reality of personified evil has simply become accustomed to magical thinking, willing to believe in anything, from demons to flying saucers; however, as we have detailed, the relationship between religiosity and paranormalism is complicated.

The key insight derived from our *bounded affinity* theory of the paranormal that led us to the curvilinear relationship between general

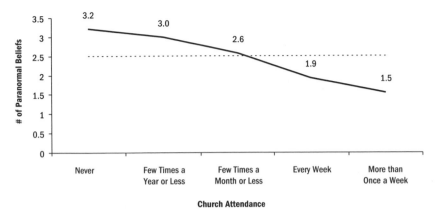

Figure 8.12. Church Attendance and Paranormalism Among Believers in an Active Satan (Chapman University Survey of American Fears 2014, n=708)

religiosity and paranormalism (see chapter 5) also provides clues for disentangling how views of religious darkness and experiences of divine light relate to paranormalism. Whether believing in the reality of active Satan on Earth or claiming intensive religious experiences go hand in hand with paranormalism depends entirely on one's level of participation in *organized* religion.

This is demonstrated by examining how belief in an active Satan impacts paranormal beliefs. Using the Chapman Survey of American Fears (2014), we determined how many of six different paranormal phenomena (Atlantis, fortune-tellers, astrology, hauntings, UFOs and Bigfoot) respondents believed in. Among respondents who believe in an active Satan, there is a clear relationship between paranormal beliefs and religious service attendance (see figure 8.12). Among *all believers* in an active Satan, the average number of paranormal beliefs is 2.5. Someone who believes in an active Satan, but never attends church, has a higher than average number of paranormal beliefs: 3.2. Among Satan believers, paranormal beliefs decrease steadily with increasing participation in organized religion. People who believe in an active Satan *and* attend about monthly are near average in their paranormal beliefs (2.6). But as Satan believers become more tightly bound to organized religion, attending every week or more, their paranormalism decreases markedly.

Put simply, believing in an active Satan is not sufficient, in and of itself, to deter paranormalism. For those who are strongly tied to institutional religion, paranormalism remains a separate sphere of the supernatural that is unlikely to hold much appeal. For those who are not tethered to the expectations and orthodoxy of organized religion, angels, demons, *and* aliens are indeed kindred spirits.[46]

9

Out on a Limb

Nearly thirty years ago I (Christopher) found myself in the passenger seat of a decrepit, rusted van as it hurtled through the woods near the town of Carson in Washington State. The driver did his best to avoid trees, boulders, ditches, and other obstacles as he navigated toward a small hunting cabin deep in the woods. Wiping mud from my eyes, I looked down, only to realize that part of the rusted floorboard had given way. I spent the remainder of the terrifying ride balancing my feet on the rough edges. Each time the van sped through a puddle, dirty water shot through the hole. Eventually the van came to a lurching stop at the bottom of a hill and the driver, Datus Perry, stepped out.

Datus was a spry, sometimes cranky, seventy-six-year-old Bigfoot witness. On this day, he wore a green winter jacket and corduroy pants that were patched in places with duct tape. Thick boots protected his feet from the mud, and a safari hat rested atop a thick mound of snowy-white hair. A long white beard completed the picture of a backwoods eccentric. A large patch on his jacket reading "Sasquatch Country" provided a clue to his particular interest.

Datus parted the brush to reveal an overgrown path heading up a hill, and we hustled away. I struggled to keep pace with a man three times my age. At frequent intervals Datus stopped to scan the nearby ridges. Suddenly he grunted and moved off the path. Standing near a large evergreen tree, he peered into the distance. Determined not to miss a potential Bigfoot sighting, I ran to his side. When I realized that Datus was urinating on the tree, I retreated to the trail, embarrassed. He snorted, giggled, zipped his fly, and resumed the hike.

A few weeks earlier, while cleaning the old cabin, Datus had spotted a nine-foot-tall, black shape in a stand of trees about 150 feet away. Assuming the shape to be a curious Bigfoot, he waved and said, "Come on down, Sasquatch!" As the creature remained motionless Datus questioned its motives. Perhaps it was a female, he thought, and he did not know how "sexy she might want to get." He decided to ignore the beast and went back to work as the creature continued to stand motionless in the distance. The stalemate continued until evening, when he lost sight of it in the enveloping darkness.

Datus stood out among Bigfoot witnesses of the time in that he claimed at least a dozen Bigfoot sightings and believed that he knew the creature's thought process. When I arrived at his home earlier that morning, he proudly retrieved from his garage a large cardboard cutout he had made of Bigfoot. Standing at least seven feet tall and in the shape of a large man, the cutout was topped off by a sharply triangular head. "That's how you know when someone is hoaxing a Bigfoot sighting," Datus told me, "because it has a sharp sagittal crest. If someone says Bigfoot doesn't have a pointy head they are a hoaxer."

This was only one of several beliefs Datus held that proved controversial in Bigfoot circles. Bigfoot has been reported in a number of different hair colors, various shades of brown or black. Even the occasional reddish and gray-colored Bigfeet have been seen. "Bigfoot only comes in black," Datus reported. All other colors people have seen are the result of the creature wearing coats made of animal skins. It was also common knowledge among Bigfoot enthusiasts that the creature has a powerful smell. "Nonsense," said Datus. "If Bigfoot smells it's because of rotten meat on the animal hides that it wears. Or maybe Bigfoot is farting."

Earlier in the day I had sat in Datus's living room as he packed his van for our trip to the cabin. In one corner of the room sat an easel with a large tablet upon it. I paged through it while waiting for Datus and found the easel filled with sketches of Bigfoot, each one captioned with the creature's thoughts. On one page was a crude drawing of the head and shoulders of an apelike creature with an astonishingly pointy head and black fur, a grimace on its face. An assortment of captions surrounding the face:

> You won't find any bigger than I am.
> I am 11 ft. tall.
> I was here FIRST. I am real.
> I don't want to be bothered. Don't pick on me little man.
> Let me eat your pig or your dog.
> I am black and very dark.

I will see you first and I'll watch you from a bush.

Throw me a fish!

On the next sheet was a full-body sketch of a Sasquatch with "I am always looking for something to eat" written sideways down the page. A profile of Bigfoot's face on the next page was titled "I am not the missing link." On the bottom of the page was Datus's attempt to spell out the way Bigfoot yells: "YEE-TEE-E-E-E-EE!!!"

When we finally reached the ramshackle cabin after our perilous van ride, we found three moss-covered walls and a collapsed door about the size of a storage unit. Datus told me about his many sightings as we stood among the trees. He claimed that the creature regularly came on to his property to steal rabbits from his pens and that he often heard it whistling and screaming in the woods surrounding his farm. His closest visual encounter with Bigfoot occurred when he was traveling in Canada and came within a few feet of a creature standing on a riverbank, but most of his other encounters took place while walking through the woods near his home, several near this cabin.

Datus had become so accustomed to Bigfoot's behaviors and habits during his many experiences that he had developed techniques for spot-

Figure 9.1. Datus Perry with his model of Bigfoot

ting the creature. And here was the purpose of our visit. We stood near the dilapidated cabin as Datus instructed me to calm my breathing and be very quiet. We needed to sit still for some time. If a Bigfoot is in the area, he instructed, it will become curious as to what encroaching humans are doing. It will stealthily follow the trespasser, staying far enough away as to avoid being seen. If a person walks around looking for Bigfoot, he will never see one, Datus told me. Should he see the person turn around, Bigfoot will stand completely still, its black fur and pointy head making it indistinguishable from the dark trees around it. Our best hope was to wait, immobile, in the hopes that a Sasquatch would become so curious as to our intentions that it would finally wander into our line of sight as it investigated.

No such luck on this day. We sat and waited. And waited. Finally Datus sighed and gave up. "They must not be around today."

We made our way back down to his van. A light rain had started as we were waiting for Bigfoot's appearance, making the downward climb treacherous and slippery. One flat tire (Datus had run over something while barreling through the woods) and a few geysers of mud through the floorboards later we arrived back at his home. "Come back again," Datus told me. "Maybe next time."

Over the next few years I did return to see Datus, but he was never able to draw Bigfoot into view. He died in the late 1990s, his passion for Bigfoot never earning him more than a reputation as a crackpot in his community and the occasional footnote in Bigfoot history.

Spending time in the realms of the paranormal in the course of writing this book led us to reflect on how much has changed since the 1980s. Back then the Internet was in its infancy, not filled with websites, blogs, and discussion forums devoted to paranormal subjects. *The X-Files* had yet to appear on television. There was no *Ghost Hunters* or *Finding Bigfoot*, let alone the seemingly endless clones and spin-offs that appeared in their wake. Since the 1980s the degree of societal interest and, perhaps more importantly, access to information about the paranormal has markedly increased.

Several decades ago an attempt to investigate the paranormal nearly always led to someone like Datus Perry. Almost every community had "that guy who sees UFOs," or the "family who thinks their house is haunted." Few people knew of the organized paranormal groups in existence at the time, such as the Mutual UFO Network and Bigfoot Field

Researchers Organization, so local inquiries usually led to colorful, eccentric dead ends.

It is clear that increased interest in the paranormal has gone hand in hand with greater media attention and the rapid diffusion of the Internet. If you live in a city or town of any size, you are likely to find an organized local or regional group of ghost hunters, a group for developing one's psychic potential, a UFO investigation club, and depending on the region, a Bigfoot hunting organization. If your area does not have its own paranormal organization or club, it is probably home to a regional chapter of a national one. Twenty years ago a visit to a reputed haunted house in a community was a lonely affair. Today one may find competition for the ghosts' attentions with a local ghost-hunting group, a documentary crew, or a radio show. Bigfoot hunters should be genuinely concerned that they are answering the wood knockings of another Bigfoot research group on the next ridge.

While we doubt many will argue with us when we claim that interest in the paranormal has increased over the last few decades, it is very difficult to prove so with any certainty. Beliefs about the paranormal have only rarely been subjected to detailed scrutiny. When survey researchers have asked Americans if they believe in paranormal topics or have had paranormal experiences, the way the questions have been asked, the population to whom the questions have been asked, and even the subjects asked about have varied so dramatically that it is impossible to know for certain how much interest in the paranormal has increased. What we can say for certainty is that we live in a paranormal America. Put another way, the paranormal is normal.

It is important that we be very clear what we mean by this statement, as it may be open to misinterpretation. Most books about the paranormal are written from a base underlying assumption regarding the reality of the phenomena under discussion. A number of skeptics and scientists have written books bemoaning increased interest in the paranormal as a sign that our culture is losing its critical reasoning skills. Michael Shermer's *Why People Believe Weird Things* and the late Carl Sagan's *The Demon-Haunted World* assume that paranormal phenomena are not objectively real and therefore try to explain what leads people to lose their common sense and believe in fallacious subjects.[1] Books written by paranormal believers attempt to present evidence, often in the form

232 | OUT ON A LIMB

of personal accounts or eyewitness testimony, in an attempt to prove the reality of the phenomenon in question. Conservative Christian authors vary—some arguing that paranormal phenomena are not real while others claim that the paranormal is a tool of Satan.

In the course of researching this book and in the wake of the publication of its first edition, we have been accused of being both (1) too skeptical by some paranormal believers who wish we would attest to the reality of UFOs or Bigfoot, and (2) not skeptical enough by some colleagues who wish we would "call out" lapses in logic among the people we have studied.

We could have presented arguments against the objective reality of UFO abductions. The first widely publicized abduction case of Betty and Barney Hill has been the subject of intense debate. For example, Betty claimed to have copied a "star map" shown to her by her abductors. Skeptics and believers have argued ever since whether the map truly displays a star system (and if so, which one) or is simply a random selection of dots produced by a deluded person.

From our perspective, there is little point in entering such debates. One aspect of the Hill case that few disagree with is that the couple truly believed themselves to have been abducted. From a sociological perspective, that is the important factor. The Hills' apparent sincerity amid their astonishing claims proved to be a formative moment in what ultimately became a popular phenomenon in the late seventies. Sociologists have long observed that people act upon their strongly held beliefs, whether those beliefs represent "reality" or not.

When we report that the paranormal is normal, therefore, it should not be taken as an implicit or explicit statement for or against the reality of UFOs, psychic phenomena, ghosts, Bigfoot, or any other paranormal topics. We simply mean that the paranormal is no longer a fringe subject. Need proof? Reflect back on the data we have presented in this book: less than half of Americans report no paranormal experiences (40%) or hold no paranormal beliefs (48%).[2] The exact percentage of Americans who believe in something paranormal will vary depending upon the number of paranormal subjects one asks about and the manner in which those questions are asked. But we see no evidence that belief in something paranormal is confined to an extremely small segment of the population.

Statistically, it is those who report *no* paranormal beliefs who are the oddballs. If we further consider strong beliefs in active supernatural religious entities and intense religious experiences the numbers are even larger. The paranormal is clearly here to stay. Whether future authors wish to lament or cheer this fact, their arguments will be strengthened by a clear understanding of who believes in and experiences the paranormal, and in what ways. This has been the goal of our project.

Key Findings

Given the diversity and amount of data we have presented, a summary of our key findings is in order.

Individual Paranormal Beliefs and Experiences

Scholars have presented contrary hypotheses regarding who should believe in paranormal subjects or report paranormal experiences. Some theorize that marginalized people (low income or education, minorities) will be more likely to believe in the paranormal, either because marginalized people have little to lose from participating in deviant beliefs or activities or because some paranormal subjects provide the believers with a sense of control over their circumstances. Other scholars suggest that paranormal interest will be more prevalent among the upper classes because they have the resources to indulge experimentation with fringe beliefs.

The correct answer appears to be much more complicated. What is clear is that it is incorrect to stereotype believers in the paranormal overall, for the people involved vary quite a bit by subject. People who believe in UFOs are not always the same types of people who believe in astrology. The following are the clear patterns we find with regard to paranormal beliefs and experiences:

- Women are more likely to believe in *enlightenment*-related paranormal topics than men, with higher levels of belief in the ability of some people to foretell the future, that places can be haunted, and astrology.
- Men are more likely to believe in *discovery*-related paranormal topics than women, with higher levels of belief in Bigfoot and UFOs.

- Economically marginalized (lower income and education) individuals gravitate towards certain paranormal beliefs, particularly belief in fortune-tellers, astrology, hauntings, and Bigfoot.
- Women are more likely to report *enlightenment* paranormal experiences than are men such as consulting a horoscope, visiting a psychic, and having had a prophetic dream.
- There is not compelling evidence that elites are more likely to report paranormal experiences. Nor is there strong evidence that paranormal experiences are entirely the province of the marginalized. Simply put— paranormal experiences are difficult to predict from status demographics.

Religious Beliefs and Paranormal Beliefs

The relationship between religious and paranormal beliefs has also been subject to competing hypotheses. Some scholars have argued that religious beliefs should open a person up to the paranormal, since someone who is willing to believe in the supernatural in one realm should be more willing to do so in another. Others have argued that religious beliefs provide a specific worldview and belief system, which is in conflict with the paranormal; therefore religious people should show lower levels of belief in paranormal topics and have fewer paranormal experiences.

We find that much of the confusion has to do with the fact that the relationship with religion and the paranormal varies by levels and types of religiosity, and also that the paranormal has previously been defined only in reference to institutional science without consideration of the relationship to institutional religions. Taking these factors into consideration, we have demonstrated the following:

- The relationship between paranormal beliefs and religiosity in general is curvilinear. People who are not at all religious (or atheists) *and* those who are deeply devoted to an exclusivist religious ideology exhibit the lowest levels of paranormal belief. The highest levels of paranormal belief appear at moderate levels of religiosity.
- The most consistent religious predictor of paranormal beliefs is religious service attendance. Those with higher levels of service attendance express lower levels of belief in all paranormal subjects.[3]
- The most consistent religious predictor of paranormal *experiences* is

biblical literalism, with literalists less likely to visit psychics or consult horoscopes, but more likely to have a prophetic dream.

Paranormal Subcultures

In chapter 6 we explored the world of paranormal subcultures and differing levels of involvement in the paranormal. Our general conclusion is that researchers should be aware of the differences between simple belief in the paranormal, research of said topics, and engaging in related activities, such as ghost hunting. Our key findings in this regard:

- Women are more interested in researching subjects related to personal *enlightenment*, such as psychics, astrology, and the New Age.
- Men are more interested in researching subjects associated with *discovery*, such as UFOs and monsters.
- The type of person interested in a paranormal subject varies depending upon level of involvement in the subject. Those who simply believe in a paranormal topic are not necessarily the same types of people who research the subject, have related experiences, or engage in related practices.

Paranormal People

In our studies of the paranormal, we were struck by the different types of people we met. We encountered some highly conventional people who believed in psychic powers, ghosts, or some other paranormal subject. Those who had more to lose by engaging in the paranormal did not necessarily avoid it altogether. Rather, these *particularists* tended to limit their beliefs. A middle-class, married banker with conventional religious beliefs may believe strongly in UFOs because of a personal interest or experience, but that same banker is unlikely to *also* believe in Bigfoot, ghosts, astrology, and psychic powers.

We met people, such as Laura, who were very unconventional and often proud of the fact that they didn't "quite fit in." Without as much to lose from embracing paranormal beliefs, such *generalists* are more willing to accept numerous paranormal topics and even claim multiple different kinds of paranormal experiences. In sum:

- In a statistical sense, it is not deviant to believe in or experience the paranormal. More than half of Americans have at least one such belief.
- Paranormal believers vary in their stakes in conformity as measured by conventional attachments, investment in conventional social status (education and income), and conventional beliefs.
- Stakes in conformity do strongly predict *how many* paranormal beliefs a person accepts. Highly conventional people report significantly fewer paranormal beliefs and experiences than unconventional people.

Darkness and Light

In chapter 8 we again examined the muddy waters between religion and the paranormal, exploring beliefs about the devil, demons, Armageddon, and hell, as well as powerful religious experiences such as speaking in tongues, miraculous healings, having a guardian angel experience, and hearing the voice of God. Patterns of belief in supernatural evil and claiming intense religious experiences include:

- People who are conservatively religious and marginalized in terms of education and income are the most likely to believe in the reality of supernatural evil forces such as Satan and demons.
- People who are conservatively religious and marginalized in terms of education and income are also the most likely to report religious experiences such as speaking in tongues and miraculous healings.
- Belief in supernatural evil is strongly related to religious experiences. In other words, those who believe in the reality of an active Satan also tend to be the same people who will speak in tongues or hear the voice of God.

Belief in supernatural evil and intensive physiological and psychological religious experiences also provide insight into patterns of paranormalism. Specifically:

- Believing in supernatural religious evil and claiming religious experiences is not associated with greater paranormalism for those with high levels of organizational religious practice; however, believing in religious evil and having religious experiences correlates with greater paranormalism for those with low levels of religious practice. In particular, views of angels and evil can be bridges to the paranormal for those who are not strongly tethered to organized religion.

- A *bounded affinity* theory of religion and the paranormal that highlights the similarities between the two, as well as the role of organized religions in defining what is considered paranormal makes sense of the wide range of complex empirical relationships between religiosity and the paranormal.

Out on a Limb

A key figure in the New Age and paranormal is actress and author Shirley MacLaine. In 1983 she released *Out on a Limb,* an autobiographical work in which she reveals how troubles in her life sparked a journey of self-exploration that led her to delve into subjects such as channeling, reincarnation, and UFOs. MacLaine was widely ridiculed and became the target of jokes on late-night talk shows, but for those in the New Age community, she was a trailblazer. Whether one considers MacLaine to be kook or a visionary, one thing is clear: releasing *Out on a Limb* was a very bold and risky move on her part.

We would like to end this journey into the paranormal with our own (relatively) risky move, predicting what the paranormal will look like in the United States in the future.

What will be the state of affairs twenty, thirty, or even forty years from now? Will people still believe? Will there be greater emphasis on paranormal beliefs? Will the level of interest in the paranormal slip? Will the ever-shifting demographic and religious composition of the U.S. population lead to a different type of paranormal? Let's get out our crystal ball and take a peek to see what the future portends.

In chapter 7 we showed that the number of paranormal beliefs a person subscribes to varies quite significantly by education, income, gender, race/ethnicity, marital status, and religiosity (see table A.6 in the appendix). Over the next twenty to forty years the sociodemographic and religious composition of the United States will change. Changing fertility patterns, increased life expectancy, changing norms regarding family structure, and immigration mean that the United States of 2040 or 2050 will not resemble the United States of today. If we hope to predict the extent of paranormal belief in the future, we will have to make some assumptions about what the demographics of the United States will look like many years from now.

The current population of the United States is approximately 323 million, and is predicted to increase to 398 million by 2050.[4] That is, by 2050, the population is projected to increase by 23%, or a net gain of 75 million people. Population projections predict an increase in the proportion of Americans who are of Hispanic ethnicity over the coming decades, but because there is a not strong association between being Hispanic and believing in the paranormal, this should have little effect on overall population rates of paranormalism. Similarly, although the age structure of the United States is projected to change, analyses of the most recent data do not show an age effect on paranormal belief. As we noted in chapter 4, there were strong age effects on belief in ghosts in data from a decade ago, but because this effect is not present in more recent data, it suggests cohort changes in paranormalism—likely related to religious change, with recent generations more likely to be outside of organized religion—rather than life course (aging) effects. As a result, changes to age structure should also have little effect on overall rates of paranormalism.

A demographic trend that may reduce the future level of paranormal belief is that of expected gains in educational attainment and subsequent gains in income. Census projections show that the share of the adult population (twenty-five and older) with a college degree is expected to increase from 22% in 2003 to 25% by 2030. Since those who have more education, on average, have higher incomes, we expect that real income should climb during that period as well. Since both of these measures are negatively related to the number of reported paranormal beliefs (see table A.6 in the appendix), then a net gain for the nation as a whole in both education and income over the next twenty to forty years should correlate with a net decline in paranormal beliefs.

As we have found, conservative religion has a dampening effect upon paranormal belief. Therefore, changes in the religious makeup of the United States should impact the paranormal. A number of studies have documented a shift in the religious landscape, particularly a decline in the Christian composition of the United States from 2007 (78%) to 2014 (70%).[5] In the last ten years the number of respondents who claim no religious affiliation has risen to over 20%; however, this increase in the nonreligious is occurring primarily among "nonaffiliated believers," rather than among non-theists (e.g., atheists or agnostics).[6] In other words, the drop in affiliation is not due to a rise in rationalism and eschewing spirituality or supernaturalism. Instead, it reflects a movement away from Christian affiliation. This is important for the paranormal moving forward, as "nonaffiliated believers" also tend to have higher levels of paranormalism. In addition, religious service attendance reduces paranormal beliefs, and there have been declines in levels of attendance, which may lead to a rise in paranormal beliefs.[7]

We also know from past research that mainline Protestant congregations have been declining in membership, and that Evangelical Christian denominations have been growing. In conjunction with these trends is an increase in the "spiritual but not religious" category.[8]

If we move forward based on such assumptions, what does it mean? Fifty-two percent of Americans currently report at least one paranormal belief. By weighting the relative importance of the demographic and religiosity variables that predict paranormal beliefs, and considering the predicted changes in the demographic and religious landscape over the next thirty to forty years, we prognosticate that, by 2050, 57.9% of Americans will report at least one paranormal belief, and that the average number of paranormal beliefs reported by respondents to surveys will be 1.35. This equates to an 11% increase in the mean number of reported paranormal beliefs in the United States.[9] As with each decennial census, we expect to continue to see modest increases in education and income over the next thirty-five years—both factors associated with a lower probability of reporting paranormal beliefs—what increases we will see in paranormal beliefs, we expect to come from the changing religious landscape.

We realize that we have gone out on the proverbial limb here by making assumptions about future changes in the United States. However, those assumptions are based upon current research on population trends, and the relationships are strong. The actual change in paranormal beliefs we experience may be slightly smaller or somewhat larger. What our models decidedly do not predict, however, is the elimination of paranormal belief, or even a dramatic reduction.

Whether we like it or not, we have become and will remain a paranormal America.

APPENDIX: METHODS AND FINDINGS

For readers concerned about methodological issues, this appendix provides details on the sources of our data—five national surveys, extensive fieldwork, and the statistical analyses that support our presentation.

SURVEY RESEARCH

In order to examine statistical patterns in paranormal beliefs and experiences, we included batteries of paranormal items on five different nationally representative surveys. Analyses presented in this volume utilize data from three waves of the Baylor Religion Survey (2005, 2011, and 2014) and two waves of the Chapman University Survey of American Fears (2014 and 2015).

Funded by the John Templeton Foundation, the Baylor Religion Survey (BRS) is a periodic in-depth survey of religious beliefs and attitudes administered to the U.S. general population. The Gallup Organization administered the Baylor Religion Surveys. Even though the BRS includes many religion questions, it was not administered only to highly religious people, or to a certain type of religious person. The Gallup Organization called a random sample of people around the country in order to solicit their participation in the survey. As such, every person in the United States with a phone or address (depending on sampling frame) had an equal chance of being selected for the survey. While Americans are overwhelmingly Christian, people of non-Christian religions and the nonreligious completed the survey as well.[1]

For Wave I (2005) and III (2011, conducted in 2010) of the Baylor Religion Survey, the Gallup Organization conducted phone recruitment, requesting participation in a survey project designed to "investigate the values and beliefs of Americans." The Gallup Organization did not indicate that the BRS was specifically about religion or that Baylor University was involved in the study for fear that this might bias the response rate. The random-digit telephone sample was drawn from telephone exchanges serving the continental United States. In order to avoid various other sources of bias, a random-digit procedure designed to provide representation of both listed and unlisted (including not-yet-listed) telephone numbers was used. The design of the sample ensures representation of all telephone numbers by randomly generating the last two digits of numbers selected on the basis of their area code, telephone exchange, and bank order. Respondents that agreed to participate in each survey are then mailed the survey instrument. Half of those who agreed to participate in the sample returned the completed survey.

Wave IV of the Baylor Religion Survey (BRS IV) is an address-based sample of households in the forty-eight contiguous states, conducted in January 2014 by the Gallup Organization. The final sample was 1,572 respondents. As with previous versions of the Baylor Religion Survey, in order to assess how well the sample compares to the general population, we compared the BRS IV to the 2014 General Social Survey on comparable measures. Demographically, the two surveys are very similar. The mean ages in the GSS 2014 and BRS IV are 46 and 45 respectively; females comprise 53% of the BRS IV and 53.8% of the GSS 2014 respectively; 18% of the GSS 2014 hold a BA degree, compared to 18.1% of the BRS IV; 45.7% of the respondents in the GSS 2014 are currently married, 26.6% are single/never married, compared to 47.1% currently married and 24.5% single/never married in the BRS IV. Given that the BRS IV is a survey on religious values and attitudes, we were concerned that the BRS data does not over-represent certain religious groups (i.e., Evangelical Christians). The BRS and GSS compare favorably among those who rarely if ever attend religious service. The BRS has a slightly higher percentage of respondents who attend church about weekly or weekly. The BRS and GSS compare favorably among very conservative respondents and liberal respondents. The BRS has a higher proportion of "conservative" respondents (21.6% vs 14.6%) and slightly fewer self-identified moderates (34.3% vs. 40.4%).

The Chapman University Survey of American Fears (CSAF) is an annual survey project housed at the Earl Babbie Research Center at Chapman University. The CSAF's primary focus is asking questions designed to determine the extent to which Americans fear or worry about life events, governmental policy, crime and victimization, natural and man-made disasters, and a host of other phenomena. While demographic items and questions about fears and worries constitute the stable core of the survey's content, each wave also includes topical modules. To date, two waves of this survey have been completed, in 2014 and 2015. Of interest to the current research, each wave includes a battery of questions on the paranormal.

These data were collected by GFK (Knowledge Networks) (www.knowledgenetworks.com), a consumer research company with expertise in probability samples. GFK maintains a probability-based web panel, KnowledgePanel, designed to be representative of the general population of the United States. The initial panel was recruited using random-digit dialing, but is maintained using the U.S. Postal Service's Delivery Sequence File, which includes households without wired telephones. Selected households are invited to participate in a web-based panel study. Potential respondents who agree to participate but lack the necessary equipment or Internet connection are provided a laptop computer and/or Internet service connection by GFK. Once recruited for the panel study, participants receive unique log-in information for accessing online surveys.

The 2014 survey was fielded to an English-speaking sample in two stages. First, GFK conducted a pre-test of 35 respondents to ensure that respondents understood the questions and that the survey was not unduly time consuming, potentially leading to subject exhaustion. This pre-test did not raise concerns, therefore, 2,500 panelists were recruited to take the survey via an email from GFK. The survey was fielded from April 15, 2014, to April 28, 2014. Of the 2,500 panelists recruited, 1,572 ultimately completed the survey, for a completion rate of 62.9%. Thus, the final sample consists of 1,572 non-institutionalized adults (18-plus years old) who reside in the United States. The 2015 CSAF was fielded from May 15, 2015, to May 26, 2015. Of the 2,660 panelists recruited, 1,541 ultimately completed the survey, for a completion rate of 58% for a final sample of 1,541 non-institutionalized U.S. adults (18-plus years old).

FIELD RESEARCH

To aid in our understanding of the subject of this book, we felt it necessary to supplement statistical findings with field research. We draw upon field research conducted by the lead researcher over the last twenty years and several new fieldwork endeavors engaged in specifically for this project.

Our methodologies varied by situation, but we most often engaged in participant observation by joining a group in its activities, whether that be a Bigfoot hunt or services at a Pentecostal church. We approached all potential subjects as social scientists interested in studying paranormal and supernatural beliefs and experiences. At no time did we present ourselves as anything other than sociologists or attempt to claim a paranormal experience in question to gain increased access to a group.

TABLE A.1. Summary of Fieldwork and Related Projects

Purpose	Location	Date(s)
Chapter 1:		
Observation of visitors at Marfa Lights viewing platform	Marfa, TX	July 2–5, 2013
Chapter 2:		
Observation/participation in the Dallas Psychic Fair*	Dallas, TX	December 7, 2008
Observation/participation in Holistic Health & Spiritual Fair	Anaheim, CA	December 12, 2015
Chapter 3:		
Observation of the UFO Contact Center International, a UFO abduction support group	Federal Way, WA	1989–1991 1997–1998 December 12, 2009
Survey of members of the UFO Contact Center International	Mailed to affiliates of the UFOCCI around the U.S.	1990
Chapter 4:		
Observation/participation in a ghost hunting course	Greenville, TN	July 31, 2007

Purpose	Location	Date(s)
Interviews with ghost hunting group	Jonesborough, TN	2010–2015
Overnight ghost watch/hunt at the Big Cypress Coffee House	Jefferson, TX	December 5–6, 2007
Evening ghost hunt at Chapman University	Orange, CA	October 21–22, 2015
Chapter 5:		
Interview with Laura Cyr, UFO Contactee	Federal Way, WA	December 12, 2009
Observation of MUFON Orange County monthly public lecture (David Jacobs)	Costa Mesa, CA	December 16, 2015
Chapter 6:		
Observations of meetings and conferences of the Texas Bigfoot Research Conservancy (now known as the NAWAC)	Tyler, TX	2005–2006
Bigfoot hunt with members of the NAWAC	Sam Houston National Forest, TX	December 8–9, 2006
Observations and survey of NAWAC Bigfoot conference	Tyler, TX	September 25–26, 2009
Observations of Sasquatch Summit conference	Ocean Shores, WA	November 21–22, 2015
Chapter 8:		
Observations of service at small Pentecostal church	Johnson City, TN	July 19, 2009
Observations of services at small Pentecostal church	Bruceville-Eddy, TX	August 26, 2009
Interviews with key figures in Paul Ingram ritual abuse case	Olympia, WA	1991
Interview with Paul Ingram	Portland, WA	July 20, 2009
Chapter 9:		
Observations of and interviews with Datus Perry	Carson, WA	1989–1990

TABLE A.1 (*Continued.*) Items marked with an asterisk indicate fieldwork that was undertaken for and discussed in the first edition of this book that are not discussed in the second edition, but are included here as they informed our conclusions.

Our descriptions of events are primarily based on our field notes. In some of these instances only one researcher was present. When more were present each took extensive field notes, which we then compared. At times our fieldwork led to other methods, such as the survey of NAWAC conference attendees described in chapters 6 and 7.

In order to avoid bogging down this book in dates and locations, we have avoided discussing the exact details of different field excursions in the main body of the text. For the interested reader, table A.1 lists key groups and locations and the dates on which we visited.

THE ANALYSES

In chapters 3 through 8 we reference analyses that are not presented in the respective chapters. In this section we include more detail on those analyses. The analyses in those chapters used a standard set of predictor variables to estimate respondents' reported paranormal beliefs, practices, and experiences. The standard model included both demographic and religiosity measures. Those measures, and their operationalization, are presented in table A.2.

TABLE A.2. Key Independent Variables

Variable	Details
Sociodemographic Measures	
Age	Measured in years
Gender	1 = Male
Race/Ethnicity	Dichotomous variables for *White (non-Hispanic)*, *Black (non-Hispanic)*, and *Hispanic*. Contrast category = *other racial/ethnic groups*.
Marital Status	Dichotomous variables for *married*, *widowed*, *divorced/separated*, and *cohabitating*. Contrast category = *never married*.
Education	1 No formal education 2 1st–4th grade 3 5th or 6th grade 4 7th or 8th grade 5 9th grade 6 10th grade 7 11th grade 8 12th grade, no diploma 9 High school diploma 10 Some college

Variable	Details
	11 Associate degree 12 Bachelor's degree 13 Master's degree 14 Professional or doctorate degree
Household Income	1 less than $10,000 2 $10k to $19,999 3 $20k to $34,999 4 $35k to $49,999 5 $50k to $99,999 6 $100k to $149,999 7 $150k or more
Region	Dichotomous variables for *Northeast, Midwest,* and *West.* Contrast category = *South.*
Political Views	1 Extremely conservative 2 Conservative 3 Leaning conservative 4 Moderate 5 Leaning liberal 6 Liberal 7 Extremely liberal

Religiosity Measures

Variable	Details
Church Attendance	1 Never 2 Less than once a year 3 Once or twice a year 4 Several times a year 5 Once a month 6 2–3 times a month 7 Weekly 8 Several times a week
Religious Tradition *This measure uses the Steensland et al. (2000) scheme.	Consists of six dichotomous variables for *Evangelical Protestant, Black Protestant, Mainline Protestant, Catholic, Jewish, Other religion.* Contrast category = *No religion.*
Biblical Literalism	Which ONE statement comes closest to your personal beliefs about the Bible? 1 The Bible is an ancient book of history and legends. 2 The Bible contains some human error. 3 The Bible is perfectly true, but it should not be taken literally, word for word. We must interpret its meaning. 4 The Bible means exactly what it says. It should be taken literally, word for word, on all subjects.

TABLE A.2 (*Continued.*)

Analyses for Chapter 3

Chapter 3 examines demographic differences in paranormal beliefs and claimed paranormal experiences. Within the chapters we present simplified analyses and charts. Our findings, however, are based upon more complex analyses in which we predict belief in paranormal topics and claimed paranormal experiences with a model that includes demographic characteristics, political preference, and measures of religiosity.

Figures 3.4, 3.5, and 3.6 examine variance in paranormal belief by gender, race, and education, respectively. Figure 3.7 provides a demographic profile for several paranormal beliefs. These figures are based upon a series of OLS regression analyses that predict responses to the following questions about paranormal belief that appeared on the Chapman University Survey of American Fears (2014):

- Ancient advanced civilizations, such as Atlantis, once existed.
- Astrologers, palm readers, tarot card readers, fortune-tellers, and psychics can foresee the future.
- Astrology impacts my life and personality.
- Houses or rooms can be haunted by spirits.
- Dreams sometimes foretell the future.
- Some UFOs are probably spaceships from other worlds.
- Bigfoot is a real creature that has yet to be discovered by science.

For each item, respondents indicated if they strongly disagree, disagree, agree, or strongly agree. Each item was coded such that higher values equal higher levels of belief. Table A.3 presents the full analysis.

Figure 3.9 presents a demographic profile of those who claim five different paranormal experiences. These analyses are also based on items from the Chapman University Survey of American Fears (2014):

As an adult, have you ever done any of the following?
- Consulted a horoscope to get an idea about the course of my life
- Called or consulted a medium, fortune-teller, or psychic
- Lived in a house or place you believed to be haunted
- Consulted a Ouija board to contact a deceased person or spirit
- Had a dream that later came true
- Witnessed an object in the sky that I could not identify (UFO)

Respondents indicated "yes" or "no" for each item. We conducted a series of binary logistic regression analyses to predict the likelihood of claiming each type of experience. The results from these analyses informed figure 3.9 (see table A.4 below).

Analyses for Chapter 6
In chapter 6 we present a contingency analysis of paranormal research activities by gender (figure 6.3) and a profile of paranormal researchers by topic. Table A.5 presents the full model on which these findings are based. This analysis uses data from the Baylor Religion Survey (2005), which asked a series of questions on paranormal research:

> Have you ever read a book on, consulted a website about, or researched:
> - Mediums, fortune-tellers, or psychics
> - UFO sightings, abductions, or conspiracies
> - Ghosts, apparitions, haunted houses, or electronic voice phenomena
> - Mysterious animals, such as Bigfoot or the Loch Ness Monster
> - Astrology
> - The prophecies of Nostradamus
> - The New Age movement in general

Binary logistic regression was used to predict the probability of researching each of these topics (see table A.5).

Analyses for Chapter 7
Table A.6 presents an analysis that is used to support the conclusions presented in chapter 7. We present a count model that estimates the number of reported paranormal beliefs, and how this varies by demographic and religiosity measures. Consistent with the conclusions presented in chapter 7, we find in the count analysis that those with more education and income report fewer paranormal beliefs, while those who are currently cohabitating have higher levels of belief. Those who attend religious services more often also report fewer paranormal beliefs. Mainline Protestants and those of "other" religions report higher levels of belief.

TABLE A.3. OLS Regressions of Paranormal Beliefs on Demographic Characteristics, Political Preference, and Religious Affiliation, Belief, and Practice (Chapman University Survey of American Fears 2014, n=1573)

	Atlantis	Fortune-Tellers	Astrology	Hauntings	Prophetic Dreams	UFOs	Bigfoot
Age	-0.025	-0.010	0.016	-0.146**	-0.156**	0.049	0.051
Gender (1=Male)	-0.030	-0.130**	-0.089**	-0.087**	-0.048	0.095**	0.079**
Race							
White	0.045	0.023	-0.052	0.099	-0.053	0.007	-0.006
Black	0.124*	0.092	0.055	0.064	0.061	-0.045	-0.023
Hispanic	0.024	-0.009	-0.036	-0.001	-0.073	0.042	-0.020
Marital Status							
Married	0.074	-0.001	-0.087*	0.079*	0.050	-0.015	0.009
Widowed	0.028	-0.008	-0.034	-0.007	0.066*	-0.046	-0.008
Div/Separated	0.025	-0.028	-0.048	0.085*	0.073*	-0.006	-0.022
Cohabitating	0.069*	0.061*	0.041	0.069*	0.056	0.052	0.074*
Income	-0.058	-0.065*	-0.064*	-0.135**	-0.040	-0.049	-0.099**
Education	-0.006	-0.129**	-0.097**	-0.062*	-0.065*	-0.058	-0.147**
Region							
Northeast	-0.028	0.016	0.019	-0.012	-0.012	0.023	0.013
Midwest	0.007	-0.028	-0.010	0.012	0.019	0.037	-0.047
West	-0.060	-0.037	-0.057	0.021	-0.005	-0.004	-0.044
Political Preference	-0.007	0.042	0.043	-0.017	-0.045	0.037	-0.012

	Atlantis	Fortune-Tellers	Astrology	Hauntings	Prophetic Dreams	UFOs	Bigfoot
Religious Tradition							
Evangelical	0.025	0.075	-0.014	0.078	0.080	-0.018	0.045
Mainline	0.114**	0.156**	0.054	0.152**	0.111**	0.060	0.097*
Black Prot	0.062	0.071	-0.008	0.110**	0.078	0.105**	0.074
Catholic	0.134**	0.147**	0.052	0.143**	0.091*	0.123**	0.079
Jewish	-0.023	0.018	-0.032	0.008	0.055	-0.054	-0.043
Other	0.064	0.141**	0.077*	0.122**	0.059	0.062	0.037
Church Attendance	-0.182**	-0.121**	-0.156**	-0.113**	-0.059	-0.205**	-0.103**
Biblical Literalism	0.004	-0.103**	-0.013	-0.011	0.061	-0.045	-0.027
N	1242	1252	1244	1249	1245	1247	1248
R^2	.055	.099	.092	.078	.063	.103	.074

TABLE A.4. Logistic Regressions of Paranormal Experiences on Demographic Characteristics, Political Preference, and Religious Affiliation, Belief, and Practice (Chapman University Survey of American Fears 2014, n=1573)

	Consulted Horoscope	Consulted Psychic	Lived in a Haunted Place	Used Ouija Board as an Adult	Had Prophetic Dream	UFO Sighting
Age	1.099*	1.169*	0.846**	1.032	0.950	1.308**
Gender (1=Male)	0.473**	0.267**	0.748	1.012	0.797*	1.280
Race						
White	0.545*	1.467	2.218*	3.125*	0.783	1.617
Black	0.507*	1.350	1.876	1.391	1.769*	1.693
Hispanic	0.579*	1.707	1.393	2.398	0.782	1.571
Marital Status						
Married	0.637*	0.809	1.893**	1.064	0.916	0.710
Widowed	0.351**	0.297*	0.784	0.863	1.263	0.105**
Div/Separated	1.165	1.113	1.951*	0.613	1.682*	0.702
Cohabitating	1.203	0.663	2.501**	2.057	1.353	1.753*
Income	0.961	1.039	0.746**	0.855*	1.003	0.919
Education	0.950	0.958	0.837**	0.946	0.965	0.949
Region						
Northeast	1.107	2.079**	1.332	1.185	1.173	1.483*
Midwest	0.758	0.581*	1.330	0.835	1.230	1.569*
West	0.674*	0.916	0.879	1.435	0.903	1.325

	Consulted Horoscope	Consulted Psychic	Lived in a Haunted Place	Used Ouija Board as an Adult	Had Prophetic Dream	UFO Sighting
Political Preference	1.263**	1.285**	1.104	1.226*	1.076	0.962
Religious Tradition						
Evangelical	0.886	0.674	1.846*	1.234	1.106	1.244
Mainline	1.530*	0.616	2.373*	1.307	1.408	1.105
Black Prot	2.402*	0.547	2.299	1.405	0.827	1.310
Catholic	1.095	0.703	1.441	1.207	1.091	0.739
Jewish	1.202	1.018	0.169	1.186	0.911	0.241
Other	1.657*	1.124	3.844**	2.301*	0.956	1.347
Church Attendance	0.974	1.052	0.871**	0.933	0.987	0.890**
Biblical Literalism	0.870*	0.783**	0.907	0.892	1.153**	1.066
N	1270	1265	1267	1265	1265	1264
Chi Square	139.91**	120.93**	116.13**	30.85	58.29**	79.03**

TABLE A.5. Logistic Regressions of Paranormal Research Topics on Demographic Characteristics, Political Preference, and Religious Affiliation, Belief, and Practice (Baylor Religion Survey 2005, n=1721)

	Psychics	UFOs	Ghosts	Monsters	Astrology	Nostradamus	New Age
Age	0.989	0.989*	0.974**	0.985**	0.986**	0.998	1.009
Gender (1=Male)	0.286**	1.856**	0.836	1.369*	0.349**	1.455**	0.459**
Race							
White	0.359**	0.552*	0.569*	0.550*	0.432**	0.602*	0.582*
Black	0.137**	0.190**	0.300**	0.232**	0.571	0.799	0.548
Marital Status							
Married	0.764	0.946	0.712*	0.778	0.511**	1.035	0.549*
Widowed	0.938	1.698	1.025	0.725	0.946	1.499	0.326*
Div/Separated	0.623	1.160	0.769	1.004	0.697	1.228	0.784
Cohabitating	1.203	1.130	0.897	0.666	0.777	1.129	0.906
Income	0.795**	0.856**	0.851**	0.900*	0.887*	1.012	0.824**
Education	1.173**	1.086*	1.037	1.067	0.995	0.957	1.179**
Region							
Northeast	1.150	1.327	0.769	1.204	1.340	0.473**	0.435**
Midwest	0.976	1.296	0.694*	0.736	1.163	0.847	0.890
West	0.833	1.206	0.804	1.192	1.239	0.621**	0.916

	Psychics	UFOs	Ghosts	Monsters	Astrology	Nostradamus	New Age
Political Affiliation	0.984	0.988	1.041	1.000	1.056	1.060*	1.078
Religious Tradition							
Evangelical	1.101	1.216	1.704*	1.396	1.466	1.503	0.612
Mainline	1.059	1.151	1.927**	1.659*	1.597	1.790*	0.520*
Black Prot	1.527	2.022	0.762	2.427	1.388	0.569	0.634
Catholic	1.628	1.028	1.748*	1.268	1.934*	2.592**	0.552*
Jewish	0.326	0.466	1.292	0.701	0.570	0.823	0.652
Other	2.237*	1.877*	2.297**	1.244	2.345**	1.850*	2.028*
Church Attendance	0.872**	0.886**	0.924**	0.934*	0.843**	0.909**	1.000
Biblical Literalism	0.703**	0.780**	0.762**	0.843*	0.798**	0.849*	0.583**
N	1328	1328	1328	1328	1328	1328	1328
Chi Square	145.12**	128.36**	138.19**	76.82**	197.22**	83.57**	147.99**

TABLE A.6. Poisson Regression: Count of Paranormal Beliefs (Chapman University Survey of American Fears 2014, n=1573)

	Estimate
Age	.003
Gender (1=Male)	.083*
Race	
White	.096
Black	.251*
Hispanic	.173
Marital Status	
Married	.014
Widowed	-.078
Div/Separated	-.043
Cohabitating	.259**
Income	-.046**
Education	-.028*
Region	
Northeast	.106
Midwest	.015
West	-.019
Political Preference	.006
Religious Tradition	
Evangelical	.049
Mainline	.156*
Black Prot	.201
Catholic	.126
Jewish	-.314
Other	.189*
Church Attendance	-.063**
Biblical Literalism	.001
N	1197
Likelihood Ratio Chi-Square	131.59**

Analyses for Chapter 9

Here we project that the percent of the population reporting at least one paranormal belief will grow from 52% to 57.9% over the next thirty-five years. We base this projection on the assumption that the relative effects of demographic and religiosity variables that predict the number of reported paranormal beliefs will continue to change over time. Working from this assumption, we create relative weights for each significant variable in table A.6 by multiplying the regression coefficient by the standard deviation of the respective variable, and dividing that product by the standard deviation of the dependent variables (number of reported paranormal beliefs). This quotient was then converted into the relative weight by estimating the total reduction in error under the null hypothesis accounted for by each significant demographic and religiosity variable.

These weights are used in standardized fixed effects regression models where we first estimate a relative factor score based on the results from the BRS. Then we adjust the effects of the relative weights based on predicted changes in the race/ethnic composition of the United States, along with changes in religious landscape, educational attainment, and income, as well as religious service attendance and biblical literalism (the latter two we set at a very conservative 3% relative drop in the next thirty to forty years). We then reestimate the model once these adjustments have been made. The last effort produced an overall 5.9% increase in the absolute value of the predicted relative factor score. If the adjustments in the demographic and religious composition of the United States occur as other scholars are predicting, then we expect that paranormal beliefs, on the aggregate level, will increase by 5% over the next thirty to forty years. We apply this factor to both the percentage who currently report believing in at least one paranormal phenomenon (52%) to arrive at our speculation that the percentage of Americans reporting paranormal experiences by year 2050 will be 57.9%.

NOTES

CHAPTER 1. THE INTERRUPTED LECTURE

1 "Bill" is a pseudonym for a Chapman professor who told the first author of this experience.

2 I have spoken to two students who were in the class in question, who corroborated Bill's story.

3 Sharon A. Hill, "Paranormal TV Show Listing," *Doubtful,* https://idoubtit.wordpress.com.

4 We have removed from these numbers shows that aired only a pilot and were not followed up by a series.

5 See *UFO Festival Roswell,* www.ufofestivalroswell.com.

6 Public lecture in Waco Texas, Baylor University Hankamer School of Business, October 2015. See "The Stephenville Lights: What Actually Happened," *Committee for Skeptical Inquiry/Skeptical Inquirer,* January/February 2009, www.csicop.org.

7 Whitcomb (2011).

8 See Barkun (2003).

9 See Goode (2000) for a discussion of popular perceptions of paranormal believers.

10 During the October 30, 2007, Democratic Party presidential debate in Philadelphia, moderator Tim Russert asked Kucinich if he had ever seen a UFO. The question was prompted by the recent release of a book by Shirley MacLaine, which reported that Kucinich witnessed a large, triangular UFO hovering over her Washington State home in the 1980s. Kucinich admitted to the experience, noting that former president Jimmy Carter had also claimed a UFO sighting.

11 Most UFO researchers trace the beginnings of the modern age of UFO sightings to the June 1947 sighting by Private Kenneth Arnold. While flying over the Cascade Mountains in Washington State, Arnold reported sighting nine delta-shaped objects flying in formation. The story received extensive press coverage at the time.

12 The anthropologist David J. Daegling (2004) concludes that the existing evidence for Bigfoot is insufficient to prove the creature's existence.

13 Detailed sampling and methodological information about the Baylor Religion Survey is available from Bader, Mencken, and Froese (2007) and in the appendix. Details about the Chapman University Survey of American Fears are also available in the appendix and at www.chapman.edu.

14 For example, Wuthnow (1978), a sample of Berkeley, California; Mears and El-
    lison (2000), a sample of Texas; Glendinning (2006), a sample of Scotland.

15 See Laubach (2004)—limited to paranormal experiences—and Bainbridge
    (2004)—a nonrandom sample.

16 See, for example, Rice (2003); Orenstein (2002); McKinnon (2003).

17 Several religious groups with UFO-based theologies appeared in the 1950s; see
    chapter 4.

18 The term "superempirical," used by Christian Smith (2003) in his theoretical
    treatise about the nature of morality and belief, is apt here.

19 See, for example, the work of philosopher and psychologist William James (1986)
    on what would now be called the "paranormal." Among contemporary theorists
    of religion, see Stark and Bainbridge (1985); Lewis and Melton (1992); Kripal
    (2010).

20 Brown (1992); Houtman and Aupers (2007); Lewis (1992).

21 Iannaccone (1995a).

22 See Fuller (1982); Moore (1977); Taves (1999).

23 Melton (1995).

24 Leslie and Adamski (1953).

25 See Sparks (2001); Orenstein (2002); or Bainbridge (2004) for an overview of
    these positions.

26 Graham (1992, 148). Note: est is a form of hypnotic therapy.

27 See Wuthnow (1978); Rice (2003).

28 See, for example, Donahue (1993); Orenstein (2002); Rice (2003); Sparks (2001).

29 Bainbridge (2004) and Orenstein (2002) have already begun to explore this pos-
    sibility.

30 See Redfern (2004).

31 We are not the first to use the metaphor of a cafeteria to refer to people who
    sample a variety of different religious and supernatural beliefs and practices. See,
    for example, Roof, Carroll, and Roozen (1995).

32 Nathan (1991).

33 For example, the McMartin daycare abuse case, which received national atten-
    tion (running from 1984 to 1990, including preliminary investigations) involved
    allegations that hundreds of children had been physically and sexually abused at
    the hands of staff involved in Satanic ceremonies at the center. The case ultimately
    cost millions of taxpayers' dollars. On moral panics about daycare centers and
    Satanic ritual abuse, see deYoung (1998).

34 The appearance of the Church of Satan in the 1960s provided the media with
    endless tales and images for use in cautionary stories about the rise of Satanism.
    Popular films such as *Rosemary's Baby* projected the image of a secretive Satanic
    cult operated by powerful members of the upper class. Tales of Satanism also
    appeared in Christian literature throughout the 1960s and 1970s, such as Mike
    Warnke's *The Satan Seller* (1972), in which he claims to have joined an under-
    ground Satanic cult in the 1960s, rising to the rank of high priest. Also famous

in panic lore is *Michelle Remembers* (1980), co-written by a medical doctor. See Russell (1991) and Stevens (1991). A classic text on Satanic panic as social phenomenon is Erikson's (1966) work on the Puritans of Salem and their infamous witch trials.

35 See, for example, Victor (1993); Richardson, Best, and Bromley (1991).

36 The most famous examples of the human costs of a Satanic panic are the 150 accused witches imprisoned during the Salem witch trials, 19 of whom were hanged.

CHAPTER 2. THE TRUTH IS WITHIN

1 Many scholars have wrestled with the difficult task of developing a definition of what beliefs and ideas are New Age. See, for example, Lewis (1992); Melton (1992); and tracing the historical roots of New Age concepts, Alexander (1992); Melton, Clark, and Kelly (1991).

2 Edmonds and Dexter (1853, 71).

3 Ibid., 32.

4 Evans (2002, 1). The cognitive anthropologist Pascal Boyer (2003; 2004) suggests that concepts such as ghosts are especially good at sticking around in people's memories as a result of their "minimally counterintuitive" nature. That is, ghosts maintain the basic features of humans with one counterintuitive feature that differs—absence of a physical body. He argues that supernatural beliefs that maintain standard cognitive templates with minor, but memorable, alterations are the ones most likely to persist across time and cultures.

5 Finucane (1984, 40–41).

6 This is not meant to suggest that there are no differences between the ghosts of today and the ghosts of yore. Some ghost motifs have fallen away over time, and the manner in which people interpret the meaning of ghosts has changed. We do not hear much today about a ghost appearing because it is angry to be sharing cemetery space with a sinner, a fairly common tale when a Christian burial was a privilege and the segregation of cemeteries common. See Finucane (1984, 43–44).

7 On the Fox sisters' role in Spiritualism, see Isaacs (1983).

8 Albanese (2007); Pike (2004). On the history of mesmermism in America, see Fuller (1982). On New Thought, see Satter (1999). Of all of these movements the one playing a central role that also stands in need of greater attention from historians is the wide-ranging influence of Swedenborg's ideas, as "Spiritualism, the most popular and widespread new religion of the mid-nineteenth century, came directly from Mesmer's and Swedenborg's teachings," putting "these ideas into a form of practice that is an important antecedent to New Age channeling and Neopagan spirit possession" (Pike 2004, 50). In their own times, these movements helped inspire progressive political movements, particularly women's rights (Braude 1989; McGarry 2008).

9 Nartonis (2010) provides an empirical assessment of the rise and initial decline of Spiritualism by tracking meetings and lectures listed in Spiritualist publications. By not setting up formal religious organizations, Spiritualism simultaneously hurt and helped the movement in the long-run; as a formal religious movement, decentralization made success all but impossible (see Nelson 1969), but in terms of diffusing the ideas of Spiritualism into American culture more broadly, the lack of formal organization has proven beneficial.

10 "Letter of Declination," *New York Times*, October 20, 1853. A reply written to the *Times* thirteen days later on behalf of the Democratic Party equated Edmonds's belief in Spiritualism with "Brigham Young's right to believe in the abominations of Mormonism," arguing for the exclusion of adherents of both movements from serving in public office (*New York Times*, November 2, 1853). Soon after, Edmonds very publically switched to the Republican Party over the impending political conflict about slavery (see *New York Times*, February 20, 1856).

11 *New York Times*, April 9, 1874.

12 To answer the reader's question before it is posed, I never saw the "ghost." I seem to have bad luck that way—Bigfoot, ghosts, UFOs, and the like are never around when I show up to see them.

13 Goode (2013); Irwin (2009).

14 Fort ([1919] 1972: 18).

15 Hitting perhaps a little too close to home, Fort ([1919] 1972) later says of the social sciences: "To be damned by slumbering giants and interesting little harlots and clowns who rank high in their profession is at least supportable to our vanity; but, we find that the anthropologists are of the slums of the divine, or of an archaic kindergarten of intellectuality, and it is very unflattering to find a mess of moldy infants sitting in judgment upon us" (178).

16 Fort ([1919] 1972, 296).

17 Fort (1923, 9).

18 Fort (1931, 31).

19 Steinmeyer (2008, xv).

20 Fort ([1919] 1972, 22).

21 Notably this means that the conceptual category of the "paranormal" requires well-established and culturally powerful institutions of science as a prerequisite (Goode 2000). Prior to the existence and cultural authority of such institutions, only the cultural designations of organized and influential religious groups could classify supernatural beliefs as illegitimate, hence the longer historical existence of the "occult" and "heresy" as cultural categories relative to the "paranormal." A related consequence of the relatively late historical development of institutional science relative to organized religion is that recently created new religious movements often have fewer friction points with institutional science because they can self-consciously incorporate contemporary scientific views into their belief systems (Rothstein 2004).

22 Bunge (1984, 39).

23 Hines (1988).

24 In many cases advocates attempt to hew closer to institutional science by pro-
actively rebranding their interests as something other than "paranormal," or by
reactively creating neologisms for topics that have become associated with the
paranormal. An interesting example of proactive rebranding is the careful deploy-
ment of "psi" by parapsychologists:

> The term *psi* denotes anomalous processes of information or energy transfer,
> processes such as telepathy or other forms of extrasensory perception that
> are currently unexplained in terms of known physical or biological mecha-
> nisms. The term is purely descriptive: It neither implies that such anomalous
> phenomena are paranormal nor connotes anything about their underlying
> mechanisms. (Bem and Honorton 1994, 4)

> An example of reactive rebranding is cryptozoology enthusiasts' neologism
> "wood ape" to refer to what is commonly called Bigfoot or Sasquatch.

25 Taves (1999; 2013).

26 Ibid., 350, emphasis in original.

27 In the long run, sectarian groups face problems institutionalizing and limiting
the disruptive potential even of the ecstatic experiences they approve, a process
Weber ([1922] 1991) referred to as the "routinization of charisma."

28 "Superstition" and "heresy" are also categories at times used by organized religion
to demarcate acceptable from unacceptable supernatural beliefs.

29 Also see Kripal (2010, 9, 39–43, 111–18, 145–47, 168–74).

30 Sociologists have noted that consumption patterns often reveal objects' structural
placement in the larger social fabric. See Bourdieu (1984).

31 Of course, certain genres complicate matters further. There have been many
academic and/or skeptical explorations of New Age beliefs such as Hines (1988),
Lewis and Melton (1992), Denzler (2001), and others that we would not consider
examples of New Age beliefs. There is also a minor genre within Christian publishing that examines New Age beliefs from a Christian perspective (often arguing
that New Age phenomena are demonic in nature). See, for example, the books
of Texe Marrs (*Mystery Mark of the New Age* [1988], *Ravaged by the New Age*
[1989], *New Age Cults and Religions* [1991], *Dark Secrets of the New Age* [2001]),
Constance Cumbey (*Hidden Dangers of the Rainbow* [1985]), and Moira Noonan
(*Ransomed from Darkness* [2005]).

32 At times New Age/paranormal topics have managed to attract the interest of
prominent institutions and academics. For example, during the 1960s and 1970s,
J. B. Rhine of Duke University conducted controlled experiments designed to test
for evidence of ESP and psychokinesis. The late John Mack, a Harvard professor of psychiatry, interviewed purported UFO abductees and reported that such
experiences could not be explained away as hallucinations or psychotic episodes
(see Mack 1994). See Northcote (2007) on the boundary maintenance between
science and the paranormal. For a general overview of the cultural boundaries of
science, see Gieryn (1999).

33 Our definition is very similar to that used by Gray (1991) and Hines (1988). Goode (2000) also notes a common thread shared by paranormal beliefs in that "traditional science regards their existence or validity as so improbable as to be all but impossible" (24).

34 Goode (2000) would disagree with us here. He distinguishes between the paranormal, which by his definition would include astrology and psychic powers, and belief in Bigfoot, which he classifies as pseudoscience. Although we see pseudoscience as useful for understanding how science marks beliefs and practices as illegitimate, we see no need to make this distinction between types of paranormalism for our purposes.

35 This is not to say that New Age beliefs or practices cannot become the focus of religious movements. Indeed, the belief in extraterrestrials has spawned several new religious movements, such as the Aetherius Society, Unarius, and the Raëlian movement. However, none of these movements have gained enough members to be a significant force in the American religious landscape.

36 For example, Evans (1984) includes a full chapter on religious visions, such as encounters with the Virgin Mary. However, he considers such visions to be similar in nature to experiences with extraterrestrials, ghosts, faeries, demons, the Men in Black, and so on. Connell (1996) recounts many of the same reported visions as Evans, but she treats such experiences as authentic encounters with the divine and proof of the tenets of Christianity. Consequently her book is filed in the religion section of most bookstores.

37 Draper and Baker (2011).

38 Intra-subculture conflict occurs when factions of believers in the same phenomenon frame their pursuits in different ways, as we found out when asking scientific-framing Sasquatch enthusiasts about the ideas of supernatural, "nature spirit" Bigfoot believers, or when we asked Christian, demonology-framing ghost hunters about the views of their crosstown neo-pagan–framing competition.

39 Even some highly skeptical institutional science advocates acknowledge this, such as Carl Sagan (1997, 285) stating his openness to (some very mild) forms of ESP, such as human thought influencing random number generators or children reporting events of past lives.

40 Haldane (1994).

41 Quote is from a handout provided by the group at its biweekly psychic fair.

42 See, for example, Melton, Clark, and Kelly (1991). Of course, there are benefits to having a committed membership over allowing experimentation. As Stark and Finke (2000) and Stark and Bainbridge (1985) note, religious organizations that require commitment from members tend to grow faster than those that do not. Making requirements of members chases away "free riders," those who want the rewards of group membership without providing anything in return (Iannaccone 1992). What remains is a committed core willing to give their time, money, and effort toward growing the organization.

43 This is not to say that people interested in the New Age never develop a commitment to a particular belief or practitioner. Many develop longtime relationships with a certain psychic or spiritual therapist. But it appears to be assumed within the subculture that such relationships are not exclusive. Someone is free to search for other sources of enlightenment, even if he has regular meetings with a particular psychic.

44 Stark and Bainbridge (1985) note that much of the interest in New Age and paranormal phenomena occurs through the mass media and within loosely organized lecture circuits, which they label as "Audience Cults" (26–27). Some beliefs gather enough momentum that they develop into "Client Cults," in which a practitioner provides a specific service (such as foretelling the future) in exchange for money (28–29).

45 Dee allowed me to tape our session. Quotes are from this recording.

46 Quotes are from a tape recording of this reading.

47 The crown chakra is an energy point or node believed to reside at the top of the skull.

48 Paulos (1991) named the effect after the famous psychic Jeane Dixon. Dixon wrote a bestselling book (*Jeane Dixon: My Life and Prophecies* [1969]), and she became famous for purportedly predicting the assassination of John F. Kennedy and consulting for Richard Nixon and the Reagans. Skeptics have long decried the fact that her many incorrect predictions (such as her prediction that World War III would start in 1958) were quickly forgotten in favor of publicizing her hits. Dixon died in 1997.

49 Cold reading is a technique used by mentalists, magicians, and some psychics, astrologers, and the like. It involves watching for very subtle cues in body language, facial expression, voice inflection, and even dress and appearance that might provide insight into the personality. A reader adept at cold reading her client would greatly cut down on incorrect statements (assuming she is not actually using psychic means to acquire information).

50 Northcote (2007, 63).

51 Ghosts were only present in the sense that some readers claimed the ability to psychically communicate with dead loved ones. UFOs sightings were not discussed, but some readers did claim to be able to channel aliens and, as noted above, one attendee was told she had experienced a past life on another planet.

52 Taves (2013, 210), summarizing the work of Subbotsky (2010) and Kripal (2010).

53 Tiryakian (1972).

54 Ben-Yehuda (1985); Gieryn (1983; 1999).

55 Weber ([1904–5] 2002); Merton (1936; 1938); cf. Becker (1986); Merton (1984).

56 On blending enlightenment and discovery, see the cases of ghosts (Baker and Bader 2014) and UFO abduction experiences (Bader 2003; Bullard 1989). For an ethnographic account of the elements of spiritual practice embedded in "ghost hunting," see Eaton (2015).

CHAPTER 3. THE TRUTH IS OUT THERE

1 See Irving ([1893] 1981, 90).
2 For example, in November 1896 a dark structure encased in bright light slowly passed over Sacramento, Folsom, and San Francisco, California. See Story (1980a, 8–9).
3 Denzler (2001, 7).
4 Ibid., 4.
5 Arnold and Palmer (1957, 10–11).
6 See Denzler (2001, 4). It should also be noted that the concept of extraterrestrial contact had a long tradition pre-Arnold. For example, some occult traditions involve the concept of communication with "spiritual masters" on other planets (see Lewis 2000, 28). Arnold's sighting, however, spurred massive public interest in the phenomenon. See Partridge (2003) for an excellent overview of extraterrestrials in occultic groups.
7 The origin of this term is also unclear (see Denzler 2001, 4).
8 As Story (1980b, 14) notes, Charles Fort, Richard Shaver, Morris K. Jessup, and others put forth the thesis that extraterrestrials had visited Earth in ancient times. According to Story, it was Louis Pauwels and Jacques Bergier who first "enumerated and synthesized" supposed examples of ancient extraterrestrial contact in their 1960 book *The Morning of the Magicians*.
9 We will not delve into the theories of author Zecharia Sitchin. Similar to Däniken, Sitchin hunts for examples of extraterrestrial intervention in Earth's history. However, he has developed a more cohesive cosmology than has Däniken. He believes that Sumerian culture is the product of interference by aliens from the planet Nibiru and who may one day return to reclaim the planet.
10 Däniken (1974b, 60).
11 For example Däniken (1974b) includes an image of a twenty-inch-tall Incan copper figure in a sun-shaped headdress. Strange features of the figure lead Däniken to an interesting conclusion. The figure has normal human proportions but "only four fingers and four toes on hands and feet. The serious scientific explanation? An adding machine!" (41).
12 See Stiebing (1984) and Story (1980b) for critical discussions of ancient astronaut claims.
13 See Harrold and Eve (1995).
14 Lemuria and Mu are two additional lost "lands." They have not gained much currency in wider popular culture but are often subjects within New Age/paranormal circles. The concept of Lemuria was originally proposed to explain the spread of species, particularly lemurs, fossils of which are found in India and Madagascar. However, this theory was rendered unnecessary with increased understanding of plate tectonics. The writings of the theosophist Helena Blavatsky resuscitated Lemuria as an occult concept. She claimed that a lost continent of Lemuria was home to a race of seven-foot-tall beings in ancient times (see Melton 1990, 258–

61). Mu was popularized through the books of James Churchward, which drew upon legend, myth, and mysterious tables he claimed to have read at a temple in India. Similar to the legend of Atlantis, Mu was supposedly an ancient advanced civilization destroyed by a natural disaster. See Churchward (1938), which has been reprinted many times.

15 See Donnelly ([1882] 1981).

16 We are indebted to J. Gordon Melton's *New Age Encyclopedia* (1990) for its excellent summary of the Atlantis myth (44–48).

17 See, for example, Greeley (1975); Ben-Yehuda (1985); Saliba (1995); Hay and Morisy (1978); Orenstein (2002); MacDonald (1995).

18 For example, Fox (1992) does not find a relationship between income, age, race/ethnicity, or marital status and the number of reported paranormal experiences. He does find that education increases the likelihood of reporting a déjà vu experience and that women, on average, report more paranormal experiences than do men. See also Mencken, Bader, and Stark (2008).

19 A number of studies utilize samples of college students. See for example Weeks, Weeks, and Daniel (2008); Bainbridge and Stark (1981).

20 See Bader, Mencken, and Froese (2007).

21 See the appendix for methodology information on the Chapman University Survey of American Fears.

22 Marx (1977, 131).

23 Legerski, Cornwall, and O'Neil (2006); Phares (2001).

24 We also recognize the possibility that those who have a strong sense of an internal locus of control are the ones who are socially successful in the first place. As with most theoretical issues in the social sciences, we have an issue of reflexivity, wherein psychological dispositions influence the external actions and the results of these actions correspondingly influence psychological dispositions and patterns.

25 Ross and Mirowsky (2002).

26 Stinchcombe (1990).

27 See Pargament (1997); Schieman and Plickert (2008); Schieman and Bierman (2007); Schieman, Nguyen, and Elliot (2003); Schieman et al. (2006). Here, we are not talking about a pure sense of fatalism, where everything is determined by fate. See Caudill (1962); Whelan (1996).

28 Stark (2008).

29 Bainbridge and Stark (1981).

30 Full analyses available in Baker (2009).

31 Chaves (2004).

32 Fox (1992).

33 Saliba (1995).

34 See Kemp (1994).

35 Women in general are more religious and spiritual than men on most measures. See Miller and Hoffman (1995); Stark (2002). Perhaps spirituality is perceived as

a form of femininity, making women more likely to embrace paranormal beliefs. See also Sjodin (2002); Stark (2002). Novel religious movements tend to be disproportionately female (Stark and Bainbridge 1985). Women may also be less stigmatized than men when they report such beliefs (Stark 200; Mears and Ellison 2000; Fox 1992).

36 Hispanics in this analysis are those of Hispanic origin, a category that was mutually exclusive from "black" or "white."

37 The Hill sighting was, in fact, investigated by Project Blue Book, a now-defunct U.S. government project to investigate UFOs based at Wright Patterson Air Force Base in Ohio. The project concluded that the Hills likely misidentified the planet Jupiter. See Clark (1996, 238).

38 See Clark (1996, 242).

39 See Fuller (1966, 87).

40 Ibid., 260.

41 The "star map" became one of the most controversial aspects of the case. In 1968 school teacher Marjorie Fish attempted to match the stars in Betty's drawing to known systems. By creating a three-dimensional representation of the map, Fish became convinced that the aliens' home planet was in the neighborhood of Zeta Reticuli 1 and 2. See Rimmer (1984, 88–92) and Klass (1989, 21–23).

42 Fuller (1966, 188).

43 Arguably the first UFO encounter involving abduction was reported by farmer Antonio Villa Boas. In 1957 he claimed that aliens pulled him aboard their ship wherein he had intercourse with a humanlike woman (see Spencer 1991). However, Boas's tale did not become widely known until after the Hills achieved fame.

44 Hopkins (1981, 401).

45 We should note a few caveats here. One early abductee, Betty Andreasson, did claim multiple contacts with the same gray beings. However, her experience was more similar to contactee tales (with friendly interactions) than to the horrifying tales of abduction that became so popular in the 1980s. Her mixture of contactee and abduction elements was more popular in the 1990s. See Fowler (1979) for a discussion of the Andreasson events (which were continued in a series of books). Further, Betty Hill did believe that she had seen alien craft after her encounter, though she never claimed another abduction-type experience (see Hill 1995, chap. 14).

46 Hopkins (1981, 214).

47 Hopkins (1987, 282).

48 See LaVigne (1995), Bryant and Seebach (1991), and Mitchell (1994) for some examples of UFO abduction therapy manuals.

49 See Pritchard et al. (1992) for the proceedings of this conference. Note that although the conference took place at MIT, most of the presenters were not, in fact, academics. Many were UFO authors or researchers such as Budd Hopkins and Jenny Randles, and/or people who claimed UFO abductions.

50 Edwards (1988, ii).

51 Brochure produced by the UFO Contact Center International, Federal Way, Washington.

52 Conroy (1989, 279).

53 The case of Betty Andreasson (see n. 45) is one of the earliest examples of a reported positive abduction-type encounter. See Fowler (1979).

54 Boylan and Boylan (1994, 4).

55 For full details of this project, see Bader (2003).

56 Our numbers for average Americans are from the 1990 General Social Survey. For full tables, see Bader (2003).

57 See Larsen (1962).

58 Historically speaking, the New Age movement represents a relatively recent idea in the American religious marketplace. While some argue that it has roots in the nineteenth-century Spiritualist movement (Hess 1993), Melton (1992) traces the modern New Age movement to the counterculture of the 1960s and the elimination in 1965 of the Asian Exclusion Act. As previously noted, what ideas and beliefs actually characterize the New Age is a matter of academic debate (Lewis and Melton 1992).

59 See Ben-Yehuda (1985); Greeley (1975); MacDonald (1995).

60 See Smelser (1962); Stark and Bainbridge (1985); Wuthnow (1978).

61 Kelly (1992) notes that new religious movements tend to be created by those that express creativity in all other fields—middle- and upper-class intellectuals. See also Mencken, Bader, and Stark (2008).

62 O'Dea (1957).

63 Alexander (1992).

64 Melton (1992).

65 See Kripal (2007) for a detailed cultural history of Esalen.

66 Adler (1979).

67 See Hirschi (1969). Hirschi's social control theory speaks to this issue (see chapter 7 for more on his work).

68 Zeleney (2008).

69 Cornwell (2003).

70 In a 2000 interview with AlienZoo.com.

71 Daymond Steer, "Clinton Promises to Investigate UFOs," *Conway Daily Sun*, December 30, 2015, www.conwaydailysun.com.

72 However, people of higher social class may be more likely to be active in subcultural communities, as we show with the example of the UFOCCI.

73 We must recognize that schizophrenics (or those with other severe mental issues) may be unlikely to complete surveys. So it is at least theoretically possible that a host of mentally unstable paranormal experiences are unaccounted for.

74 Lofland and Stark (1965) outline a step-by-step process by which a person would be likely to affiliate with a deviant religious group. They note that the potential convert must be at a "turning point"—a time in which their life is undergoing dramatic changes that may lead to the search for answers. For example, the death

of a loved one might lead one to search for new answers to the meaning of life. By observing some of the original converts to the Unification Church (popularly known as the Moonies), Lofland and Stark outlined seven progressive steps necessary for conversion. Brainwashing is not one of them. More recently see Cowan and Browley (2008) and Anthony and Robbins (2004).

CHAPTER 4. THE THRILL OF THE HAUNT

1 See Durkheim ([1912] 1995, 242–75) and Lévy-Bruhl ([1927] 1966) for classical accounts, and Boyer (2003), Cohen (2007), and Delaplace (2012, S131) for contemporary work on the anthropology of spirits.

2 Bloom (2004; 2007); Cohen et al. (2011).

3 Derrida (1994).

4 The amount of paranormal content available on television at any given time is actually much larger, given the frequency with which networks air repeats of current or concluded paranormal shows and one-time specials about the paranormal. If fictional movies and television shows with paranormal themes, such as the *Paranormal Activity* (2007–12) and *Last Exorcism* series (2010–13), are included, the paranormal has become a near ubiquitous feature of American popular culture.

5 Kwilecki (2009). On the relationship between paranormal media consumption and belief, see Sparks and Miller (2001).

6 See Molle and Bader (2013).

7 Ben Hansen also informed me that some ghost investigators believe that a spirit might simply use the energy produced by a spirit box to speak, producing a voice that emerges from the spirit box, but is *not* composed of snippets from the radio stations.

8 I reconstructed the events that occurred in Smith Hall by interviewing several of those present at the time, and also by using the observations and field notes of L. Ed Day, a fellow sociologist at Chapman who accompanied the team into Smith Hall.

9 Many ghost hunters believe that the presence of a ghost may cause part of a room to become colder in temperature. This phenomenon is often reported to be quite localized, with the rest of the room remaining at normal temperature. It is believed that ghosts may draw energy from a room to manifest, thereby causing the "cold spot."

10 A number of factors contributed to Jefferson's decline, including the development of the railroads and the removal of an enormous blockade of trees from the Red River by the U.S. Army Corps of Engineers. This last dropped the water level of the Big Cypress Bayou enough to make its use by large ships dangerous.

11 Wlodarski and Wlodarski (2001, 121).

12 Duane labels himself a high priest of Wicca and uses the spiritual name of "Gwydian," which means "storm brewer."

13 In our experience, photos of "orbs" are the evidence most commonly produced by ghost hunters. Searching the Internet for orb photos produces thousands of hits. Skeptics often contend that photos of orbs are the result of a camera flash or natural light reflecting off of dust particles.

14 On the role of deathlore in ghost narratives, see Montell (1975).

15 There are, however, some rare cases where non-believers in religious supernatural concepts hold interests in ghosts. Typically these individuals are interested in ghost hunting as a spiritual practice (see Eaton 2015, 398).

16 See Baker and Bader (2014) for greater detail on these themes and a comparative analysis of the ghost hunting group from Jefferson with two groups located in southern Appalachia.

17 Childs and Murray (2010).

18 Ramsey, Venette, and Rabalais (2011).

19 See Yamane (2000) on the role of narrative in religious experiences.

20 These results are from models controlling for other sociodemographic and religious variables correlated with paranormalism. Full models are available in Baker and Bader (2014).

21 See Bader, Baker, and Molle (2012, 716). The age pattern is less prevalent in data from the 2014 Chapman Survey of American Fears, suggesting a generational cohort, rather than life course, effect.

22 Bubandt (2012); McCorristine (2010).

CHAPTER 5. ROUND TRIP TO HELL IN A FLYING SAUCER?

1 On the decline in affiliation, see Baker and Smith (2015).

2 However, Americans also overreport how much they attend religious services, due to social desirability (Brenner 2011; Hadaway, Marler, and Chaves 1993).

3 Estimates for the proportion in Christian traditions and levels of religiosity are from the 2014 General Social Survey.

4 Leslie and Adamski (1954, 172).

5 Ibid., 188.

6 Ibid., 194–95.

7 Ibid., 197.

8 Clark (1992, 3).

9 Adamski recounts details of this meeting in his final book, *Flying Saucers Farewell* (1961). Adamski also claimed to have met Pope John XXIII in May 1963, but the Vatican denied such a meeting occurred. See Clark (1992, 4).

10 Adamski (1961, 110).

11 Clark (1992, 4).

12 In addition to the examples provided in this chapter, there were dozens of contactees. Some of the more famous examples include Howard Menger, Orfeo Angelucci, Frank Stanges, Robert Short, Cedric Allingham, and Buck Nelson.

13 See Tumminia (2005, 3) for a detailed definition of UFO contactee religion.

14 King formed the Aetherius Society (www.aetherius.org) in 1956 after claiming that a "Master of Yoga" had helped him develop the ability to communicate with a Venusian named Aetherius. See Saliba (2003, 129) and Scribner and Wheeler (2003, 157).

15 See King (1961, 11) for this tale.

16 Brown (1992) notes that New Age belief systems draw upon many religious traditions, including Eastern and Judeo-Christian beliefs.

17 Stark and Iannaccone (1997).

18 Bushman and Bushman (1999).

19 The LDS Church grew by over 45% in the United States alone between 2000 and 2010, placing it in the top ten fastest-growing denominations in the United States for that time period. See "U.S. Membership Report," *Associated of Religion Data Archives*, 2010 www.thearda.com.

20 Palmer (2004).

21 See Goode (2000) and Bainbridge (2004).

22 Iannaccone is one of several scholars that have developed the so-called rational choice perspective on religion. See Iannaccone (1992; 1995a; 1995b); Stark and Bainbridge (1987); Stark and Finke (2000).

23 Iannaccone (1995a, 285).

24 Ibid., 288.

25 We will provide a different perspective on the holding of diverse religious portfolios in chapter 7—another reason why people may experiment with the paranormal is having a low stake in conformity, of which religion plays a part.

26 Iannaccone (1992; 1995a).

27 Iannaccone (1995a, 287).

28 Of course, there are some paranormal writers who believe that UFOs are mentioned throughout the Bible.

29 Bainbridge (2004).

30 A host of books from a Christian perspective address the perceived threat of the paranormal including *The Paranormal Conspiracy: The Truth about Ghosts, Aliens and Mysterious Beings* (Dailey 2015) and *The Dark Side of the Supernatural: Uncovering God's Truth* (Myers and Wimbish 2012).

31 Rabey (1988).

32 Rhodes (1998, 198–99). Emphases and quotes in original.

33 See, for example, Larson (1997) and Bates (2004).

34 Lesage (1998).

35 Hutchings, Spargimino, and Glaze (2000, 156).

36 Historically, African American denominations, such as the African Methodist Episcopal Zion Church, tend to be theologically conservative but socially progressive. Approximately one-fourth (26%) of Americans do not belong to a Christian denomination but (see the chart) are Jewish, profess another religion such as Hinduism, Buddhism, Islam, or any number of small, religious movements, or claim no religion.

37 See Steensland et al. (2000).

38 Stark and Bainbridge (1980) hypothesized that Christian and paranormal beliefs are negatively related and found that paranormal beliefs tend to be strongest in areas where traditional Christianity tends to be weak and vice versa. Wuthnow (1978) and Hess (1993) make similar arguments.

39 The full model of controls for this graph is available in Baker and Draper (2010). Here we have also included belief in Armageddon and the Rapture as part of the religious beliefs index, items which were not included in the original study, hence the slight difference in the graph here and the one presented in Baker and Draper's article.

CHAPTER 6. PARANORMAL SUBCULTURES

1 See Glock and Stark (1965, 23–35).

2 Organizations such as the Committee for Skeptical Inquiry (www.csicop.org) are devoted to trying to inject skeptical discourse about the paranormal into the public sphere. There are also a number of celebrities, such as James Randi (The Amazing Randi) and Benjamin Radford, who regularly appear as the skeptical voice on programs related to paranormal subjects. The late Philip J. Klass was a thorn in the side of UFO believers for years.

3 Daegling (2004, 233–34).

4 See Coleman (2003) for an overview of Native American traditions related to Bigfoot. See also Rigsby (1977).

5 Eberhart (2002, 473). See also Strain (2008).

6 Bord and Bord (1982, 17) includes an excellent historical overview of Bigfoot sightings reported in the 1800s.

7 Roosevelt's book is the only original source for this tale, and he did not provide a full name for Bauman or his partner. The story has been repeated countless times in books about Bigfoot.

8 This version of the tale is from Roosevelt (1927).

9 Beck's encounter was first reported by the Portland *Oregonian* on July 13, 1924, under the title "Fight with Big Apes Reported by Miners." The article was reproduced in Green (1980, 45). In 1967 Beck self-published his own version of the events. The above quote is from Beck (1967, 2).

10 Beck (1967, 4).

11 For example, those who desire to see Ape Canyon can visit the Ape Canyon Trail in the Gifford Pinchot National Forest.

12 The Bigfoot researcher John Green was contacted by Albert Ostman in 1957, after Ostman saw stories written by Green in the newspaper.

13 This tale is repeated in several Bigfoot-related books, including Coleman (2003) and Green (1980).

14 The contractor on the Klamath job was Ray Wallace. As Coleman (2003, 66–74) notes, Wallace ultimately became notorious for his Bigfoot hoaxes.

15 Indeed, much of Bigfoot's earlier history coalesced after the Crew incident, as people who claimed pre-1958 experiences came forward and Bigfoot enthusiasts scanned newspaper archives. See Daegling (2004, 24–33).

16 For reasons of space we cannot adequately cover Bigfoot's history. For example, entire books have been devoted to the dissection of a film of a purported Bigfoot taken by Roger Patterson and Bob Gimlin in 1967. See also Patterson and Murphy (2005) and Long (2004). For histories of Bigfoot, interested readers are referred to Green (1978), Coleman (2003), Buhs (2009), McLeod (2009), and Daegling (2004).

17 Eberhart (2002, 52).

18 "Report #45918," *Bigfoot Field Researchers Organization*, August 13, 2015, www.bfro.net.

19 Bigfoot's reported appearance has changed over time. Some of the earliest reported encounters (such as the Ape Canyon incident) feature creatures that could best be described as Neanderthal in appearance. Today Bigfoot is typically reported with more gorilla-like features.

20 For example, the film taken by Patterson and Gimlin shows a hairy creature with obvious breasts (see n. 16). The late William Roe provided a sworn account of his sighting of a female Bigfoot in British Columbia (see Green 1978, 52–56).

21 Homepage, *Bigfoot Field Researchers Organization*, www.bfro.net.

22 See Farnsworth (1996), Murphy (2006), Opsasnick (2004), Holyfield (1999), Michael (undated), J. Smith (2003), and Green (2002), respectively.

23 The late Grover Krantz of Washington State University and Jeffrey Meldrum of Idaho State University, both physical anthropologists, are among the few academics who have openly supported the possibility of Bigfoot's existence.

24 See Quast (2000).

25 Baylor Religion Survey (2005).

26 Unfortunately, we can only speculate (although this seems fitting) as to whether much of this interest in Nostradamus occurred at the turn of the millennium in 1999, as we did not ask about dates people researched paranormal topics.

27 See Mears and Ellison (2000) and Denzler (2001).

28 Of course, the fact that the hunts for Bigfoot and UFOs have not, to date, provided conclusive physical evidence is one of the primary arguments against their reality used by skeptics.

29 As of this writing the most recent UFO Con: The Experiencer Event took place October 24–25, 2015, in Sacramento.

30 L. Edward Day, chair of the Sociology Department at Chapman University.

31 Cantrall (2012; 2013).

32 Simmons (2015).

33 Bindernagel (2010).

34 This, of course, is no different than a typical academic conference.

35 Many Bigfoot books provide an account of the Patterson-Gimlin encounter. See for example, Patterson and Murphy (2005, 184–87).

36 Various Bigfoot experts (skeptical, believers, and undecided) have attempted to estimate the height of the creature in the Patterson-Gimlin film via various

means. Their estimates range from the late Grover Krantz's calculation of 6 feet to Jeff Glickman's estimate of 7.3 feet. See Patterson and Murphy (2005, particularly 234) for a discussion of varying height estimates. See also Long (2004, 383–84).

37 Patterson died in 1972.

38 For Morehead's account of these events, see Morehead (2012).

39 See "Sasquatch Phonetic Alphabet and Transcription Standard," *Bigfoot Encounters*, www.bigfootencounters.com.

40 For example, the Skeptical Humanities website (http://skepticalhumanities.com) added Nelson to its "Linguistic Hall of Shame" and *Scientific American* featured a skeptical take on Nelson's work on its blog (see Stollznow 2013).

41 MMORPGs are massively multiplayer online role-playing games, or games in which the player connects to a server hosting the game and creates a character. He then plays the game alongside other players—in most cases fighting monsters in a fantasy world to acquire treasure and become more powerful. *World of Warcraft* is the most popular such game (so far) with several million players. In turn-based combat, combat takes place in turns or rounds with the focus upon strategy. In real-time combat all participants attack simultaneously, thus there is a greater focus upon speed and movement.

42 A residual haunting is akin to a videotape—it is believed that a traumatic event might somehow be imprinted upon an environment and "replayed" at particular times. The ghosts involved in residual hauntings are not assumed to have independent thought. Intelligent hauntings involve ghosts that are aware of their surroundings. Here, a ghost could theoretically choose when, where, and to whom it appears. Human entities are assumed to be the ghosts of deceased humans. Inhuman entities are assumed to be demons or elementals. Many ghost hunters carry handheld tape recorders around haunted sites hoping that EVPs (electronic voice phenomena) will appear on their recordings.

43 Bigfoot author Thom Powell told of an incident where a colleague's son found a pair of expensive sneakers left in the same location where the group had previously left out some tomatoes as a gift for Bigfoot. See Powell (2015, 131).

44 At the time of this conference the NAWAC went by the name Texas Bigfoot Research Conservancy or TBRC. To ease confusion, we refer to the group as the NAWAC throughout.

45 "New Name, Same Mission," *North American Wood Ape Conservancy*, http://woodape.org.

46 The Ohio Howl was recorded by Bigfoot researchers Matt Moneymaker and Jamie Watson in Columbiana County, Ohio and can be heard at: http://www.bfro.net/avevid/mjm/ohrec.asp.

47 The Skookum Cast was taken in September 2000 in the Gifford Pinchot National Forest in Washington State by a team from the Bigfoot Field Researchers Organization. The group tried to entice Bigfoot into leaving footprints by dropping fruit into the center of a patch of muddy ground. Later, investigators found the large impression of an animal at the edge of the mud wallow. Supporters see the

imprints of Bigfoot's arm, thighs, buttocks, and heel and theorize that Bigfoot avoided leaving footprints by reclining outside the mud and reaching its arms toward the fruit.

48 The *Memorial Day Bigfoot Film* was taken by Lori Pate during a family fishing trip at Chopaka Lake, Washington, on May 26, 1996.

49 The NAWAC helped us to prepare this list.

50 By our accounting Keith personally consumed five large sausages, two packages of beef jerky, and a rack of ribs in twenty-four hours. He earned the appellation "Dr. Meat."

51 David had warned us several times about the bitter cold we would experience, but we never spent the evening outdoors in a Texas winter.

52 "NAWAC Investigators Hear a Number of Close Knocks and Discover Fresh Tracks the Next Day," *North American Wood Ape Conservancy*, December 9, 2006, http://woodape.org.

53 Ibid.

CHAPTER 7. PARANORMAL PEOPLE

1 Email correspondence with Laura Cyr.

2 Ibid.

3 See Buhs (2009, 199–203) for a discussion of this issue.

4 Meldrum (2006, 45).

5 This speaker shall remain unnamed in order to avoid creating conflict.

6 Johnson and Shapiro (1987, 10).

7 Ibid., 28.

8 Many of the arguments made by believers in a biological version of Bigfoot highlight that they believe there are only a handful of these creatures in existence. To this they add that the animals would presumably be found in very densely forested areas uninhabited by humans, and that the Bigfeet are very intelligent, purposefully avoiding humans. Additionally they point to the immense number of sightings as evidence that humans have in fact encountered these creatures at various points.

9 Several other Bigfoot researchers have hypothesized that the creature is not simply an undiscovered ape. For example, Jack Lapseritis claims to have developed a psychic link with both friendly Bigfoot creatures and extraterrestrials (see Lapseritis 2005). Clark and Coleman (2006) outline several cases in which a Bigfoot emerged from a flying saucer or appeared to exhibit the ability to disappear into thin air.

10 For instance, anthropologist Jeff Meldrum has endured ridicule and ostracism within the scientific establishment for his interest in Bigfoot.

11 For example, we attended a November 2006 monthly meeting of what was then the TBRC in Tyler, Texas. A good portion of the meeting was devoted to relating the case of a man who believed that a camera he had placed near a deer feeder

had captured pictures of a Bigfoot's eyes glowing in the darkness. TBRC investigators were able to demonstrate that the "eyes" were merely reflections off of the
deer feeders.

12 Zahn and Sagi (1987) and Jenkins (1994).

13 See Canter, Missen, and Hodge (1996) and Fox and Levin (1999).

14 Taylor and Sorenson (2002).

15 Hirschi (1969).

16 Hirschi's control theory owes a particular debt to the works of Reiss (1951), Nye
(1958), Reckless (1962), and Toby (1957).

17 The concept of a "stake in conformity" first appeared in Toby's (1957) study of
academic achievement. Toby argued that youth who are doing poorly in school
would be more likely to break the law. Students with low academic achievement,
he argued, risk less by engaging in deviance than students who perform well in
school. Therefore, such students will be more likely to give in to the temptation
to engage in deviance. A key predictor of deviance then, is the extent to which a
person is invested in conformity. The greater someone's "stake in conformity," the
more they risk by engaging in deviance, and the less attractive deviance becomes.

18 In contrast to Hirschi's (1969, 3–4, 225; 1979) view of other theories of deviance
and crime as mutually exclusive of control theories, our explicit application of
social control theory does not preclude the application of other theories to help
explain patterns of paranormalism. In particular, much of our descriptive analyses
and fieldwork implicitly operate on the logic of subcultural theories of deviance
and religion, which outline how belief systems and their related practices are
embedded in social networks and the interpersonal relations maintained therein
(also see Baker and Smith 2015, 34–44).

19 Wu and Hart (2002); Sherman et al. (1992).

20 Abramowitz and Saunders (2006).

21 See, for example, Greeley (1995); Stark (2001); Bader and Froese (2005); Froese
and Bader (2007; 2008); Froese, Bader, and Smith (2008).

22 See the discussion in Vold, Bernard, and Snipes (1998).

CHAPTER 8. DARKNESS AND LIGHT

1 God's team.

2 For example, in *Spellbound: The Paranormal Seduction of Today's Kids*, Montenegro (2006) notes that the purported effects of Ouija boards may be the result of
the unconscious mind or involuntary body movements by the participants. She
then puts forth another possibility: "[another] view should be the biblical one—
that in some cases, the responses are from fallen angels. This would explain some
of the strange and dangerous experiences people have had when using the board"
(187).

3 "Saddleback Presidential Candidates Forum," *CNN Transcripts*, August 17, 2008,
http://transcripts.cnn.com.

4 See Wilcox, Linzey, and Jelen (1991) and Wilson and Huff (2001). Swatos (1988) found the belief that Satan is responsible for pornography is related to the picketing of stores carrying erotic materials.

5 About 43% of Americans believe in Bigfoot (11.4%), modern alien visitations (18.1%), and psychic powers (13.9%) combined. Chapman Survey of American Fears (2015).

6 Baylor Religion Survey (2014).

7 See Krause and Chatters (2005); Pargament (1997); Pargament and Hahn (1986); Spilka et al. (2003).

8 Lupfer, Tolliver, and Jackson (1996).

9 See Morone (2003); Poole (2009).

10 Jensen (2007).

11 Erikson (1966) provides an excellent overview of the Salem witch trials, as well as a classic study in theories of deviance. In seventeenth-century Massachusetts almost everyone followed strict codes of conduct, and there was little fear of violence or crime within the community. However, this bucolic life fostered the birth of a wholly fictitious moral enemy—the dreaded witch. Yet instead of tearing the community apart, Erikson argues that these acts of betrayal and murder strengthened the unity and resolve of the "good" colonists.

12 See Goode and Ben-Yehuda (1994).

13 Sarah Good, Sarah Osborne, and a slave named Tituba were the first to be accused of being witches. Good was impoverished and often begged neighbors for food. Osborne rarely attended the local church and had married her servant. Tituba was dark skinned and of Caribbean descent, adding rumors that she practiced voodoo to her already outcast racial and social statuses.

14 Jensen (2007, 218), quoting Silverman (1985, 110–11).

15 Jensen (2007, 221).

16 For a detailed comparison of the similarities and differences between the Salem witch trials and the Satanic panic of the 1980s, see Jensen (2007, 233–37).

17 Wright (1994, 24–25).

18 Ibid., 59.

19 Thurston County Sheriff's Office (1989a).

20 Thurston County Sheriff's Office (1988, 14).

21 In his report, Ofshe (1989) notes that prior to the charges against her father, Erika made a charge of improper sexual advances against a church youth counselor while at a church retreat. Curiously, Erika reported the advances to Jim Rabie, who at that time was head of the Thurston County sex crimes department. She eventually dropped the charges against the counselor.

22 Ofshe (1989, 2–3).

23 Ibid., 7.

24 Thurston County Sheriff's Office (1988b, 14).

25 Ibid., 48.

26 Expletives replaced with asterisks.

27 Jacobsen (1989, 1).

28 This interview took place on July 20, 2009.

29 The authors would like to thank Paul Ingram for reviewing and updating his current status for this volume.

30 See Russell (1991), Stevens (1991), and Victor (1993) for historical overviews of Satanism and witchcraft panics.

31 See Goodman (1972) for a cross-cultural analysis of glossolalia.

32 Woodberry and Smith (1998).

33 Pentecostals are often confused with charismatics. Both Pentecostals and charismatics have a strong focus upon personal religious experiences, but the two movements have different histories. The Pentecostal movement began in the early 1900s with the ministry of the Rev. Charles Parham of Topeka, Kansas. It ultimately spawned several distinct denominations, such as the Assemblies of God, Church of God Mountain Assembly, and Holiness Church of God, among others. See Cox (1995) for an overview of the Pentecostal movement. Any congregation—regardless of affiliation—might contain a charismatic movement. For example, in 1959 a small group of Episcopalians in a California church began speaking in tongues, ultimately resulting in the First National Episcopal Charismatic Conference in 1973 (Rosten 1975, 591; see also Melton and Baumann 2002).

34 See Melton (2003) and Poloma (1989).

35 Both the 1990 National Survey of Religious Identity (Kosmin and Lachman 1993) and the 2001 American Religious Identity Survey (Kosmin, Mayer, and Keysar 2001) included a question that asked respondents if they identify with the label "Pentecostal/charismatic." This resulted in an estimated 3.2 million in 1990, and 4.4 million by 2001 (about 1.8% of the adult population and 2.1% of the Christian population in 1990, 2.1% of the adult population and 2.8% of the Christian population in 2001). The 2014 Chapman Survey of American Fears found that 4.8% of Americans indicate that "Pentecostal" describes their religious identity.

36 The experiences examined here are all "intense" religious experiences that involve the direct intervention of the supernatural in the physical world or an experience that transcends religious feeling alone. Other experiences such as "being filled with the spirit" or "feeling called by God to do something" deserve inquiry in their own right but will not be considered here. See Baker (2009) for a discussion of the distinction between deviant and normative religious experiences and multivariate analyses of the social patterns of both.

37 For example, only 11% of those who never attend church reported one or more of these experiences, compared to nearly 65% of those who attend more than once a week.

38 We use pseudonyms for the name of the church and its members.

39 Stark and Bainbridge (1987).

40 For an introduction to this line of inquiry see Chaves (2004); Iannaccone (1988); Niebuhr ([1929] 1957); Troeltsch ([1912] 1932); Weber ([1922] 1991).

41 Baylor Religion Survey (2011). Following testimonies are quoted from this survey.

42 See Boyer (2003); Kaneko (1990); Scott (1977); Trachtenberg ([1939] 2004); Williams (1980).

43 See Draper and Baker (2011) for more in-depth analyses of the predictors of angelic beliefs and experiences.

44 Baylor Religion Survey (2005).

45 For definitions and discussions of what constitutes religious experiences, cf. Hood et al. (1996); Glock and Stark (1965); James ([1902] 1961); Poloma (1995); Proudfoot (1985); Yamane (1998, 2000).

46 We found a parallel pattern among those claiming intensive religious experiences and paranormalism at different levels of religious service attendance. These results all point to the need for a more complete incorporation of the study of the paranormal into disciplines focused on examining religion.

CHAPTER 9. OUT ON A LIMB

1 See Sagan (1997) and Shermer (2002).

2 See chapter 7.

3 Having a prophetic dream is an exception, but this stems from the overlap between the importance of prophetic dreams in both religious and paranormal subcultures.

4 "Release of 2014 U.S. and State Population Estimates on American FactFinder and Monthly Population Estimates to Jan. 1, 2015," U.S. Census Bureau, January 22, 2015, www.census.gov.

5 "America's Changing Religious Landscape," Pew Research Center, May 12, 2015, www.pewforum.org.

6 Baker and Smith (2015).

7 On declining attendance, see Chaves (2011).

8 Ibid.

9 We have tempered our prediction in growth of paranormal beliefs since our initial projections with 2005 data. This is primarily because the driving force of population change over the next thirty years is Hispanic population growth and white population decline (as a percentage of the total population). However, our data do not show any differences in these two transitional race/ethnicity categories when it comes to paranormal beliefs. We find no projections which indicate that African Americans, the race/ethnic group currently with the highest number of reported paranormal beliefs, will increase in population representation over the next thirty-five years.

APPENDIX: METHODS AND FINDINGS

1 For details of the methodology behind the Baylor Religion Survey, see Bader, Mencken, and Froese (2007).

REFERENCES

Abramowitz, Alan J., and Kyle L. Saunders. 2006. "Exploring the Bases of Partisan-
ship in the American Electorate: Social Identity vs. Ideology." *Political Research
Quarterly* 59: 175–87.

Adamski, George. 1955. *Inside the Space Ships.* New York: Abelard-Schuman.

———. 1961. *Flying Saucers Farewell.* New York: Abelard-Schuman.

Adler, Margot. 1979. *Drawing Down the Moon: Witches, Druids, Goddess-Worshippers,
and Other Pagans in America Today.* New York: Penguin.

Albanese, Catherine E. 2007. *A Republic of Mind and Spirit.* New Haven, CT: Yale
University Press.

Alexander, Kay. 1992. "Roots of the New Age." In *Perspectives on the New Age,* ed. James
R. Lewis and J. Gordon Melton, 30–58. Albany: State University of New York Press.

Angelucci, Orfeo. 1955. *The Secret of the Saucers.* Amherst, WI: Amherst Press.

Anthony, Dick, and Thomas Robbins. 2004. "Conversion and 'Brainwashing' in New
Religious Movements." In *The Oxford Handbook of New Religious Movements,* ed.
J. R. Lewis, 243–97. New York: Oxford University Press.

Arnold, Kenneth, and Ray Palmer. 1957. *The Coming of the Saucers.* Boise, ID, and
Amherst, WI: self-published.

Auerbach, Loyd. 2003. *How to Investigate the Paranormal.* Berkeley, CA: Ronin.

Bader, Christopher. 2003. "Supernatural Support Groups: Who Are the UFO Abductees
and Ritual Abuse Survivors?" *Journal for the Scientific Study of Religion* 42(4): 669–78.

Bader, Christopher, Joseph O. Baker, and Andrea Molle. 2012. "Countervailing Forces:
Religiosity and Paranormal Belief in Italy." *Journal for the Scientific Study of Religion*
51(4): 705–20.

Bader, Christopher, and Paul Froese. 2005. "Images of God: The Effect of Personal Theologies on Moral Attitudes, Political Affiliation, and Religious Behavior." *Interdisci-
plinary Journal of Research on Religion* 1, article 11.

Bader, Christopher D., F. Carson Mencken, and Paul Froese. 2007. "American Piety
2005: Content and Methods of the Baylor Religion Survey." *Journal for the Scientific
Study of Religion* 46(4): 447–63.

Baer, Randall N. 1989. *Inside the New Age Nightmare.* Lafayette, LA: Huntington House.

Bainbridge, William Sims. 2004. "After the New Age." *Journal for the Scientific Study of
Religion* 43: 381–94.

Bainbridge, William Sims, and Rodney Stark. 1980. "Scientology: To Be Perfectly
Clear." *Sociological Analysis* 41: 128–36.

———. 1981. "The Consciousness Reformation Reconsidered." *Journal for the Scientific Study of Religion* 20(1): 1–16.

Baker, Joseph. 2008a. "An Investigation of the Sociological Patterns of Prayer Frequency and Content." *Sociology of Religion* 69(2): 169–85.

———. 2008b. "Who Believes in Religious Evil? An Investigation of Sociological Patterns of Belief in Satan, Hell, and Demons." *Review of Religious Research* 50(2): 206–20.

———. 2009. "The Variety of Religious Experiences." *Review of Religious Research* 51(1): 39–54.

Baker, Joseph O., and Christopher D. Bader. 2014. "A Social Anthropology of Ghosts in Twenty-First-Century America." *Social Compass* 61(4): 569–93.

Baker, Joseph O,. and Scott Draper. 2010. "Diverse Supernatural Portfolios: Certitude, Exclusivity, and the Curvilinear Relationship between Religiosity and Paranormal Belief." *Journal for the Scientific Study of Religion* 49(3): 413–424.

Baker, Joseph O., and Buster G. Smith. 2015. *American Secularism: Cultural Contours of Nonreligious Belief Systems*. New York: New York University Press.

Balzano, Christopher. 2009. *Picture Yourself Ghost Hunting*. Boston: Course Technology.

Barker, Gray. 1956. *They Knew Too Much about Flying Saucers*. New York: University Books.

Barkun, Michael. 2003. *A Culture of Conspiracy: Apocalyptic Visions in Contemporary America*. Berkeley: University of California Press.

Barrett, Greg. 2001. "Can the Living Talk to the Dead?" *USA Today*, June 20.

Bates, Gary. 2004. *Alien Intrusion*. Green Forest, AK: Master Books.

Baxter, Marla. 1958. *My Saturnian Lover*. New York: Vantage.

Baylor Religion Survey. 2005. *The Baylor Religion Survey, Wave I*. Waco, TX: Baylor Institute for Studies of Religion.

———. 2008. *The Baylor Religion Survey, Wave II* (conducted in 2007). Waco, TX: Baylor Institute for Studies of Religion.

———. 2011. *The Baylor Religion Survey, Wave III* (conducted in 2010). Waco, TX: Baylor Institute for Studies of Religion.

———. 2014. *The Baylor Religion Survey, Wave IV*. Waco, TX: Baylor Institute for Studies of Religion.

Beck, Fred. 1967. *I Fought the Apemen of Mt. St. Helens*. Kelso, WA: R. A. Beck.

Becker, George. 1986. "The Fallacy of the Received Word: A Reexamination of Merton's Pietism-Science Thesis." *American Journal of Sociology* 91(5): 1203–18.

Bem, Daryl J., and Charles Honorton. 1994. "Does Psi Exist? Replicable Evidence for an Anomalous Process of Information Transfer." *Psychological Bulletin* 115(1): 4–18.

Ben-Yehuda, Nachman. 1985. *Deviance and Moral Boundaries*. Chicago: University of Chicago Press.

Bender, Albert K. 1962. *Flying Saucers and the Three Men*. Clarksburg, WV: Saucerian Books.

Berger, Peter L. 1967. *The Sacred Canopy: Elements of a Sociological Theory of Religion*. New York: Anchor Books.

Berger, Peter L., and Thomas Luckmann. 1967. *The Social Construction of Reality: A Treatise in the Sociology of Knowledge*. Garden City, NY: Doubleday.

Berlitz, Charles, and William L. Moore. 1980. *The Roswell Incident*. New York: Grosset & Dunlap.

Bindernagel, John A. 2010. *The Discovery of Sasquatch: Reconciling Culture, History, and the Discovery Process*. Courtenay, British Columbia: Beachcomber Books.

Birnes, William. 2002. "The Day after Corso." In *MUFON 2002 International UFO Symposium Proceedings*, ed. Barbra Maher and Irena Scott, 33–49. Morrison, CO: Mutual UFO Network.

Bivins, Jason. 2008. *Religion of Fear: The Politics of Horror in Conservative Evangelicalism*. New York: Oxford University Press.

Bloom, Paul. 2004. *Descartes' Baby*. New York: Basic Books.

———. 2007. "Religion Is Natural." *Developmental Science* 10(1): 147–51.

Bord, Janet, and Colin Bord. 1982. *The Bigfoot Casebook*. Harrisburg, PA: Stackpole Books.

Bourdieu, Pierre. 1984. *Distinction: A Social Critique of the Judgment of Taste*. Trans. R. Nice. Cambridge, MA: Harvard University Press.

Boyer, Pascal. 2003. "Religious Thought and Behaviour as By-products of Brain Function." *Trends in the Cognitive Sciences* 7(3): 119–24.

———. 2004. *Religion Explained: The Evolutionary Origins of Religious Thought*. New York: Basic Books.

Boylan, Richard J., and Lee K. Boylan. 1994. *Close Extraterrestrial Encounters: Positive Experiences with Mysterious Visitors*. Tigard, OR: Wild Flower.

Braude, Ann. 1989. *Radical Spirits*. Boston, MA: Beacon Press.

Brenner, Philip S. 2011. "Exceptional Behavior or Exceptional Identity? Overreporting of Church Attendance in the US." *Public Opinion Quarterly* 75(1): 19–41.

Bromley, David. 1991. "Satanism: The New Cult Scare." In *The Satanism Scare*, ed. James T. Richardson, Joel Best, and David G. Bromley, 49–72. New York: Aldine de Gruyter.

Brown, Susan L. 1992. "Baby Boomers, American Character, and the New Age: A Synthesis." In *Perspectives on the New Age*, ed. James R. Lewis and J. Gordon Melton, 87–96. Albany: State University of New York Press.

Bryant, Alice, and Linda Seebach. 1991. *Healing Shattered Trauma: Understanding Contactee Trauma*. Tigard, OR: Wild Flower.

Bubandt, Nils. 2012. "A Psychology of Ghosts: The Regime of the Self and the Reinvention of Spirits in Indonesia and Beyond." *Anthropological Forum* 22(1): 1–23.

Buhs, Joshua Blu. 2009. *Bigfoot: The Life and Times of a Legend*. Chicago: University of Chicago Press.

Bullard, Thomas E. 1989. "UFO Abduction Reports: The Supernatural Kidnap Narrative Returns in Technological Guise." *Journal of American Folklore* 102(404): 147–70.

Bunge, Mario. 1984. "What Is Pseudoscience?" *Skeptical Inquirer* 9: 36–46.

Bushman, Claudia L., and Richard L. Bushman. 1999. *Building the Kingdom: A History of Mormons in America*. New York: Oxford University Press.

Canter, David, Christopher Missen, and Samantha Hodge. 1996. "A Case for Special Agents?" *Policing Today* 2: 23–27.

Cantrall, Thom. 2012. *Sasquatch: The Living Legend*. Charleston, SC: self-published (CreateSpace).

———. 2013. *Sasquatch: Search for a New Man*. Charleston, SC: self-published (CreateSpace).

Carey, Thomas J., and Donald R. Schmitt. 2007. *Witness to Roswell: Unmasking the Sixty-Year Cover-Up*. Franklin Lakes, NJ: New Page Books.

Caudill, Harry. 1962. *Night Comes to the Cumberlands: A Biography of a Depressed Area*. Boston: Little, Brown.

Chaves, Mark. 2004. *Congregations in America*. Cambridge, MA: Harvard University Press.

———. 2011. *American Religion: Contemporary Trends*. Princeton, NJ: Princeton University Press.

Chapman University. 2014. *The Chapman University Survey of American Fears, Wave I*. Orange, CA: Earl Babbie Research Center.

———. 2015. *The Chapman University Survey of American Fears, Wave II*. Orange, CA: Earl Babbie Research Center.

Cheeseman Day, Jennifer, and Kurt J. Bauman. "Have We Reached the Top? Educational Attainment Projections of the U.S. Population." Population Division, U.S. Bureau of the Census. May 2000. Population Division Working Paper 43.

Childs, Carrie, and Craig D. Murray. 2010. "'We All Had an Experience in There Together': A Discursive Psychological Analysis of Collaborative Paranormal Accounts by Paranormal Investigation Team Members." *Qualitative Research in Psychology* 7(1): 21–33.

Churchward, James. 1938. *The Lost Continent of Mu*. New York: Washburn.

Clark, Jerome. 1992. *The Emergence of a Phenomenon: UFOs from the Beginning through 1959. The UFO Encyclopedia*, vol. 2. Detroit, MI: Omnigraphics.

———. 1996. *High Strangeness: UFOs from 1960 through 1979. The UFO Encyclopedia*, vol. 3. Detroit, MI: Omnigraphics.

Clark, Jerome, and Loren Coleman. 2006. *The Unidentified and Creatures from the Outer Edge*. San Antonio: Anomalist Books.

Cohen, Emma. 2007. *The Mind Possessed: The Cognition of Spirit Possession in an Afro-Brazilian Religious Tradition*. New York: Oxford University Press.

Cohen, Emma, Emily Burdett, Nicola Knight, and Justin Barrett. 2011. "Cross-Cultural Similarities and Differences in Person-Body Reasoning: Experimental Evidence from the United Kingdom and Brazilian Amazon." *Cognitive Science* 35(7): 1282–1304.

Coleman, Loren. 2003. *Bigfoot! The True Story of Apes in America*. New York: Paraview Pocket Books.

Connell, Janice T. 1996. *Meetings with Mary: Visions of the Blessed Mother*. New York: Ballantine.

Conroy, Ed. 1989. *Report on Communion*. New York: Avon.

Cornwell, Rupert. 2003. "In God He Trusts—How George Bush Infused the White House with a Religious Spirit." *Independent*, September 21.

Corso, Philip J., and William J. Birnes. 1997. *The Day after Roswell*. New York: Pocket Books.

Cowan, Douglas E., and David G. Browley. 2008. *Cults and New Religions: A Brief History*. Malden, MA: Blackwell.

Cox, Harvey. 1995. *Fire from Heaven: The Rise of Pentecostal Spirituality and the Reshaping of Religion in the Twenty-First Century*. Cambridge, MA: Da Capo.

Daegling, David J. 2004. *Bigfoot Exposed: An Anthropologist Examines America's Enduring Legend*. New York: AltaMira.

Dailey, Timothy J. 2015. *The Paranormal Conspiracy: The Truth about Ghosts, Aliens and Mysterious Beings*. Bloomington, MN: Chosen Books.

Däniken, Erich von. 1974a. *The Gold of the Gods*. New York: Bantam.

———. 1974b. *In Search of Ancient Gods: My Pictorial Evidence for the Impossible*. New York: G. P. Putnam's Sons.

Dean, Jodi. 1998. *Aliens in America: Conspiracy Cultures from Outerspace to Cyberspace*. Ithaca, NY: Cornell University Press.

Delaplace, Grégory. 2012. "Parasitic Chinese, Vengeful Russians: Ghosts, Strangers, and Reciprocity in Mongolia." *Journal of the Royal Anthropological Institute* 18(S1): S131–44.

Denzler, Brenda. 2001. *The Lure of the Edge: Scientific Passions, Religious Beliefs, and the Pursuit of UFOs*. Berkeley: University of California Press.

Derrida, Jacques. [1993] 1994. *Specters of Marx*, trans. Peggy Kamuf. New York: Routledge.

deYoung, Mary. 1998. "Another Look at Moral Panics: The Case of Satanic Day Care Workers." *Deviant Behavior* 19(3): 257–78.

Donahue, Michael J. 1993. "Prevalence and Correlates of New Age Beliefs in Six Protestant Denominations." *Journal for the Scientific Study of Religion* 32(2): 177–84.

Donnelly, Ignatius. [1882] 1981. *Atlantis: The Antediluvian World*. New York: Harper's.

Dougherty, Kevin D., Christopher D. Bader, Paul Froese, Edward C. Polson, and Buster G. Smith. 2009. "Religious Diversity in a Southern Baptist Congregation." *Review of Religious Research* 50(3): 321–34.

Draper, Scott, and Joseph O. Baker. 2011. "Angelic Belief as American Folk Religion." *Sociological Forum* 26(3): 623–43.

Durkheim, Emile. [1912] 1995. *The Elementary Forms of Religious Life*. Trans. Karen E. Fields. New York: Free Press.

Eaton, Marc A. 2015. "'Give Us a Sign of Your Presence': Paranormal Investigation as a Spiritual Practice." *Sociology of Religion* 76(4): 389–412.

Eberhart, George M. 2002. *Mysterious Creatures: A Guide to Cryptozoology*, vol. 2, M–Z. Santa Barbara, CA: ABC-CLIO.

Edgar Cayce Foundation. 1987. *Gems and Stones: Based on the Edgar Cayce Readings*. Virginia Beach, VA: A.R.E.

Edmonds, John W., and George T. Dexter. 1853. *Spiritualism*. New York: Partridge & Brittan.

Edwards, Aileen. 1988. *On the (UFO) Road Again: Case Histories of Close Encounters of the Third Kind*. Seattle: UFO Contact Center International.

Erikson, Kai T. 1966. *Wayward Puritans: A Study in the Sociology of Deviance*. New York: Macmillan.

Evans, Hilary. 1984. *Visions, Apparitions, Alien Visitors: A Comparative Study of the Entity Enigma*. Northamptonshire, UK: Aquarian.

———. 2002. *Seeing Ghosts: Experiences of the Paranormal*. London: John Murray.

Farnsworth, Susan A. 1996. *The Mogollon Monster: Arizona's Bigfoot*. Mesa, AZ: Southwest.

Finucane, R. C. 1984. *Appearances of the Dead: A Cultural History of Ghosts*. Buffalo, NY: Prometheus Books.

Fort, Charles. [1919] 1972. *The Book of the Damned*. New York: Ace Books.

———. 1923. *New Lands*. New York: Boni & Liveright.

———. 1931. *Lo!* New York: Claude Kendal.

Fowler, Raymond E. 1979. *The Andreasson Affair*. New York: Bantam.

Fox, James Alan, and Jack Levin. 1999. "Serial Murder: Popular Myths and Empirical Realities." In *Homicide: A Sourcebook of Social Research*, ed. M. Dwayne Smith and Margaret A. Zahn, 167–75. Thousand Oaks, CA: Sage.

Fox, John W. 1992. "The Structure, Stability, and Social Antecedents of Reported Para-normal Experiences." *Sociological Analysis* 53(4): 417–31.

Frazier, E. Franklin. 1963. *The Negro Church in America*. New York: Schocken Books.

Friedman, Stanton T., and Don Berliner. 1992. *Crash at Corona: The U.S. Military Retrieval and Cover-up of a UFO*. St. Paul, MN: Paragon House.

Froese, Paul, and Christopher D. Bader. 2007. "God in America: Why Theology Is Not Simply the Concern of Philosophers." *Journal for the Scientific Study of Religion* 46(4): 465–81.

———. 2008. "Unraveling Religious Worldviews: The Relationship Between Images of God and Political Ideology in a Cross-cultural Analysis." *Sociological Quarterly* 49(4): 689–718.

Froese, Paul, Christopher D. Bader, and Buster Smith. 2008. "Political Tolerance and God's Wrath in the United States." *Sociology of Religion* 69(1): 29–44.

Fukuyama, Francis. 1995. *Trust: The Social Virtues and the Creation of Prosperity*. New York: Free Press.

Fuller, John G. 1966. *The Interrupted Journey: Two Lost Hours "Aboard a Flying Saucer."* New York: Dial.

Fuller, Robert C. 1982. *Mesmerism and the American Cure of Souls*. Philadelphia: University of Pennsylvania Press.

Geertz, Clifford. 1973. *The Interpretation of Cultures*. New York: Basic Books.

Gieryn, Thomas F. 1983. "Boundary-Work and the Demarcation of Science from Nonscience: Strains and Interests in Professionalization Ideologies of Scientists." *American Sociological Review* 48(6): 781–95.

———. 1999. *Cultural Boundaries of Science: Credibility on the Line*. Chicago: University of Chicago Press.

Glendinning, Tony. 2006. "Religious Involvement, Conventional Christian, and Unconventional Nonmaterialist Beliefs." *Journal for the Scientific Study of Religion* 45(4): 585–95.

Glock, Charles Y., and Rodney Stark. 1965. *Religion and Society in Tension.* Chicago: Rand McNally.

Goldberg, Robert A. 2001. *Enemies Within: The Culture of Conspiracy in Modern America.* New Haven, CT: Yale University Press.

Goode, Erich. 2000. *Paranormal Beliefs: A Sociological Introduction.* Prospect Heights, IL: Waveland.

———. 2013. "Paranormalism and Pseudoscience as Deviance." In *Philosophy of Pseudoscience: Reconsidering the Demarcation Problem,* ed. Massimo Pigliucci and Maarten Boudry, 145–64. Chicago: University of Chicago Press

Goode, Erich, and Nachman Ben-Yehuda. 1994. "Moral Panics: Culture, Politics, and Social Construction." *Annual Review of Sociology* 20: 149–71.

Goodman, Felicitas D. 1972. *Speaking in Tongues: A Cross-Cultural Study of Glossolalia.* Chicago: University of Chicago Press.

Graham, Billy. 1977. *Angels.* New York: Simon & Schuster.

———. 1992. *Storm Warning.* Dallas: Word.

Gray, William D. 1991. *Thinking Critically about New Age Ideas.* Belmont, CA: Wadsworth.

Greeley, Andrew. 1975. *The Sociology of the Paranormal.* Studies in Religion and Ethnicity, vol. 3. Beverly Hills, CA: Sage.

———. 1995. *Religion as Poetry.* New Brunswick, NJ: Transaction.

Green, John. 1978. *Sasquatch: The Apes among Us.* Blaine, WA: Hancock House.

———. 1980. *On the Track of Sasquatch,* Book 1. British Columbia: Cheam.

Green, John C., James L. Guth, Corwin E. Smidt, and Lyman A. Kellstedt. 1996. *Religion and the Culture Wars.* Lanham, MD: Rowman & Littlefield.

Green, Mary A. 2002. *Fifty Years with Bigfoot: Tennessee Chronicles of Co-Existence.* Cookeville, TN: Green and Coy Enterprises.

Hadaway, C. Kirk, Penny L. Marler, and Mark Chaves. 1993. "What the Polls Don't Show: A Closter Look at U.S. Church Attendance." *American Sociological Review* 58(6): 741–52.

Haldane, David. 1994. "Crystal Clear: New Age Center Decides It Must Rechannel Energy to the Mainstream." *Los Angeles Times,* August 2. http://articles.latimes.com.

Harrold, Francis B., and Raymond A. Eve, eds. 1995. *Cult Archeology and Creationism: Understanding Psuedoscientific Beliefs about the Past.* Iowa City: University of Iowa Press.

Hay, David, and Ann Morisy. 1978. "Reports of Ecstatic, Paranormal, or Religious Experience in Great Britain and the United States." *Journal for the Scientific Study of Religion* 17(3): 255–68.

Heelas, Paul. 1996. *The New Age Movement: The Celebration of Self and the Sacralization of Modernity.* Oxford: Blackwell.

Hess, David J. 1993. *Science in the New Age: The Paranormal, Its Defenders and Debunkers, and American Culture.* Madison: University of Wisconsin Press.

Hill, Betty. 1995. *A Common Sense Approach to UFOs*. Greenland, NH: self-published.

Hines, Terence. 1988. *Pseudoscience and the Paranormal: A Critical Examination of the Evidence*. Buffalo, NY: Prometheus Books.

Hirschi, Travis. 1969. *Causes of Delinquency*. Berkeley: University of California Press.

————. 1979. "Separate and Unequal Is Better." *Journal of Research in Crime and Delinquency* 16(1): 34–38.

Hofstadter, Richard. 1966. *The Paranoid Style in American Politics and Other Essays*. New York: Knopf.

Holyfield, Dana. 1999. *Swamp Bigfoot: Tales of the Louisiana Honey Island Swamp Monster*. Pearl River, LA: Honey Island Swamp Books.

Hood, Ralph W., Jr., Peter C. Hill, and W. Paul Williamson. 2005. *The Psychology of Religious Fundamentalism*. New York: Guilford.

Hood, Ralph W., Jr., Bernard Spilka, Bruce Hunsberger, and Richard Gorsuch. 1996. *The Psychology of Religion: An Empirical Approach*, 2nd ed. New York: Guilford.

Hopkins, Budd. 1981. *Missing Time: Documented Stories of People Kidnapped by UFOs and Then Returned with Their Memories Erased*. New York: Richard Marek.

————. 1987. *Intruders: The Incredible Visitations at Copley Woods*. New York: Ballantine.

Hout, Michael, and Claude S. Fischer. 2002. "Why More Americans Have No Religious Preference: Politics and Generations." *American Sociological Review* 67(2): 165–90.

Houtman, Dick, and Stef Aupers. 2007. "The Spiritual Turn and the Decline of Tradition: The Spread of Post-Christian Spirituality in 14 Western Countries, 1981–2000." *Journal for the Scientific Study of Religion* 46(3): 305–20.

Hutchings, Noah, Larry Spargimino, and Bob Glaze. 2000. *Marginal Mysteries: A Biblical Perspective*. Oklahoma City: Hearthstone.

Iannaccone, Laurence R. 1988. "A Formal Model of Church and Sect." *American Journal of Sociology* 94: S241–S268.

————. 1992. "Sacrifice and Stigma: Reducing Free Riding in Cults, Communes and Other Collectives." *Journal of Political Economy* (April): 271–91.

————. 1995a. "Risk, Rationality and Religious Portfolios." *Economic Inquiry* 23: 285–95.

————. 1995b. "Voodoo Economics? Reviewing the Rational Choice Approach to Religion." *Journal for the Scientific Study of Religion* 34(1): 76–89.

Irving, Washington. [1893] 1981. *The Life and Voyages of Christopher Columbus*. Boston: Twayne.

Irwin, Harvey J. 2009. *The Psychology of Paranormal Belief: A Researcher's Handbook*. Hatfield: University of Hertfordshire Press.

Isaacs, Ernest. 1983. "The Fox Sisters." In *The Occult in America: New Historical Perspectives*, ed. Howard Kerr and Charles L. Crow, 79–110. Urbana: University of Illinois Press.

Jacobsen, Judith A. 1989. *Medical Report of Erika Ingram*. Seattle, WA: Harbourview Hospital.

James, William. [1902] 1961. *Varieties of Religious Experience: A Study in Human Nature*. New York: Collier Macmillan.

———. 1986. *Essays in Psychical Research*. Cambridge, MA: Harvard University Press.

Jenkins, Philip. 1994. *Using Murder: The Social Construction of Serial Homicide*. Hawthorne, NY: Aldine de Gruyter.

Jensen, Gary. 2007. *The Path of the Devil: Early Modern Witch Hunts*. Lanham, MD: Rowman & Littlefield.

Johnson, Stan, and Joshua Shapiro. 1987. *The True Story of Bigfoot*. Pinole, CA: J&S Aquarian Networking.

Jung, Carl G. 1979. *Flying Saucers: A Modern Myth of Things Seen in the Sky*. Princeton, NJ: Princeton University Press.

Kaneko, Satoru. 1990. "Dimensions of Religiosity among Believers in Japanese Folk Religion." *Journal for the Scientific Study of Religion* 29(1): 1–18.

Kelly, Aidan A. 1992. "An Update on Neopagan Witchcraft in America." In *Perspectives on the New Age*, ed. James R. Lewis and J. Gordon Melton, 136–51. Albany: State University of New York Press.

Kemp, Alice Abel. 1994. *Women's Work: Degraded and Devalued*. Englewood Cliffs, NJ: Prentice Hall.

King, George. 1961. *The Twelve Blessings: The Cosmic Concept as Given by the Master Jesus*. London: Aetherius.

Klass, Philip J. 1989. *UFO Abductions: A Dangerous Game*. Buffalo, NY: Prometheus.

Knight, Peter. 2002. "Introduction: A Nation of Conspiracy Theorists." In *Conspiracy Nation: The Politics of Paranoia in Postwar America*, ed. Peter Knight, 1–20. New York: New York University Press.

Kosmin, Barry A., and Seymour P. Lachman. 1993. *One Nation under God: Religion in Contemporary Society*. New York: Harmony.

Kosmin, Barry A., Egon Mayer, and Ariela Keysar. 2001. *American Religious Identification Survey*. New York: Graduate Center of New York University.

Krause, Neal, and Linda M. Chatters. 2005. "Exploring Race Differences in a Multi-Dimensional Battery of Prayer Measures among Older Adults." *Sociology of Religion* 66(1): 23–43.

Kripal, Jeffrey J. 2007. *Esalen: American and the Religion of No Religion*. Chicago: University of Chicago Press.

———. 2010. *Authors of the Impossible: The Paranormal and the Sacred*. Chicago: University of Chicago Press.

Kwilecki, Susan. 2009. "Twenty-First-Century American Ghosts: The After-Death Communication—Therapy and Revelation from beyond the Grave." *Religion and American Culture: A Journal of Interpretation* 19(1): 101–33.

Lapseritis, Jack. 2005. *The Psychic Sasquatch and Their UFO Connection*. Mills Spring, NC: Wild Flower.

Larsen, Otto N. 1962. "Innovators and Early Adopters of Television." *Sociological Inquiry* 32(S): 16–23.

Larson, Bob. 1997. *UFOs and the Alien Agenda*. Nashville: Thomas Nelson.

Laubach, Marty. 2004. "The Social Effects of Psychism: Spiritual Experience and the Construction of Privatized Religion." *Sociology of Religion* 65(3): 239–63.

LaVigne, Michelle. 1995. *The Alien Abduction Survival Guide*. Newberg, OR: Wild Flower.

Legerski, Elizabeth, Marie Cornwall, and Brock O'Neil. 2006. "Changing Locus of Control: Steelworkers Adjusting to Forced Unemployment." *Social Forces* 84: 1521–38.

Legget, Mike. 2009. "Texas Bigfoot Conference More Boring than You Would Think." *Austin-American Statesman*, October 4.

Lesage, Julia. 1998. "Christian Media." In *Media, Culture, and the Religious Right*, ed. L. Kintz and J. Lesage, 21–50. Minneapolis: University of Minnesota Press.

Leslie, Desmond, and George Adamski. 1953. *Flying Saucers Have Landed*. New York: British Book Centre.

Lévy-Bruhl, Lucien. [1927] 1966. *The "Soul" of the Primitive*. Chicago: Henry Regnery.

Lewis, James R. 1992. "Approaches to the Study of the New Age Movement." In *Perspectives on the New Age*, ed. James R. Lewis and J. Gordon Melton, 1–14. Albany: State University of New York Press.

———, ed. 2000. *UFOs and Popular Culture: An Encyclopedia of Contemporary Myth*. Santa Barbara, CA: ABC-CLIO.

Lewis, James R., and Gordon Melton, eds. 1992. *Perspectives on the New Age*. New York: State University of New York Press.

Lincoln, C. Eric. 1974. *The Black Church Since Frazier*. New York: Schocken Books.

Lincoln, C. Eric, and Lawrence H. Mamiya. 1990. *The Black Church in the Africa-American Experience*. Durham, NC: Duke University Press.

Lofland, John, and Rodney Stark. 1965. "Becoming a World-Saver: A Theory of Conversion to a Deviant Perspective." *American Sociological Review* 30: 862–74.

Long, Greg. 2004. *The Making of Bigfoot: The Inside Story*. Amherst, NY: Prometheus Books.

Lupfer, Michael, Donna Tolliver, and Mark Jackson. 1996. "Explaining Life-Altering Occurrences: A Test of the 'God-of-the-Gaps' Hypothesis." *Journal for the Scientific Study of Religion* 35(4): 379–91.

MacDonald, William L. 1995. "The Effects of Religiosity and Structural Strain on Reported Paranormal Experiences." *Journal for the Scientific Study of Religion* 34(3): 366–76.

Mack, John E. 1994. *Abduction: Human Encounters with Aliens*. New York: Charles Scribner's Sons.

MacLaine, Shirley. 1986. *Out on a Limb*. New York. Bantam Books.

Marx, Karl. 1977. *Critique of Hegel's "Philosophy of Right."* London: Cambridge University Press.

Mason, Fran. 2002. "A Poor Person's Cognitive Mapping." In *Conspiracy Nation: The Politics of Paranoia in Postwar America*, ed. Peter Knight, 40–56. New York: New York University Press.

Maudlin, Michael G. 1989. "Holy Smoke! The Darkness Is Back." *Christianity Today* 15 (December): 58–59.

McAndrew, James. 1997. *The Roswell Report: Case Closed*. Washington, DC: U.S. Government Printing Office.

McCorristine, Shane. 2010. *Spectres of the Self: Thinking about Ghosts and Ghost-Seeing in England, 1750–1920*. New York: Cambridge University Press.

McGarry, Molly. 2008. *Ghosts of Futures Past*. Berkeley, CA: University of California Press.

McKinnon, Andrew. 2003. "The Religious, the Paranormal, and Church Attendance: A Response to Orenstein." *Journal for the Scientific Study of Religion* 42(2): 299–303.

McLeod, Michael. 2009. *Anatomy of a Beast: Obsession and Myth on the Trail of Bigfoot*. Oakland, CA: University of California Press.

Mears, Daniel P., and Christopher G. Ellison. 2000. "Who Buys New Age Materials? Exploring Sociodemographic, Religious, Network, and Contextual Correlates of New Age Consumption." *Sociology of Religion* 61(3): 289–314.

Meldrum, Jeff. 2006. *Sasquatch: Legend Meets Science*. New York: Tom Doherty Associates.

Melley, Timothy. 2000. *Empire of Conspiracy: The Culture of Paranoia in Postwar America*. Ithaca, NY: Cornell University Press.

———. 2002. "Agency Panic and the Culture of Conspiracy." In *Conspiracy Nation: The Politics of Paranoia in Postwar America*, ed. Peter Knight, 57–84. New York: New York University Press.

Melton, J. Gordon. 1990. *New Age Encyclopedia*. Detroit: Gale Research.

———. 1992. "New Thought and the New Age." In *Perspectives on the New Age*, ed. J. Lewis and G. Melton, 15–29. Albany: State University of New York Press.

———. 1995. "The Contactees: A Survey." In *The Gods Have Landed: New Religions from Other Worlds*, ed. James R. Lewis, 1–13. Albany: State University of New York Press.

———. 2003. "Pentecostal Family." *The Encyclopedia of American Religions*, 7th ed. Detroit: Gale Research.

Melton, J. Gordon, and Martin Baumann. 2002. *Religions of the World: A Comprehensive Encyclopedia of Beliefs and Practices*. Santa Barbara, CA: ABC-Clio.

Melton, J. Gordon, Jerome Clark, and Aidan Kelly. 1991. *New Age Almanac*. Canton, MI: Visible Ink.

Mencken, F. Carson, Christopher Bader, and Ye Jung Kim. 2009. "Round Trip to Hell in a Flying Saucer: The Relationship between Conventional Christian and Paranormal Beliefs in the United States." *Sociology of Religion* 70(1): 65–85.

Mencken, F. Carson, Christopher Bader, and Rodney Stark. 2008. "Conventional Christian Beliefs and Experimentation with the Paranormal." *Review of Religious Research* 50: 194–205.

Menger, Howard. 1959. *From Outer Space to You*. Clarksburg, WV: Saucerian Books.

Merton, Robert K. 1936. "Puritanism, Pietism, and Science." *Sociological Review* 28(1): 1–30.

———. 1938. "Science, Technology and Society in Seventeenth Century England." *Osiris* 4: 360–632.

_____. 1984. "The Fallacy of the Latest Word: The Case of 'Pietism and Science.'" *American Journal of Sociology* 89(5): 1091–1121.

Michael, Jay. Undated. *Bigfoot in Mississippi*. Laurel, MS: self-published.

Miller, Alan S., and John P. Hoffman. 1995. "Risk and Religion: An Explanation in Gender Differences in Religiosity." *Journal for the Scientific Study of Religion* 34(1): 63–75.

Mitchell, Karyn K. 1994. *Abductions: Stop Them, Heal Them, Now!* St. Charles, IL: Mind Rivers.

Molle, Andrea, and Christopher D. Bader. 2013. "The Birth of 'Paranormal Science' in Italy." In *Paranormal Cultures*, ed. Olu Jenzen and Sally R. Munt, 121–38. London: Ashgate.

Montenegro, Marcia. 2006. *Spellbound: The Paranormal Seduction of Today's Kids*. Colorado Springs, CO: Cook Communications Ministries.

Montell, William L. 1975. *Ghosts along the Cumberland: Deathlore in the Kentucky Foothills*. Knoxville: University of Tennessee Press.

Moore, Laurence R. 1977. *In Search of White Crows: Spiritualism, Parapsychology, and American Culture*. New York: Oxford University Press.

Morehead, Ron. 2012. *Voices in the Wilderness*. n.l.: self-published.

Morone, James A. 2003. *Hellfire Nation: The Politics of Sin in American History*. New Haven, CT: Yale University Press.

Moseley, James. W., and Karl T. Pflock. 2002. *Shockingly Close to the Truth!* Buffalo, NY: Prometheus Books.

Murphy, Christopher L. 2006. *Bigfoot Encounters in Ohio: Quest for the Grassman*. Blaine, WA: Hancock House.

Mustapa, Margit. 1960. *Spaceship to the Unknown*. New York: Vantage.

_____. 1963. *Book of Brothers*. New York: Vantage.

Myers, Bill, and David Wimbish. 2012. *The Dark Side of the Supernatural: Uncovering God's Truth*. Grand Rapids, MI: Zondervan.

Nartonis, David K. 2010. "The Rise of 19th-Century American Spiritualism, 1854–1873." *Journal for the Scientific Study of Religion* 49(2): 361–73.

Nathan, Debbie. 1991. "Satanism and Child Molestation: Constructing the Ritual Abuse Scare." In *The Satanism Scare*, ed. James T. Richardson, Joel Best, and David G. Bromley, 75–94. New York: Aldine de Gruyter.

National Geographic. 2012. "Aliens among Us." Survey conducted by Kelton Research, May 21–29, 2012.

Nelson, G. K. 1969. *Spiritualism and Society*. London: Routledge & Kegan Paul.

Newport, Frank. 1997. "What If Government Really Listened to the People?" www.gallup.com.

Niebuhr, H. Richard. [1929] 1957. *The Social Sources of Denominationalism*. New York: Meridian Books.

Northcote, Jeremy. 2007. *The Paranormal and the Politics of Truth: A Sociological Account*. Charlottesville, VA: Imprint-Academic.

Nye, F. Ivan. 1958. *Family Relationships and Delinquent Behavior*. New York: John Wiley and Sons.

O'Dea, Thomas F. 1957. *The Mormons*. Chicago: University of Chicago Press.

Ofshe, Richard. 1989. Report from Dr. Richard Ofshe to Gary Tabor, Prosecutor. Olympia, WA.

Opsasnick, Mark. 2004. *The Maryland Bigfoot Digest: A Survey of Creature Sightings in the Free State*. n.l.: self-published (Xlibris).

Orenstein, Alan. 2002. "Religion and Paranormal Belief." *Journal for the Scientific Study of Religion* 41(2): 301–12.

Pagels, Elaine. 1995. *The Origin of Satan*. New York: Random House.

Palmer, Susan J. 2004. *Aliens Adored: Raël's UFO Religion*. New Brunswick, NJ: Rutgers University Press.

Pargament, Kenneth I. 1997. *The Psychology of Religion and Coping: Theory Research, Practice*. New York: Guilford.

Pargament, Kenneth I., and June Hahn. 1986. "God and the Just World: Causal and Coping Attributions to God in Health Situations." *Journal for the Scientific Study of Religion* 25(2): 193–207.

Parish, Jane, and Martin Parker, eds. 2001. *The Age of Anxiety: Conspiracy Theory and the Human Sciences*. Oxford: Oxford University Press.

Partridge, Christopher. 2003. "Understanding UFO Religions and Abduction Spiritualities." In *UFO Religions*, ed. Christopher Partridge, 3–42. London: Routledge.

Passel, Jeffrey S., and D'Vera Cohn. 2008. *U.S. Population Projections: 2005–2050*. Washington, DC: Pew Research Center. www.pewresearch.org.

Patterson, Roger, and Christopher Murphy. 2005. *The Bigfoot Film Controversy*. Blaine, WA: Hancock House.

Paulos, John Allen. 1991. *Beyond Numeracy*. New York: Vintage.

Phares, Jerry. 2001. "Locus of Control." In *The Corsini Encyclopedia of Psychology and Behavioral Science*, vol. 2, ed. W. E. Craighead and C. B. Nemeroff, 889–91. New York: John Wiley and Sons.

Pike, Sarah M. 2004. *New Age and Neopagan Religions in America*. New York: Columbia University Press.

Pipes, Daniel. 1997. *Conspiracy: How the Paranoid Style Flourishes and Where It Comes From*. New York: Simon & Schuster.

Poloma, Margaret. M. 1989. *The Assemblies of God at the Crossroads: Charisma and Institutional Dilemmas*. Knoxville: University of Tennessee Press.

———. 1995. "The Sociological Context of Religious Experience." In *Handbook of Religious Experience*, ed. R. W. Hood Jr., 161–82. Birmingham, AL: Religious Education Press.

Poole, W. Scott. 2009. *Satan in America: The Devil We Know*. Lanham, MD: Rowman & Littlefield.

Powell, Thom. 2015. *Edges of Science*. West Linn, OR: Willamette City Press.

Pritchard, Andrea, David E. Pritchard, John E. Mack, Pam Kasey, and Claudia Yapp, eds. 1992. *Alien Discussions: Proceedings of the Abduction Study Conference Held at MIT, Cambridge, MA*. Cambridge, MA: North Cambridge Press.

Proudfoot, Wayne. 1985. *Religious Experience*. Berkeley: University of California Press.

Putnam, Robert D. 2000. *Bowling Alone: The Collapse and Revival of American Community*. New York: Simon & Schuster.

Quast, Mike. 2000. *Big Footage: A History of Claims for the Sasquatch on Film*. Moorhead, MN: self-published.

Quine, Williard V., and J. S. Ullian. 1978. *The Web of Belief*. New York: Random House.

Rabey, Steve. 1988. "Spiritual Warfare, Supernatural Sales." *Christianity Today* 9 (December): 69.

Raboteau, Albert J. 1997. "The Black Experience in American Evangelicalism: The Meaning of Slavery." In *African-American Religion*, ed. Timothy E. Fulop and Albert J. Raboteau, 89–106. New York: Routledge.

Ramsey, Matthew C., Steven J. Venette, and Nicole Rabalais. 2011. "The Perceived Paranormal and Source Credibility: The Effects of Narrative Suggestions on Paranormal Belief." *Atlantic Journal of Communication* 19(2): 79–96.

Reckless, Walter C. 1962. "A Non-Causal Explanation: Containment Theory." *Excerpta Criminologica* 2: 131–32.

Redfern, Nick. 2004. *Three Men Seeking Monsters: Six Weeks in Pursuit of Werewolves, Lake Monsters, Giant Cats, Ghostly Devil Dogs, and Ape-Men*. New York: Pocket Books.

Reiss, Albert J. 1951. "Delinquency as the Failure of Personal and Social Controls." *American Sociological Review* 16(2): 196–207.

Rhodes, Ron. 1998. *Alien Obsession*. Eugene, OR: Harvest House.

Rice, Tom W. 2003. "Believe It or Not: Religious and Other Paranormal Beliefs in the United States." *Journal for the Scientific Study of Religion* 42(1): 95–106.

Richardson, James T., Joel Best, and David G. Bromley. 1991. *The Satanism Scare*. New York: Aldine de Gruyter.

Rigsby, Bruce. 1977. "Some Pacific Northwest Native Language Names for the Sasquatch Phenomenon." In *The Scientist Looks at Sasquatch*, ed. Roderick Sprague and Grover S. Krantz, 31–37. Moscow: University of Idaho Press.

Rimmer, John. 1984. *The Evidence for Alien Abductions*. Northamptonshire, UK: Aquarian.

Roof, Wade C. 1999. *Spiritual Marketplace: Baby Boomer and the Remaking of American Religion*. Princeton, NJ: Princeton University Press.

Roof, Wade Clark, Jackson W. Carroll, and David A. Roozen. 1995. "Conclusion: The Post-War Generation-Carriers of a New Spirituality." In *The Postwar Generation and Establishment Religion: Cross-Cultural Perspectives*, ed. Wade Clark Roof, Jackson W. Carroll, and David A. Roozen, 243–55. Boulder, CO: Westview.

Roosevelt, Theodore. 1927. *Hunting Adventures in the West*. New York: Putnam.

Ross, Catherine, and John Mirowsky. 2002. "Households, Employment, and the Sense of Control." *Social Psychology Quarterly* 55(3): 217–35.

Rosten, Leo. 1975. *Religions of America: Ferment and Faith in an Age of Crises*. New York: Simon and Schuster.

Rothstein, Mikael. 2004. "Science and Religion in the New Religion." In *Oxford Handbook of New Religious Movements*, ed. James R. Lewis, 99–118. New York: Oxford University Press.

Russell, Jeffrey. 1991. "The Historical Satan." In *The Satanism Scare,* ed. James T. Richardson, Joel Best, and David G. Bromley, 41–48. New York: Aldine de Gruyter.

Sagan, Carl. 1997. *The Demon-Haunted World: Science as a Candle in the Dark.* New York: Ballantine.

Saler, Benson, Charles A. Ziegler, and Charles B. Moore. 1997. *UFO Crash at Roswell: The Genesis of a Modern Myth.* Washington, DC: Smithsonian Institution Press.

Saliba, John. 1995. "Religious Dimensions of the UFO Phenomenon." In *The Gods Have Landed: New Religions from Other Worlds,* ed. James R. Lewis, 15–64. Albany: State University of New York Press.

———. 2003. "The Earth Is a Dangerous Place: The Worldview of the Aetherius Society." In *Encyclopedia Sourcebook of UFO Religions,* ed. James R. Lewis, 123–42. Amherst, NY: Prometheus.

Satter, Beryl. 1999. *Each Mind a Kingdom.* Berkeley, CA: University of California Press.

Schieman, Scott, and Alex Bierman. 2007. "Religious Activities and Changes in the Sense of Divine Control." *Sociology of Religion* 68(4): 361–81.

Schieman, Scott, Kim Nguyen, and Diana Elliot. 2003. "Religiosity, Socioeconomic Status, and the Sense of Mastery." *Social Psychology Quarterly* 66(3): 202–21.

Schieman, Scott, and Gabriele Plickert. 2008. "How Knowledge Is Power: Education and the Sense of Control." *Social Forces* 87(1): 153–83.

Schieman, Scott, Tetyana Pudrovska, Leonard I. Pearlin, and Christopher G. Ellison. 2006. "The Sense of Divine Control and Psychological Distress: Variations by Race and Socioeconomic Status." *Journal for the Scientific Study of Religion* 45(4): 529–49.

Schuessler, John F. 2000. *Public Opinion Surveys and Unidentified Flying Objects: 50+ Years of Sampling Public Opinions.* Morrison, CO: Mutual UFO Network.www. nidsci.org.

Scott, James C. 1977. "Protest and Profanation: Agrarian Revolt and the Little Tradition, Part I." *Theory and Society* 4(1): 1–38.

Scribner, Scott, and Gregory Wheeler. 2003. "Cosmic Intelligences and their Terrestrial Channel." In *Encyclopedic Sourcebook of UFO Religions,* ed. James R. Lewis, 157–71. Amherst, NY: Prometheus Books.

Sherkat, Darren E. 2001. "Tracking the Restructuring of American Religion: Religious Affiliation and Patterns of Religious Mobility, 1973–1998." *Social Forces* 79(4): 1459–93.

———. 2008. "Beyond Belief: Atheism, Agnosticism, and Theistic Certainty in the United States." *Sociological Spectrum* 28(5): 438–59.

Sherman, Lawrence W., Douglas A. Smith, Janell D. Schmidt, and Dennis P. Rogan. 1992. "Crime, Punishment, and Stake in Conformity: Legal and Informal Control of Domestic Violence." *American Sociological Review* 57(5): 680–90.

Shermer, Michael. 2002. *Why People Believe Weird Things: Pseudoscience, Superstition, and Other Confusions of Our Time.* New York: Holt.

Silverman, Kenneth. 1985. *The Life and Times of Cotton Mather.* New York: Columbia University Press.

Simmons, Lori. 2015. *Tracking Bigfoot: The Journey Continues.* Ellensburg, WA: Rhettman.

Sjodin, Ulf. 2002. "The Swedes and the Paranormal." *Journal of Contemporary Religion* 17(1): 75–85.

Slate, Bobbie Ann, and Al Berry. 1976. *Bigfoot*. New York: Bantam.

Smelser, Neil J. 1962. *Theory of Collective Behavior*. Glencoe, NY: Free Press.

Smith, Christian. 2003. *Moral, Believing Animals: Human Personhood and Culture*. New York: Oxford University Press.

Smith, James M. 2003. *Sasquatch: Alabama Bigfoot Sightings*. Wadley, AL: self-published.

Southall, Richard. 2003. *How to Be a Ghost Hunter*. Woodbury, MN: Llewellyn.

Sparks, Glenn. G. 2001. "The Relationship between Paranormal Beliefs and Religious Beliefs." *Skeptical Inquirer* 25: 50–56.

Sparks, Glenn G., and Will Miller. 2001. "Investigating the Relationship between Exposure to Television Programs That Depict Paranormal Phenomena and Beliefs in the Paranormal." *Communication Monographs* 68(1): 98–113.

Spencer, John. 1991. *The UFO Encyclopedia: A to Z Guide of Extraterrestrial Phenomena*. New York: Avon.

Spilka, Bernard, Jr., Ralph W. Hood, Bruce Hunsberger, and Richard Gorsuch. 2003. *The Psychology of Religion: An Empirical Approach*, 3rd ed. New York: Guilford.

Stark, Rodney. 1996. *The Rise of Christianity*. Princeton, NJ: Princeton University Press.

———. 2001. "Gods, Rituals, and the Moral Order." *Journal for the Scientific Study of Religion* 40(4): 619–36.

———. 2002. "Physiology and Faith: Addressing the 'Universal' Gender Difference in Religious Commitment." *Journal for the Scientific Study of Religion* 41(3): 495–508.

———. 2004. *Exploring the Religious Life*. Baltimore: Johns Hopkins University Press.

———. 2008. *What Americans Really Believe*. Waco, TX: Baylor University Press.

Stark, Rodney, and William Sims Bainbridge. 1980. "Networks of Faith: Interpersonal Bonds and Recruitment to Cults and Sects." *American Journal of Sociology* 85(6): 1376–95.

———. 1985. *The Future of Religion: Secularization, Revival and Cult Formation*. Berkeley: University of California Press.

———. 1987. *A Theory of Religion*. New York: Peter Lang.

Stark, Rodney, and Roger Finke. 2000. *Acts of Faith: Explaining the Human Side of Religion*. Berkeley: University of California Press.

Stark, Rodney, and Laurence Iannaccone. 1997. "Why the Jehovah's Witnesses Grow So Rapidly: A Theoretical Application." *Journal of Contemporary Religion* 12(2): 133–57.

Steensland, B., J. Z. Park, M. D. Regnerus, L. D. Robinson, W. B. Wilcox, and R. D. Woodberry. 2000. "The Measure of American Religion: Toward Improving the State of the Art." *Social Forces* 79(1): 291–318.

Steinman, William S., and Wendelle C. Stevens. 1987. *UFO Crash at Aztec: A Well Kept Secret*. Tucson, AZ: UFO Photo Archives.

Steinmeyer, Jim. 2008. *Charles Fort: The Man Who Invented the Supernatural*. New York: Penguin.

Stevens, Phillip. 1991. "The Demonology of Satanism: An Anthropological View." In *The Satanism Scare,* ed. James T. Richardson, Joel Best, and David G. Bromley, 21–40. New York: Aldine de Gruyter.

Stiebing, William H., Jr. 1984. *Ancient Astronauts, Cosmic Collisions and Other Popular Theories about Man's Past.* Buffalo, NY: Prometheus Books.

Stinchcombe, Arthur. 1990. *Information and Organizations.* Berkeley: University of California Press.

Stollznow, Karen. 2013. "(Big)foot in Mouth: Bigfoot Language." *Scientific American.* July 24. http://blogs.scientificamerican.com.

Story, Ronald. 1980a. *The Encyclopedia of UFOs.* New York: Doubleday.

———. 1980b. *Guardians of the Universe?* New York: St. Martin's.

Strain, Kathy M. 2008. *Giants, Cannibals and Monsters: Bigfoot in Native Culture.* Blaine, WA: Hancock House.

Stranges, Frank E. 1967. *The Stranger at the Pentagon.* Van Nuys, CA: I.E.C.

Strieber, Whitley. 1987. *Communion: A True Story.* New York: William Morrow.

Subbotsky, Eugene. 2010. *Magic and the Mind: Mechanisms, Functions, and Development of Magical Thinking and Behavior.* Oxford: Oxford University Press.

Swatos, William H. 1988. "Picketing Satan Enfleshed at 7-Eleven: A Research Note." *Review of Religious Research* 30(3): 73–82.

Taves, Ann. 1999. *Fits, Trances, and Visions: Experiencing Religion and Explaining Experience from Wesley to James.* Princeton, NJ: Princeton University Press.

———. 2013. "The Power of the Paranormal (and Extraordinary)." *History of Religions* 53(2): 205–11.

Taylor, Catherine, and Susan B. Sorenson. 2002. "The Nature of Newspaper Coverage of Homicide." *Injury Prevention* 8(2): 121–27.

Thomas, William I., and Dorothy Swain Thomas. 1928. *The Child in America: Behavior Problems and Programs.* New York: Knopf.

Thurston County Sheriff's Office. 1988. Transcript of interview with Paul Ingram, conducted by Joe Vukich and Brian Schoening. Olympia, WA.

———. 1989a. Transcript of interview with Sandra Ingram, conducted by Loreli Thompson. Olympia, WA.

———. 1989b. Transcript of interview with Chad Ingram, conducted by Dr. Richard Peterson and Detective Brian Schoening. Olympia, WA.

Tiryakian, Edward A. 1972. "Toward a Sociology of Esoteric Culture." *American Journal of Sociology* 78(3): 491–512.

Toby, Jackson. 1957. "Social Disorganization and Stake in Conformity: Complementary Factors in the Predatory Behavior of Hoodlums." *Journal of Criminal Law, Criminology and Police Science* 48 (May/June): 12–17.

Torres, Noe, and Ruben Uriarte. 2008. *The Other Roswell: UFO Crash on the Texas-Mexico Border.* n.l.: Roswellbooks.com.

Trachtenberg, Joshua. [1939] 2004. *Jewish Magic and Superstition: A Study in Folk Religion.* Philadelphia: University of Pennsylvania Press.

Troeltsch, Ernst. [1912] 1932. *The Social Teaching of the Christian Churches*. New York: Macmillan.

Tumminia, Diana G. 2005. *When Prophecy Never Fails: Myth and Reality in a Flying-Saucer Group*. New York: Oxford University Press.

Valerian, Valdamar. 1988. *The Matrix*. Stone Mountain, GA: Arcturus Book Service.

Victor, Jeffrey S. 1993. *Satanic Panic: The Creation of a Contemporary Legend*. Chicago, IL: Open Court.

Vigil, Delfin. 2006. "Conspiracy Theories Propel AM Radio Show into Top 10." *San Francisco Chronicle*, November 12.

Vold, George B., Thomas J. Bernard, and Jeffrey B. Snipes. 1998. *Theoretical Criminology*, 4th ed. New York: Oxford University Press.

Wallis, Roy. 1974. "The Aetherius Society: A Case Study in the Formation of a Mystagogic Congregation." *Sociological Review* 22(1): 27–44.

Warnke, Mike. 1972. *The Satan Seller*. South Plainfield, NJ: Bridge Books.

Weaver, Richard L., and James McAndrew. 1995. *The Roswell Report: Fact vs. Fiction in the New Mexico Desert*. Washington, DC: U.S. Government Printing Office.

Weber, Max. [1904–5] 2002. *The Protestant Ethic and the Spirit of Capitalism*. Trans. Talcott Parsons. New York: Routledge.

———. [1922] 1991. *The Sociology of Religion*. Trans. Ephraim Fischoff. Boston: Beacon.

Weeks, Matthew, Kelly P. Weeks, and Mary R. Daniel. 2008. "The Implicit Relationship between Religious and Paranormal Constructs." *Journal for the Scientific Study of Religion* 47(4): 599–611.

Whelan, Christopher. 1996. "Marginalization, Deprivation, and Fatalism in the Republic of Ireland: Class and Underclass Perspectives." *European Sociological Review* 12(1): 33–51.

Whitcomb, Jonathan D. 2011. *Live Pterosaurs in America*, 3rd ed. Charleston, SC: CreateSpace Independent Publishing.

Wilcox, Clyde, Sharon Linzey, and Ted G. Jelen. 1991. "Reluctant Warriors: Premillennialism and Politics in the Moral Majority." *Journal for the Scientific Study of Religion* 30(3): 245–58.

Williams, Peter W. 1980. *Popular Religion in America: Symbolic Change and the Modernization Process in Historical Perspective*. Englewood Cliffs, NJ: Prentice Hall.

Williamson, W. Paul, and Ralph W. Hood Jr. 2004. "Differential Maintenance and Growth of Religious Organizations Based Upon High-Cost Behaviors: Serpent Handling within the Church of God." *Review of Religious Research* 46(2): 150–68.

Williamson, W. Paul, and Howard R. Pollio. 1999. "The Phenomenology of Religious Serpent Handling: A Rationale and Thematic Study of Extemporaneous Sermons." *Journal for the Scientific Study of Religion* 38(2): 203–18.

Willman, Skip. 2002. "Spinning Paranoia: The Ideologies of Conspiracy and Contingency in Postmodern Culture." In *Conspiracy Nation: The Politics of Paranoia in Postwar America*, ed. Peter Knight, 21–39. New York: New York University Press.

Wilson, Keith M., and Jennifer L. Huff. 2001. "Scaling Satan." *Journal of Psychology* 135(3): 292–300.

Wlodarski, Robert, and Anne Powell Wlodarski. 2001. *A Texas Guide to Haunted Restaurants, Taverns, and Inns*. Plano: Republic of Texas Press.

Woodberry, Robert D., and Christian Smith. 1998. "Fundamentalism et al.: Conservative Protestantism in America." *Annual Review of Sociology* 24: 25–56.

Wright, Lawrence. 1994. *Remembering Satan*. New York: Knopf.

Wu, Zheng, and Randy Hart. 2002. "The Effects of Marital and Nonmarital Union Transition on Health." *Journal of Marriage and Family* 64(2): 420–32.

Wuthnow, Robert. 1978. *Experimentation in American Religion*. Berkeley: University of California Press.

———. 1987. *Meaning and Moral Order: Explorations in Cultural Analysis*. Berkeley: University of California Press.

Yamane, David. 1998. "Experience." In *Encyclopedia of Religion and Society*, ed. William H. Swatos Jr., 179–82. Walnut Creek, CA: AltaMira.

———. 2000. "Narrative and Religious Experience." *Sociology of Religion* 61(2): 171–89.

Zahn, Margaret A., and Philip C. Sagi. 1987. "Stranger Homicide in Nine American Cities." *Journal of Criminal Law and Criminology* 78(2): 377–97.

Zeleney, Jeff. 2008. "Obama, in His New Role as President-Elect, Calls for Stimulus Package." *New York Times*, November 7.

INDEX

Adamski, George, 16, 108–10, 165; *Flying Saucers Farewell*, 109–10, 271n9; *Flying Saucers Have Landed*, 109; *Inside the Spaceships*, 109; *Pioneers of Space*, 110

Aetherius Society, 16, 272n14

African Americans: Christians, 272n36; paranormal beliefs, 59–60, 280n9; UFO abductions, 73. *See also* racial/ethnic minorities

African Methodist Episcopal Zion Church, 272n36

age: and belief in evil, 200; and ghost beliefs, 105; and intense religious experiences, 216; and paranormal beliefs and experiences, 77, 141, 238, 267n18, 271n21; as a subculture, 145–46; and UFO beliefs, 61

alien abductions. *See* UFO abductions

Alien Obsession (Rhodes), 120

aliens: belief in alien intervention, 49–54; as demons and devils, 120; friendly contact with (*see* UFO contactees); and ghost lights, 6; Grays, 66, 69, 72, 76, 268n45; hierarchy of beings, 69. *See also* UFOs

amateur science, 46–47. *See also* pseudoscience

ancient astronaut thesis, 50–54

Andreasson, Betty, 268n45, 269n53

angels, 32, 98, 105, 167; as bridge between religion and paranormal, 222–23, 236–37; guardian angel encounters, 194, 220–24, 236; as space people, 110

animal psychics, 36–40

Ape Canyon, 133, 273n11, 274n19

argot (specialized vocabulary): of Bigfoot hunters, 148–49, 152; of ghost hunters, 98–100, 149

Armageddon, 198, 200, 202, 236

Arnold, Kenneth, 49–50, 259n11, 266n6

astrology: belief in, 44, 167; and enlightenment, 45; and gender, 59; and ghost beliefs, 98, 100; horoscopes, 77–79; research on, 138, 141; ridicule of, 75

atheists, 121, 126, 184–85, 220, 222, 234, 239

Atlantis, 122, 267n16; belief in, 59–63; Plato's reference to, 54

Atlantis (Donnelly), 54

attachments (social control theory), 179–82

automatic writing, 167

Auxerre, France, 23–26

Baker, Tom, 170–71

ball lightning, 6

Barwood, Frances Emma, 75–76

Bauman (Bigfoot spotter), 132, 273n7

Baylor Religion Survey (BRS), 7, 9, 55, 241–42, 249; on religious experiences, 57

Beck, Fred, 132–33, 135

Beckjord, Jon-Erik, 18, 174–75

belief, 129–31; conventional, 182–84. *See also* paranormal beliefs and experiences

beliefs (social control theory), 179–80, 182–84

believers. *See* paranormal people

ABOUT THE AUTHORS

CHRISTOPHER D. BADER is Professor of Sociology and is affiliated with the Institute for Religion, Economics and Culture (IRES) at Chapman University. He is Associate Director of the Association of Religion Data Archives (www.theArda.com), the world's largest archive of religion survey data, funded by the John Templeton Foundation and Lilly Foundation.

JOSEPH O. BAKER is Associate Professor in the Department of Sociology and Anthropology at East Tennessee State University, and Senior Research Associate for the Association of Religion Data Archives. He is the author of *American Secularism* (NYU Press).

F. CARSON MENCKEN is Professor and Chair, Department of Sociology, Baylor University. He is former Director of the Baylor Religion Survey. His research has focused on religion and social trust, religious tension, and non-traditional supernatural beliefs, as well as the role of religious organizations in promoting and sustaining civil society and economic development. His research has appeared in such journals as *Journal for the Scientific Study of Religion*, *Sociology of Religion*, *Review of Religious Research*, *Sociological Perspectives*, and *Rural Sociology*. His research has been funded by the John Templeton Foundation, U.S. Department of Agriculture, U.S. Department of Justice, and U.S. Department of the Interior.